Going Remote

Going Remote

HOW THE FLEXIBLE WORK ECONOMY
CAN IMPROVE OUR LIVES AND OUR CITIES

Matthew E. Kahn

UNIVERSITY OF CALIFORNIA PRESS

University of California Press
Oakland, California

Library of Congress Cataloging-in-Publication Data
    Names: Kahn, Matthew E., 1966– author.
    Title: Going remote : how the flexible work economy can improve our
lives and our cities / Matthew E. Kahn.
    Identifiers: LCCN 2021039067 (print) | LCCN 2021039068 (ebook) |
ISBN 9780520384316 (cloth) | ISBN 9780520384323 (epub)
    Subjects: LCSH: Telecommuting—United States. | Quality of work life—
United States. | Work-life balance—United States.
    Classification: LCC HD2336.35.U6 K34 2022 (print) | LCC HD2336.35.
U6 (ebook) | DDC 658.3/123—dc23
    LC record available at https://lccn.loc.gov/2021039067
    LC ebook record available at https://lccn.loc.gov/2021039068

31 30 29 28 27 26 25 24 23 22
10 9 8 7 6 5 4 3 2 1

Contents

Introduction

No Going Back

We are not going back to the work world of January 2020. Going forward, perhaps as many as 35 percent of the workforce will work from home at least a few days a week.[1] Nobody anticipated this shift in our work arrangements.

In recent years, major companies such as Amazon, Apple, Facebook, and Google have built new corporate campuses. They hired leading architects to design buildings and outdoor spaces where people would want to spend time, and in doing so, remove both the real and self-defined walls that often separate work, socializing, wellness, and creativity. One Apple executive told *Wired Magazine*, "We don't want you to feel like you're in a casino. We want you to know what time of day it is, what temperature it is outside. Is the wind really blowing? That was Steve's original intention, to sort of blur that line between the inside and outside. It sort of wakes up your senses." Apple built a 2.8 million–square-foot building that cost billions of dollars. The 175-acre Cupertino campus, Apple Park, opened in 2017 and was filled with 12,000 people.[2]

For much of 2020 and 2021, these buildings have been quiet. The sudden onset of the COVID-19 pandemic in 2020 sent tens of millions of workers home. A "silver lining" of this national emergency is that millions of workers and many firms have learned how to continue to be productive while working from home (WFH). Such workers have experienced how working from home affects their productivity and their quality of life. The lessons learned in the recent past will influence how workers configure their lives in our post-COVID economy.[3] In this sense, WFH is an "experience good." This economics term refers to situations where we underestimate how much we value an experience until we try it. When the first *Star Wars* movie was released in 1977, I could never have imagined how much I would enjoy it. A written explanation of the plot would not have conveyed its power and excitement.

This book explores how our recent nationwide experiment with WFH will influence our nation's economic geography over the next decades. We are more likely to unlock the full potential of this new opportunity if we can anticipate the opportunities and challenges posed for workers, firms, and local governments by the WFH option.

Just before the COVID crisis hit in early 2020, we faced four social challenges. First, we spent too much time commuting. Second, rents were too high in America's most productive cities. Third, local economies were stagnant in many rural places and in postindustrial cities such as Baltimore. Fourth, many women and many minorities did not have the same economic success and access to opportunities as white men. This book explores how the rise of WFH can improve our quality of life and help us to overcome each of these four challenges.

The gains from WFH differ depending on one's life goals and responsibilities. As I discuss in chapter 1, a young ambitious person who is eager to make her mark will continue to value the face-to-face interactions at work as she seeks to build up her skill set, network, and reputation. At the same time, a middle-aged worker who has an aging mother in Iowa may greatly benefit from the flexibility offered by engaging in remote work. These two examples highlight a central theme of this book. We differ with respect to what we gain from working from home. No one expected that millions of us would have the opportunity to engage in WFH. Over the next few years, workers who anticipate having the option to engage in WFH on at least a part-time basis will have strong incentives to reconfigure their plans and to invest in the skills to make the most of this new opportunity.

While the rise of WFH offers potentially large benefits for eligible workers, it also could impose costs on US workers. Such workers will face greater international competition as US workers compete with international remote workers. Economic analysis offers insights here about how younger workers can position themselves in terms of human capital investment to better adapt to the new "rules of the game."

Economists are debating how our economy will look in the aftermath of the pandemic. Nobel laureate Paul Krugman has argued that our cities and our urban work life will basically return to our pre-pandemic experience. He writes: "So the best bet is that life and work in, say, 2023 will look a lot like life and work in 2019, but a bit less so. We may commute to the office less than we used to; there may well be a glut of urban office space. But most of us won't be able to stay very far from the madding crowd."[4]

On one level, I agree with him. Through billions of dollars of past investment in tall buildings and urban infrastructure (including the electricity grid, transit systems, and sewage systems), we have built up durable capital in major hubs like Boston, New York

City, and San Francisco. This durable capital has not been fully utilized in 2020 and 2021 but the excitement and buzz of cities will certainly return. As some people choose to move to more far-flung areas and engage in WFH there, center cities will become more affordable and attract younger people who want to be closer "to the action." In our diverse society, some people will respond to the rise of WFH and move farther from city centers, but at the same time a type of "musical chairs" occurs that creates new opportunities for those who want to live in center cities. In an economy that is continually upgrading old housing and building new housing, this does not have to be a zero-sum game. The economic geography of our cities shifts over time in response to supply and demand forces.

This book traces the emerging improvements in quality of life made possible by having more freedom over how we allocate our scarce time. On any given day and at any given hour, many people will be working from home. They will have control over their schedules and their lives that will significantly increase their flexibility as to how they live. On a snowy day in February in Chicago, some may choose to work from home. On a March day, a suburban dad may attend his son's play and work from home that afternoon.

In the recent past, we spent too much time commuting. WFH opens up new possibilities for productively doing our job while making the most of our scarce time. My teacher, Nobel laureate Gary Becker, emphasized the central role of how we spend our time in determining our health and our quality of life. I will argue that the rise of WFH creates new quality-of-life opportunities for workers who do not work from home. WFH workers represent a large enough share of the population such that their choices will shift real estate prices both within and across cities and regions.

As some WFH workers spread out, this creates new opportunities for service-sector workers to move to such areas, which will both lower the rents they pay for housing and expand their menu of lifestyle possibilities.

In the recent past, the United States featured too few centers of economic growth. I will argue that the rise of WFH increases these points on the map. Where exactly these new growth hubs emerge depends on several factors ranging from their "God-given" quality of life (weather, mountains, beauty) and local land use decisions. Will the incumbent property owners welcome new construction or will they use zoning land use rules to limit economic growth? In this sense, both demand- and supply-side conditions determine the emerging new menu of geographic possibilities created by a more footloose workforce. The economic perspective offers new insights here for anticipating shifts in our nation's economic geography.

Short-Run Gains for Workers

WFH workers will gain from having more control over their commuting schedule and by having the option to completely avoid commuting on some days. The time savings will be the greatest for those who have chosen to live the farthest from their place of work. Working parents will be able to spend more time at home, which means children will spend more time with their parents. Most couples wrestle with household "chore wars." Reduced weekday commuting creates new possibilities for couples to revisit their individual efforts in contributing to the needs of the household. As people spend more time in their home communities rather than at work, people will be more civically engaged.

Those with greater job flexibility will be better able to cope and adapt to the various risks each of us faces, which includes shocks to our own health and shocks to local economies. Over the course of our life, our personal circumstances change as we are confronted with unexpected challenges in coping with our own needs, our children's needs, and our parents' needs. The United States is a large nation and people often have family and friends scattered across it. A company's physical location on the map ties down a worker to that location and raises the transportation and psychic costs of maintaining ties with the other people in one's life. The possibility of having the option to telecommute creates a new level of freedom and flexibility for meeting all of our life goals and responsibilities.

For decades, young people have chosen to live in cities to engage in a more organic search for job opportunities, friends, romantic relationships, and places to shop and eat. I can imagine a type of science fiction AI world where advanced algorithms quickly figure out the right matches, and young people rarely have to leave their homes to find the right foods and friends and experiences that would be suggested for them. Such a powerful algorithm, combined with internet delivery of services, would substitute for directly experiencing the city. At the early stage of his career, my twenty-year-old son would turn down this offer. While he has the skills to be eligible to work from home, he would rather be close to the action and meet other young people, to network and build up his reputation amidst the challenging and exciting trial-and-error of urban life.

Post-COVID there will continue to be a demand for face-to-face interaction, especially among the young who do not have a rolodex of social capital built up to rely on now while navigating endless zoom calls. Young people's creativity, and their ability to inspire and be inspired by others, still relies on in-person communication. Cities facilitate such interaction both at work and at play. The young do not need much private housing space, and they will have an edge and a desire to live in high density to facilitate their ability to meet and interact with each other. In contrast to her grandson, my eighty-year-old mother has thrived while working at home in 2020 as a lawyer in New York City.

Medium-Term Gains for Workers

WFH does not mean that we are going to abandon urban buildings such as New York City's Empire State Building. While some of us may "head for the hills," as I will discuss below, many of us will continue to seek out urban life (for both career concerns and amenities). Instead, I will argue that our personal freedom has greatly expanded. In the past, the choices of where to work and where to live were almost always bundled into one "all or nothing" choice because commute times were typically so long (see chapter 2). A key point that I will return to again and again relates to contingencies. While a person who loves California will be willing (if she can afford it) to live and work there, life always features contingencies (taking care of a sick mother, attending a class reunion, or watching a child's annual school play), and it is because of such contingencies that one would greatly value the flexibility to keep working even when physically distant from the workplace. This is just one example of the new freedom WFH eligible workers now have.

Urban economists study the interplay between where workers and firms locate within and across cities. This book explores how the rise of WFH will affect the economic geography of our cities and suburbs and will affect the choices made by different types of workers and firms. In the "old" urban economics model, workers know where they work and must choose where to live as they are well aware of the time and transportation costs and agony of the daily commute.

WFH workers have new freedoms to go where they want to go and where they need to go to take care of their family responsibilities. Firms will decide where to locate their companies and how much office space to access. They will face the tradeoff between, on the one hand, the benefits of saving money on office rent and reducing their workforce's time commuting and, on the other, the challenges of maintaining their organization's morale and encouraging synergistic teamwork given that a large percentage of their workforce will be geographically dispersed. Firms will need to learn how to reconfigure their operations to continue to be productive while allowing workers to have greater flexibility. For-profit firms retain the option to bring workers back to working full-time at headquarters if such firms are unable to maintain their culture, focus, and profitability when many workers work from home.

In 2019, an ambitious worker was expected to be at the office roughly 200 days a year for twelve-hour stretches of work and commuting. Considering the physical location of offices—such as finance in New York and tech in San Francisco—and the slow commute speeds into and within cities, this worker would have very limited options when deciding where to live. In other words, the traditional pattern of commuting to work demands that an employee live close to a single point on the map, namely the physical location of the employer. When engaging in WFH, the worker is "liberated" and can go where she wants to go or go where she needs to go to take care of family issues and challenges. This reduces stress and improves her quality of life.

How much one values the right to engage in WFH depends on many factors. Those who live farther from their place of work save more time when they can engage in WFH. In several of America's most productive cities, like San Francisco and New York City, the local area features high home prices due to high demand to live near a very productive vibrant city and too little new housing being constructed. Middle-class people who work in these productive core areas face high home prices and they are stuck in traffic at rush hour. A commuter moving at a speed of thirty miles per hour who is only willing to commute one and a half hours round trip per day must search for housing within twenty-two miles of where he works. In an expensive local real estate market, this is a costly constraint as the menu of affordable neighborhoods is limited.

WFH workers are no longer tethered to choosing among homes close to where they work. This newfound freedom expands their menu of where they will live. Some will choose to move out to the distant suburbs where homes are newer, larger, and cheaper. In more remote places, real estate developers often have more freedom to build than in center cities that often feature litigious neighbors who block new construction. Other WFH workers will be more adventurous and will move to places that meet their own personal needs. Environmentalists may head to the mountains to be able to spend more leisure time in nature and to live close to like-minded people. Those with responsibilities caring for aging parents may move closer to where their parents live. Those with strong ties to their birthplace community may move back home now that their workplace location no longer acts as such a strong magnet.

The rise of WFH could shrink the gender gap in earnings as women will be better able to remain attached to the labor market. The flexibility offered by WFH will encourage more mothers of young children to engage in part-time work. Such a commitment to the workforce will encourage employers to invest more effort in training such workers. The ability to engage in WFH will increase the set of jobs for eligible women and this will increase workforce attachment. Young women will anticipate that the option to engage in WFH in later life provides an incentive to invest more in skills that offer greater future economic returns.

Remote work creates new employment opportunities for minorities. Cities like Baltimore, Cleveland, and Detroit are home to hundreds of thousands of African Americans. In recent years, these cities have not featured strong private-sector job prospects, but many people have built up social networks there and their families have lived there for generations. Access to remote jobs creates new opportunities for minorities to continue to live in cities where they feel more comfortable and where they have roots while working remotely. The expectation that this new option is created by WFH provides an incentive for young minorities to invest in the necessary skills to compete for these high-paying positions.

How will the quality of life of non-WFH workers be affected by the life choices made by millions of WFH workers? Many less skilled workers are employed in the service sector. Such individuals are often paid close to minimum wages and cannot afford good housing in American's most productive cities because rents are so high in these cities. As WFH workers spread out across the nation, this creates local demand for services provided by non-WFH workers. These WFH workers will need people to clean their homes and take care of their gardens and babysit their children. Locations far from core cities feature cheaper rents. Low rents effectively raise the purchasing power of non-WFH workers. This example highlights the interdependencies in our economy where richer people demand nontradable services.

The New Geography of Firm Locational Choice

Many prominent American firms have made large recent investments in corporate campuses. Given the billions that were invested, these firms were making a large place-based bet that their companies would be more profitable by locking into that specific location and that amount of physical space. Going forward for both America's greatest companies and for medium- and small-sized firms, how does the rise of WFH affect where they locate their offices and how much space they demand?

Each firm faces a tradeoff. Given the cost of real estate in America's greatest cities, firms will reduce their demand for such space if these costs exceed the benefits these firms anticipate they will gain. If most eligible workers are working from home at least two days a week, then overall demand for such real estate will decline.

Startup firms face a key decision regarding where to locate as they seek to achieve several goals. They need access to finance to launch their ideas. They need access to a talent pool to hire the right people. They need to network with industry leaders to build a reputation, and they need to tap into a city's professional services to have access to lawyers and other service providers to protect their intellectual property. Many startups seek to be in the "middle of the action." Such proximity offers greater learning and networking opportunities.

Worker compensation is a firm's major cost expenditure. The nominal earnings of WFH workers are likely to decline as such workers will enjoy greater hourly flexibility and as they compete with international "offshored" workers for these WFH jobs. The probability that more jobs will be offshored hinges on how domestic workers compete with foreign workers.[5] The ability to engage in WFH in a national economy featuring many cities, including some with lower home prices, allows US workers to be more competitive with their cheaper foreign rivals and this helps to maintain our domestic jobs base.

Annual pay is just one part of a worker's compensation. Workers also value their career development opportunities. WFH potentially poses risks here if the absence of daily face-to-face contact at the office reduces altruism and loyalty within the organization. A firm that anticipates this challenge can adapt by relying on its real-time worker productivity metric data to track how different workers are performing. By experimenting with different strategies for bringing workers together, such a firm will figure out ways to balance the benefits of WFH while reducing the costs such isolation can create for a firm's culture. A key issue that arises concerns whether face-to-face interaction on a daily basis is key to an organization's success. Alternatively, there may be a quantity versus quality tradeoff as, during a typical month, workers gain from engaging in WFH most of the time but then are expected to spend a few intense days of interaction at headquarters. Firms have strong incentives to experiment with different working arrangements to optimize their new work rules. Firms that are sluggish in adapting their work rules will lose talent, have to pay a "combat pay" wage premium, and will be less profitable.

Will the Rise of Remote Work Weaken Superstar Cities?

Cities compete against each other for footloose educated people and the firms that hire them. In recent decades, New York City, San Francisco, and other cities boomed. Going forward, how will the rise of WFH affect the demand to live in the "superstar cities" versus postindustrial cities such as Baltimore, Cleveland, and Detroit? I examine the emerging competition that will play out between places ranging from Baltimore to Boise to Bozeman as they compete for workers and jobs that in the recent past were concentrated in superstar cities.

Billions of dollars have been invested in durable commercial real estate in major cities such as Boston and Manhattan, with the expectation that major firms and startups would continue to rent expensive space in commercial towers. While WFH is likely to reduce each firm's demand for commercial real estate, commercial real estate will continue to be demanded. Face-to-face communication continues to be essential for sealing deals, earning a reputation, making new connections, and meeting with the press.

In recent years, in cities like San Francisco and Seattle, the tech boom has led to high local rents, which has displaced local renters. Worried about the negative effects of a boom on local resident quality of life, local elected officials in major tech cities such as San Francisco and Seattle have sought to enact new taxes on major local companies to collect revenue to use for pro-redistribution purposes. As these cities raise their taxes and regulations on local tech firms, this creates a "push incentive" for such firms to threaten to downsize locally. In recent years, members of Seattle's city council have sought to impose new taxes on Amazon to collect roughly $500 million a year to fund transfers to the poor. The ability to hire more remote workers (rather than hiring workers who will work in Seattle at Amazon) gives Amazon executives a credible threat in this firm's ongoing negotiations with the Seattle city council.

America's most productive cities tend to be located along the coasts, and these beautiful areas continue to have great consumer city and tourism appeal. If these cities lose mobile WFH workers, the new city would feature a younger population paying more affordable rents. High-amenity cities have proven to be remarkably resilient when hit with major shocks. In recent decades, Manhattan has rallied back several times when it was hit with the job loss it experienced starting in the 1950s as manufacturing jobs vanished and after the damage and horror caused by the 9/11/2001 terrorist attacks. In contrast, other cities such as Detroit have had more trouble rallying after the decline of the local car industry.

New Opportunities for Other Areas

WFH-eligible workers can move to many possible destinations across the United States. Some will seek out the distant suburbs of their employer's metropolitan area. Others will be more adventurous and move to the mountains or to places close to water. Some may simply seek out low-tax areas such as Florida and Texas that do not have a state income tax. Others may move back to their birthplace area. This migration will spread out talent across the United States.

As WFH workers shop around for where to live, cities and jurisdictions that seek to lure them can reposition themselves by making a set of strategic investments. While a city cannot build mountains, it can have good schools and safe streets and enforce environmental regulations. A city can offer reliable internet connections and its region can have good airports to allow for easy direct flight access to an HQ. High-amenity places that in the past were not major productivity hubs could enjoy a surge of new local growth. Local land use zoning rules will play a key role in determining whether beautiful areas will become "the next Nashville" or whether a type of moat will be built around the area that limits growth and inflates local real estate prices as buyers bid up the price of relatively few homes.

Beautiful areas often attract environmentalists and nature lovers who may want to preserve their paradise and not change the local culture or its current scale of activity. Incumbent homeowners often vote for land use regulations to slow new construction in order to boost the value of their homes. If a coalition of incumbent homeowners and environmentalists are able to block new real estate development in desirable areas, then the rise of remote work will lead to even higher home prices in such areas.

By influencing the geography of where successful people live across the United States, the rise of WFH creates new possibilities for economic growth to take place in areas that have lagged for decades. Both rural areas and postindustrial cities such as Baltimore have lost population in recent decades. Some WFH workers will reconsider moving to these areas now that they can live in these affordable and familiar places without suffering an earnings penalty. If more college-educated African Americans settle in Baltimore because they can engage in WFH, then a socially beneficial by-product of their own choice is to make Baltimore a more vibrant area as the city, which has been shrinking in population for cities, attracts role models and people with purchasing power who would have been less likely to have moved there if they did not have the ability to engage in WFH.

In recent decades, rural area quality of life has declined as economic insecurity has increased and local deaths from despair associated with drug addiction and substance abuse have increased. The rise in political polarization has increased as many residents of these areas feel that the American Dream is no longer attainable for them or their children. The rise of WFH creates new possibilities for such areas as some urbanites seek out new lifestyle opportunities in the countryside. On the whole, this creates new possibilities for a rural resurgence featuring a more diversified rural economy.

As the Biden administration makes new investments in the nation's infrastructure, this is a key time to consider the synergies between private investments and public-sector investments. Upgrades of our transportation infrastructure (highways, airports) and internet infrastructure (broadband internet being expanded into rural areas) help to unlock the full potential of WFH to improve worker quality of life.

Finding Freedom and "The Good Life"

At any point in time, our lives can be described by points on a map that include where we live, where we work, places where we enjoy taking leisure, and the locations of our friends and family. Before WFH, we faced the challenge that slow commuting speeds constrained us to live in a handful of affordable places close to where we work. This impinges on our personal freedom because we would really like to locate closer to the other points on the map that we care about, such as living close to our parents.

The rise of WFH increases our personal freedom. Given that each of us has a different conception of "the good life," the rise of telecommuting raises the possibility that more of us can achieve our life goals. This increases our personal freedom, allowing us more adaptation pathways to cope with new challenges that arise, ranging from sick family members to local labor market recessions and even natural disaster shocks. In our increasingly uncertain world, we need more flexibility so that we can adapt to "new news." WFH offers such increased flexibility because one can continue to work for the same employer while physically moving to another distant area or one can search for new work using the ever more sophisticated internet work platforms that match workers with firms seeking to hire them.

The rise of WFH poses new risks for US workers as they compete with foreign workers. Such head-to-head competition can lower US worker earnings. I discuss several new Big Data benchmarks for judging quality-of-life progress for those who do and do not qualify to work in WFH jobs. The quality of life of both sets of workers is interconnected because when WFH workers move to new parts of major cities (such as the New York City distant suburbs) or to Montana, this creates new local service-sector jobs and these will be filled by other workers. This rising local demand for less skilled workers in low-cost areas creates the possibility that the rise of WFH raises the real earnings of those with talents that WFH workers need to help them in their daily lives.

The Living Standards Debate

A few years ago, the economist Robert Gordon pessimistically argued that recent inventions have not greatly improved our quality of life. "Invention since 2000 has centered on entertainment and communication devices that are smaller, smarter, and more capable, but do not fundamentally change labor productivity or the standard of living in the way that electric light, motor cars, or indoor plumbing changed it."[6] He wrote this back in 2012. While I will not rank WFH as the equal of electric light or the motor car, I do argue that WFH will increase the quality of our leisure time and raise the real earnings of many service-sector workers.

Economists have written extensively about how we gain from the introduction of new goods. Many richer people are enjoying driving a Tesla more than other luxury vehicles. The Tesla is a new good with features that other vehicles do not have. The cell phone was a significant upgrade over pay phones. Diet Coke offers the great taste of Coke without the sugar and the calories. Honey Nut Cheerios is a tastier cousin of the traditional Cheerios. In each of these cases, for-profit firms are incurring costs to create a new product for which they believe there is a market willing to pay a premium.

WFH is an especially important new work arrangement because tens of millions of American workers engage in it—and we spend much more of our time working than we do eating breakfast or driving around. I predict that the rise of WFH will improve the quality of life of both those who engage in it and even those who do not engage in it due to market pricing effects. Firms could learn that their productivity greatly declines when workers are not in the office five days a week. Workers could learn that being "out of the loop" and away from co-workers and bosses slows down their career prospects and these losses exceed the benefits of commuting less. In truth, I expect that relatively few firms and workers will want to turn back the clock and return to our 2019 work arrangements.

Put simply, the rise of WFH increases our personal freedom. The ability to work for an employer but to live where one wants to live opens up so many new quality-of-life opportunities. Our nation is huge and offers a great variety of experiences. Our workforce is highly diverse with different tastes and talents. Our labor markets solve a spatial assignment problem as workers reveal who they want to work for and where they want to live. Our population's diversity highlights the importance of creating work rules that allow "different strokes for different folks." This book explores how our new freedoms will shift America's economic geography in many surprising ways.

I *Workers*

1   *Short-Run Gains for Workers*

In his 2020 annual statement to his Berkshire shareholders, Warren Buffett wrote, "A lot of people have learned that they can work at home, or that there's other methods of conducting their business than they might have thought from what they were doing a couple of years ago. When change happens in the world, you adjust to it."[1]

The next two chapters focus on Buffett's word "adjust." While his quote suggests a seamless transition that anyone can make, in truth at any given point in time we may differ in our ability and our desire to adapt to new circumstances. Over time, whether we can make the most of a new opportunity hinges on our choices and how we reconfigure our lives.

Who Can Zoom to Work?

Nick Bloom, an economist at Stanford, has been conducting surveys during 2020 to quantify who is working from home and what, going forward, are their expectations about future WFH. The more educated are more likely to engage in WFH. Among those who are working from home in 2020, 53 percent are college graduates. There is a wide range of preferences in the number of days people want to work from home, with 11 percent never wanting to WFH to 27 percent wanting to WFH all the time. The average person wants to work from home two days per week.[2]

One research team concludes that 32 percent of all US jobs can be performed almost entirely at home, although this varies significantly based on the industry. For example, while 74 percent of jobs in finance and insurance are "teleworkable," as are 93 percent of jobs in data processing, only 11 percent of retail trade jobs can be WFH.[3] This research team ranked eighty-eight industries with respect to what percentage of their jobs can be done by remote work. Their data can be used to calculate what share of a county's jobs can be done remotely. The County Business Patterns (an annual series produced by the US Census Bureau) provides data listing the employment count for each county divided into those eighty-eight different industries. By combining these data with the national data on the share of jobs in that industry that can be done remotely, I calculate the share of a county's jobs that can be done remotely. Intuitively, if a county features a large share of jobs in finance and insurance, then this county will have a higher overall average share of WFH jobs than a county whose employment is concentrated in retail trade.

The top ten remote work–friendly counties in the United States feature a jobs base such that 45–51.9 percent of the jobs can be done remotely. The top five are well known: Arlington and Fairfax Counties, New York County, and Santa Clara and San Francisco Counties. The top three WFH industries are in finance and data analysis; for these industries, over 90 percent of the jobs can be done at home. Counties with more than 250,000 people that have low rates of WFH do not include any famous areas. One example of such a county is Stanislaus, California, with a WFH rate of 25.7 percent.

Who Wants (and Does Not Want) to Work Remotely?

Most young people do not want to engage in WFH. They have not yet established a reputation. Face-to-face communication facilitates both personal growth and spreading the word about one's skills. Young people switch employers multiple times at the start of their career as they seek to learn about their tastes and talents in order to find a good company match.[4] Most young workers need face-to-face interactions so they can "learn the ropes." Working at a company provides them with valuable experience. They need to be mentored and this requires face-to-face interaction. Young people need to network and build up work social capital. This takes time. Research on the earnings dynamics of young men documents that two-thirds of their lifetime job changes occur during their first ten years of work experience. Roughly one-third of their wage growth during these first ten years can be attributed to job changes.[5]

If young workers could simply "zoom in" to a sequence of employers, they would face low switching costs for trying out different jobs. In truth, such remote workers would have trouble learning each firm's culture. These workers would be unlikely to be loyal to any one firm because they have never been an insider. In this "gig economy," a firm's workers would almost resemble a type of Uber driver as they provide a given service that is demanded. Such a transactional relationship will be acceptable for some workers, but younger workers and those who seek connection and to be part of a larger mission will be less likely to find such work emotionally satisfying. Face-to-face interaction on a regular basis helps to build up workplace social capital and firm loyalty.

Consider twenty-five-year-old Allie Micka. Micka moved from Boston to Washington, DC, to start a new job as a solutions engineer at a tech firm—one she admired for its highly social culture. Micka imagined going out for after-work drinks and making lifelong friends. And the office was just as she had imagined—for exactly ten days, before the coronavirus pandemic descended. Her now-virtual contact with her co-workers feels much too transactional. "As friendly as everyone is, it's hard to just say 'hi' to get to know someone when you have no purpose for reaching out," Micka said.[6] Such young workers are well aware that at the office one learns by osmosis and one can network and sometimes have the opportunity to attend impromptu meetings with higher-ups at the firm.

Middle-aged people who have established a reputation do not need to go to the office for networking. They will have a greater demand for the opportunity to work from home. Many tenured college professors get more work done when they do not go to the office. Unlike untenured professors, the tenured faculty have a promise of lifelong employment at their home institution. They do not have to engage in office politics to earn the friendship of the department leadership. While bumping into colleagues is fun and informative, it can also be distracting and the day can pass by without having long periods of uninterrupted thought.

My mother was born in 1941 and continues to practice law in New York City. My father was born in 1939 and continues to practice medicine in New York City. They have quickly learned the benefits of zoom interactions. My father's patients tend to be older and they do not have to commute to the hospital to see him. My mother can access all of her legal records electronically and is not tethered to an office desk. Improvements in information technology allow for easy access to records and she subcontracts to outside record-formatting companies to make her briefs comply with the expected standards featuring hyperlinks and bookmarks. Her clients are happy to speak to her by zoom or phone because they do not have to travel to meet with her.

As older workers consider their pathways to retirement, they are well aware that retirement contributes to cognitive decline and frankly to boredom for many.[7] An alternative to transitioning to full-time retirement is the option to engage in WFH. This pathway to retirement provides seniors with intellectual stimulation, a source of income, and a source of life satisfaction. Sociologists have worried about the isolation and loneliness that many seniors experience. The ability to continue to contribute and to feel valued is very important for every person. One's personal dignity is tied to having control over one's life.

Older workers who are eligible to engage in WFH can choose to migrate to warmer, more pleasant areas earlier in their lives. Many successful New Yorkers retire and move to Florida. In the new WFH economy, these individuals do not have to wait. Qualified older people can have a much better quality of life in their early sixties by relocating and continuing to work on at least a part-time basis for their original employer. This process means that retirement is less abrupt and less dramatic and likely to be less stressful and disruptive. Economists have noted that seniors' expenditures on food decline when they retire.[8] In our new Big Data economy, we need more real-time indicators of senior quality of life to measure their life satisfaction and the stress they are under. The ability to engage in WFH should reduce their stress by giving them a sense of purpose, allowing them to move to a place where they are comfortable, and giving them the option to retire later on. WFH also allows for an easier transition into retirement because their jobs would be more flexible.[9]

True Grit: The Personality Types Who Thrive While Working from Home

In recent years the field of behavioral economics has enjoyed a boom, a striking example of which was Richard Thaler being honored with the 2017 Nobel Prize in Economics for his behavioral research. One topic that behavioral researchers study is the causes and consequences of self-control problems. Working from home creates a kind of high-stakes laboratory for the further testing of such behavioral economics ideas.

In 2020, as millions of people have gained experience with working from home, many authors write on platforms such as Medium to report "dos and don'ts" for how to be an effective WFH worker. These pieces often offer tips for achieving good mental health in the face of workplace loneliness and how to develop self-control. Basic advice is offered, such as not working in one's pajamas and not working in bed and avoiding constant snacking. Some of the writing suggests that many Americans are having trouble "just saying no" to temptation while at home. Such self-control challenges suggest that these workers may be better suited to a more organized formal workplace environment where they know that their boss and co-workers are watching them. A worker with some self-awareness will know what she gains from engaging in WFH.

Spending Less Time Stuck in Traffic

In the United States, roughly 80 percent of the population live in a metropolitan area and 20 percent in rural places. Those who do not live in a rural area must choose where they live and work within the metro area. When I was a child in the 1970s, we lived in the suburbs of New York City (Westchester County) and my father commuted to Manhattan. Those who live in the suburbs and work in the center city face the longest commutes. Given that transit speeds are higher in the suburbs, those who live and work in the suburbs spend less time commuting. Urban economists have documented the rise of reverse commuting, where, for example, a person lives in downtown San Francisco and commutes to Silicon Valley firms closer to San Jose. Such commuters value the amenities of urban life and have access to major suburban employers like Google and Apple.

In America's most productive cities, many middle-class people commute for a long time. Cities such as Seattle, Portland, Boston, and San Francisco do not build much new housing and they do not charge a time-varying price for accessing the roads during rush hour. The net effect of these two policies is to create enormously high home prices close to the city. Middle-class people, and young people without housing equity, must put up with long commutes to gain access to the productive core. This dynamic lowers the real incomes of the middle class who work in these cities and pushes many young workers with families to the distant suburbs.

In major cities, the average commute time soars. A large number of Americans can be classified as "super-commuters," those workers whose place of work is the center city of a metropolitan area and place of home is outside of that metropolitan area. In 2010, 13 percent of the workforce of Dallas (180,000 people) and Houston (255,000) lived outside their respective metro areas. While only 3 percent of Manhattan's workforce were "super-commuters" in 2010, the number of these commuters grew by 70 percent from 2002 to 2010 to a total of 63,000 workers. This increase was partly driven by a sharp rise in the number of workers living in the Boston (162 percent increase) and Washington, DC (167 percent increase) metropolitan areas and working in Manhattan. These "super-commuters" (that is, people who commute more than ninety minutes each way to and from work) have become increasingly common in the Northeast corridor and the Pacific Northwest.[10]

Central Valley metros near the San Francisco Bay Area have seen significant increases in the number of "super-commuters"— 44.7 and 40.9 percent in Stockton and Sacramento, respectively, since 2005. For many middle-class people, these long commutes allow them to take advantage of lower real estate prices in the Central Valley and higher wages in the Bay Area, at the expense of less leisure time and greater expenditure on transportation.

In major cities such as Boston, Chicago, New York City, and Philadelphia, commuters who work in the center city often use public transit. While public transit is cheaper and greener than commuting by car, it both takes more time and is more physically uncomfortable as one must wait on crowded platforms for a subway or a bus. When one is dressed in business clothes on a hot day or a cold or rainy day, this can be quite unpleasant. WFH reduces the grind of the daily commute that involves public transit.

In 2018, 85.3 percent of American commuters commuted by car, but this average masks huge spatial variation. In the center cities of Atlanta, Boston, Chicago, Los Angeles, and New York City, the respective percentages were 71, 45, 58, 79, and 27.[11] During 2020 my brother, who lives in New Jersey, was able to avoid a ninety-minute one-way commute to Manhattan that involves driving to a train, taking the train to the city, and then a subway to his office.

Low traffic speeds and long mileage commutes emerge as a byproduct of there being too little housing available close to employment centers, and not introducing road pricing as a policy to reduce traffic congestion. While traffic congestion frustrates drivers, each individual driver has no incentive to recognize that as she gets on the road to go where she wants to go, she slows down every other driver by taking up space on the road during a peak demand time. Each driver views herself as too small to be responsible for clogging the road, but during weekday rush hours the result is a congested road.

In my past research, I have studied household decisions over where to live, what transport mode to use to commute to work, and what type of house to live in. Those who live in a city center and work in a city center are more likely to live in an apartment building and to commute by public transit. Those who live and work in the suburbs tend to have faster commutes by car. In the suburbs, there is less traffic congestion and one drives at higher speeds.

Real estate in highly productive and high-amenity center cities such as Boston and San Francisco becomes even more valuable when suburban residents face challenges in commuting to such places. The laws of supply and demand teach us that when there are few housing units and there is high demand for such real estate, real estate prices will soar. The owners of such properties gain a huge asset value windfall while those who have not accumulated wealth face higher housing prices. Researchers have documented that high rents in productive places such as Silicon Valley mean that local workers are not earning as high an income as an outsider might think because a large share of their after-tax earnings is spent on local housing.[12]

The straightforward solution to reducing traffic congestion is to charge drivers a fee (the congestion charge) during peak demand times. Commuters by car both seek to quickly arrive at their destination and to find a parking spot at the location. Dynamic pricing for parking would assure that during times of peak demand, the price of parking would rise so that demand would equal supply and there would be less cruising for free parking (another cause of traffic congestion).[13] The dynamic fees for road access and parking would provide an incentive to commuters to drive during off-peak times and would encourage some to instead use public transit. The net effect of adopting this policy would be higher road speeds and shorter commute times.

Cities such as Singapore and Stockholm have implemented such road pricing and have demonstrated that this incentive helps to increase road speeds and generates new revenue for the governments that implement it. The Stockholm case study is informative. Back in 2006, Stockholm introduced a toll system for seven months after which citizens voted on its permanent adoption. A research study of the resulting voting patterns reveals a type of "experience good" effect as those who enjoyed the greatest reductions in commute times due to road pricing were more likely to subsequently vote for continuing the road pricing policy.[14]

The lessons learned from these cities have not created a domino effect such that other cities have tried it. This fact has puzzled urban and transport economists. Of course, people like "free goods" and do not want to pay for accessing the roads, but if we do not pay using money for road access then we will pay using our scarce time as we are stuck in traffic. This logic suggests that we are already paying for the traffic congestion. Over time, as our wages rise, the loss to drivers from being stuck in traffic increases. The extra hours we lose in traffic jams could be more productively used for other activities.

Another strategy for reducing road traffic congestion is to improve public transit. Based on my past research, I found that light rail transit investment costs billions of dollars to build and in most cases the main effect of such investments in cities such as Los Angeles is to encourage bus riders to substitute to rail rather than to nudge car commuters to commute by public transit.[15] In dense urban corridors such as Boston, New York City, and Washington, DC, heavy rail continues to have a large market share, but even in cities such as Chicago, Philadelphia, and San Francisco that have subway systems, the majority of commuters commute by private vehicle.

The rise of WFH will help to improve worker quality of life in these superstar cities as they can structure their daily commute to avoid rush hour road-pricing spikes by working at home during the peak hours and traveling off-peak. Such a dynamic would reduce road congestion for everyone else who does need to commute during peak hours. This is an example of how the rise of WFH affects everyone else in the economy.

The option to engage in remote work two to three days a week effectively reduces one's weekly commuting time by 50 percent. Commuters care about more than their average commute time to work. Road accidents or severe weather can lead to commuting spikes of twice the usual length of time. Those with the WFH option can choose to work from home on such terrible commute days or restructure their day such that they start out working at home and then travel in when the traffic clears. This ability to adapt in real time to emerging challenges reduces stress and raises productivity. For people who live in cities with challenging winters such as Boston or Chicago, the ability to engage in remote work allows them to avoid commuting on the worst weather days such as during snowstorms.

As WFH workers commute less often to center city employment hubs, traffic congestion for everyone else may decrease. Transport economists caution that the "fundamental law of traffic congestion" lurks. Such economists predict that as the roads become less clogged at rush hour, there are always other drivers who will now make discretionary trips because the time price of such trips has declined. While this claim makes sense, in the case of rush hour trips I do believe that WFH will help to reduce road congestion. With the exception of workers, who else must travel to the downtown at 8:30 a.m. on a weekday? There are no sports events or cultural events at those times. There are exciting retail stores in the city center, but shopping at such luxury stores is a rare event. A legacy of China's communist past is that the best schools in the major cities are located in the center cities. This means that many children and their parents get stuck in traffic as suburban parents take their children to elite schools. In contrast in the United States, a vast majority of suburban children attend suburban schools. These points suggest that non-WFH workers who work in center cities and live in the suburbs will enjoy a reduction in commute times. This predicted spillover gain for everyone else merits measurement.

When I grew up in Scarsdale, New York (a suburb twenty miles north of Manhattan), my father was one of the public transit commuters as he took a 6 a.m. train to the city. In major metropolitan areas such as New York City, San Francisco, Boston, Chicago, and Washington, DC, an elaborate set of public transit trains and buses is geared to meet peak rush-hour demand in the morning and the early evening. These progressive cities feature billions of dollars of public transit contracts hiring unionized employees and purchasing transport capital (buses and trains and maintaining tunnels) to deliver these services. If the rise of WFH shifts the daily commute flows, an interesting issue will arise concerning how much less revenue these public transit authorities will receive and whether the public-sector unions will allow workers to be redeployed to new uses rather than having bus drivers drive less filled buses at peak times. An open question asks: How quickly will local governments reoptimize the supply of transit services as the overall quantity of demand and the timing of demand (shaved peaks) arises because of the rise of WFH?

The Gain from Commuting Less

There are roughly 158 million Americans who work. If one-third are eligible to engage in WFH and if each of those who are eligible works from home two days a week, then 104 million round trip commutes are avoided each week because of WFH. If each commuter has a round trip commute of one hour, then we collectively avoid 104 million hours of commuting each week. Each of us has our own vision for how to use this windfall of extra time. A major research agenda in social science studies how we use our time as we allocate it across many at-home activities ranging from exercise, to time with family, learning, home improvement, and recreation.[16]

The ability to work from home two or three days a week represents a type of pay increase![17] In an urban economics class, the teacher discusses the tradeoff that workers face. Housing closer to a major work center is more expensive but features a shorter commute. The worker only has twenty-four hours in the day and her daily leisure equals the time she does not spend working and commuting.

Middle-class people tend to have the longest commute to work, especially when they work in a center city as they commute from the suburbs to the city. Since home prices decline as a function of distance to major employment centers, the middle class are more likely to choose to commute longer in return for a cheaper, larger home. The ability to avoid commuting every day to work saves such individuals more time than a person who can walk to a nearby work location.

Time is our scarcest asset and WFH gives us more of it. For workers who now have an extra 1.5 hours per day, what will they do this with new time? The American Time Use Survey from 2019 provides some clues. On the days they did household activities, women spent an average of 2.5 hours on these activities, while men spent 1.9 hours.[18] Watching TV was the leisure activity that occupied the most time (2.8 hours per day), accounting for just over half of all leisure time, on average. Socializing and visiting with friends or attending or hosting social events accounted for an average of 38 minutes per day, and was the next most common leisure activity after watching TV. Adults living with young children spent an average of 2.2 hours per day providing primary childcare. Adults living in households where the youngest child was between the ages of 6 and 17 spent less than half as much time providing primary childcare to household children (48 minutes per day).

Raising children is both time-intensive and expensive. The ability to telecommute creates the possibility of a more equitable sharing of these responsibilities. This is likely to strengthen a marriage and reduce stress.[19] Most couples wrestle with dividing up time spent tending to the needs of the household; the so-called chore wars.[20] Reduced weekday commuting creates new possibilities for couples to revisit household responsibilities.[21] Those working at home can save extra time by multitasking. Household chores ranging from doing laundry to preparing meals to cleaning the house can all be simultaneously done while working when work involves steps such as running a statistical model or thinking about a specific problem.

One study set in China found that people are willing to give up five minutes of leisure for every one minute they can reduce their commute time.[22] If this large effect holds true in other nations, then this suggests that the stress effects of commuting are large. The disutility of commuting differs by income group and one's personal tastes. A person who loves his sports car may actually enjoy his commute as he listens to books on tape.[23]

To measure how much different workers gain from WFH requires special data. Ideally, a researcher could observe objective indicators of each worker's well-being when she is engaging in work from home and these same indicators for the same worker if she is not allowed to engage in work from home. Such great data would allow the researcher to measure how much each person gains from having greater freedom. Unfortunately, we face a missing data problem. For those select workers who now engage in WFH, we could ask them retrospective questions such as, "How much has your quality of life improved by engaging in WFH?"

Recent research has helped to fill this data gap. One recent field experiment set in China documented that those with a longer commute to their workplace value the right to work from home more than workers with a shorter commute. A Stanford research team accessed data for a major Chinese firm called CTrip, a 16,000-employee, NASDAQ-listed Chinese travel agency. Call center employees who volunteered to WFH were randomly assigned to work from home or in the office for nine months. Those who lived farther from the workplace were more likely to ask to continue to work from home when the experiment ended. Most of the call center workers were younger employees. This fact can create a concern that these individuals will shirk if a monitoring supervisor is not around. Perhaps surprisingly, employees who worked at home saw a 13 percent performance increase, mainly from an increase in time spent working during a shift and decreased sick days and time off. Interviewed workers reported fewer distractions and greater convenience when working from home. They also reported higher levels of work satisfaction and had their attrition rate fall by half. However, their promotion rate fell, possibly because they were out of sight of managers. The firm improved their productivity by 20 to 30 percent and saved an estimated $2,000 per year for each WFH employee. Following the experiment, the company allowed workers to reselect whether they wanted to continue WFH, with over half of them switching, leading to 22 percent of employees working from home.[24] This last fact about "switchers" raises an important point. WFH is an experience good. Each worker must experience WFH before they can declare "I love it" or "I hate it." Given our diverse talents and interests, some gain more than others from having this option. In a fair society, individuals are exposed to it on a trial basis and then reserve the option to "lock in" and engage in more WFH if this work arrangement improves their quality of life.

While the Chinese firm CTrip's workers gained from WFH, one should not extrapolate and jump to the conclusion that every firm's overall productivity will grow by allowing some of their workers to engage in WFH. Labor economists are partnering with major firms to use their administrative data to study worker productivity under different work configurations. Intuitively, we would like to observe the same worker's output per hour when she works from home versus when she works at an office. Ideally, we would also like to measure her well-being under both work configurations. The extreme conditions of 2020 sent many workers home, and this variation allows researchers to conduct a "before versus after" comparison to measure worker productivity dynamics. One recent study used data from a firm that is one of the world's largest IT services companies.[25] They have over 150,000 employees who work with clients across the globe. Most work in the home country, a rapidly developing Asian nation. In response to the COVID shock, the company abruptly switched all employees to WFH in March 2020. The company provided worker-level data for a large sample of more than 10,000 employees, for seventeen months before and during WFH, from its personnel records. The researchers document that the WFH workers work more hours and their output did not increase. This means that their productivity per hour worked declined. The researchers argue that dispersed WFH workers face higher communication and coordination costs.

These two case studies from Asia raise several key points. First, there is no "iron law" that WFH must raise each worker's productivity at a point in time or over time. Workers differ with respect to their skills, their ambitions, and under what environmental conditions they thrive. A key economic point is that workers know themselves! If firms create the work conditions (i.e., the menu of opportunity) to allow different workers to choose their own work arrangements, workers are more likely to choose the right fit for them as they understand that they must play by their "firm's rules" in order to continue to be employed. A second point to note in the case of the large Asian IT firm is that the finding of low WFH worker productivity in 2020 is a short-term result. The COVID crisis of 2020 was a surprise and firms had little time to optimize their operations. Going forward, I predict that firms will use their administrative data to help them to configure WFH to achieve the "win-win" of happy and productive workers. Families faced unique stresses in 2020 (as children could not go to school) that going forward stay-at-home workers will not face. In this sense, our 2020 experience with WFH that featured a bundle of the dread of a global pandemic and children stuck at home provides a "worst case" scenario preview of our future work experience with WFH as part of the "new normal."

Gains for Children

The children of parents who can engage in WFH will see more of their parents and their parents will be there for key events such as a child's sports competition or a music recital. Two-parent working households will gain more as the couple can mix and match times when each will be home and other times when they coordinate their respective activities. When I was a child growing up in the suburbs of New York City, my father never attended a single weekday school event because he was always in New York City at the hospital where he worked. In a WFH economy, one can adjust one's schedule to be more involved in a child's life in her residential community.

Children whose parents have divorced may now see more of each parent, as their activities and handoffs can be better coordinated given that they live in separate homes that are not likely to be close to each other. Remote work increases the likelihood that children have dinners with their parents. Such quality time can help children toward achieving their full potential. The ability of WFH workers to spend more time with their children raises the concern of an increase in inequality as the children of workers whose parents cannot engage in WFH (often the less educated) will not receive this benefit.[26]

Building Up Social Capital in the Residential Community

Leisure is more enjoyable when such time is spent with friends and family who share one's interests and hobbies. The joy of being with friends and engaging in a favorite group activity is even larger on a pleasant, low-pollution day.[27] As WFH workers spend more time in their residential communities, this strengthens these communities. Such social engagement builds up local social capital and this results in trust and greater understanding and empathy for one's neighbors. In geographic areas where there is more social capital, people are less likely to free ride and they will be more civically engaged.[28] For example, more people will vote, and will be more likely to protect common property and this reduces concerns about the "Tragedy of the Commons." In cities such as Rome, Italy, urban residents are strangers and invest little time disposing of dog waste or used cigarettes. Such litter degrades the commons as strangers do not think about the social consequences of their actions.

In his influential book *Bowling Alone*, Robert Putnam argues that Americans are engaging less with each other as they watch more television.[29] After reading Putnam's work, Dora Costa and I explored whether the rise of women's labor force participation reduced local social capital as women tended to be the backbone of such volunteer organizations because many mothers in the 1970s and 1980s were not working.[30] With the rise of remote work, people spend more time in and have and a greater incentive to invest in the social fabric of their residential communities because they have a greater stake in the community.

In 2021, the modern equivalent of the claim that we are not interacting face to face is that we are so addicted to our cell phones that we have substituted a virtual life for face-to-face communication. The rise of WFH will mean that such workers will spend more time online during working hours but they will actually have more free time to spend in their residential communities and with family.

With the rise of weekly remote work, people will be spending more time in their residential community and they will see more of their neighborhood friends. The residential community as a whole gains from such investments of time. As people invest more time getting to know each other, the community becomes stronger. People plant roots and are less likely to migrate away.[31]

Even on weekdays, WFH workers will not be rushing home from New York City to get back to the suburbs of New Jersey or

Connecticut. The same hour of leisure has differential effects on our well-being: for example, spending that hour on a crowded commuter train versus spending that hour resting after a good workday at home and then perhaps entertaining friends on a weekday or pursuing a hobby with some of them in your nearby residential area. As more neighbors are home during weekdays, neighbors will get to know each other better and this can even improve intergenerational connections as adults come to better know their neighbors' kids.

Face-to-face meetings with neighbors and friends are even more pleasant in temperate, low-pollution places. Over the last few decades, both air pollution and water pollution have sharply declined across the United States. The cause of such progress is due to the decline in industrial activity, cleaner automobiles (due to the Clean Air Act), and the sharp reduction in coal use for generating electric power. As environmental quality improves across America's cities, it is more enjoyable to spend more time outside and this leisure time is even more enjoyable when one can coordinate activities with friends. This further increases the joy of living in a residential community where you have friends. In a recent study set in China, we document that on polluted days people do not want to go out to restaurants because they would be exposed to more pollution. People are happier on a low-polluted day when they can go out and socialize with their friends.[32]

I have focused on WFH workers investing their time in making friends with their residential neighbors. Over the course of our lives, we make friends at every stage such as when we attend school or where we grew up when we were young. When one friend engages in WFH and one worker does not, the former can visit the latter. This life flexibility creates many new opportunities to remain in touch. When both friends engage in WFH, this creates even more opportunities to travel together and explore tourist destinations, while at the same time putting in the necessary hours to do one's job. For adults who are not responsible for young children, this new freedom offers exciting possibilities that improve our mental health and well-being.

Opportunities to Earn Extra Income and to Try New Jobs

During an economic boom, many people seek to work more hours.[33] By moonlighting, industrious people can earn more income or they can branch out and try something new to learn about their tastes and talents. This possibility of using remote work to experiment means that workers will have fewer life regrets about early life choices that locked them into a path. The desire, and the ability, to reinvent themselves can be good for people's mental health. Before 2020, moonlighting workers had to commute from their home to a second job and this additional commute discouraged them from engaging in extra work. Such workers were also limited in their ability to choose from interesting second jobs because they had to select among open jobs that were in their commuting range. WFH moonlighting relaxes both of these physical constraints.

WFH opens up opportunities for freelancers to do more contract work. They can decide what mix of tasks they like and then contract these out to firms and do the work remotely, as do the copy editor and indexer of this book. The growth of people who want to supply their services creates a two-sided platform and an opening for matching firms like Upwork. Such internet search firms have incentives to improve their algorithms for matching task demanders and task "doers" if there is an increase in people seeking such employment and entities seeking tasks to be completed. To appreciate this point, suppose that there were only ten people in the United States seeking moonlighting work to do copyediting while working at home. In this case, no good computer programmer would devote her time to develop the platform to match such individuals with people who are willing to pay to have another person read and edit their work. In contrast, if there are thousands of people who differ in their talents (can they translate Croatian?), then it becomes lucrative to design the matching software to make this new market work. Note the chicken and egg issue here. If a good computer programmer codes up a better algorithm for matching workers to the right jobs, then more potential employers will be drawn to the website because they anticipate that they will be happy with the workers they hire on that platform. Workers with the skills will anticipate that they will find a good job on the platform. This anticipation creates an incentive for workers to build up these skills and then use this platform. The net effect of this dynamic is a more vibrant internet labor economy.

A key geographic point arises here. In the pre-WFH economy, ambitious workers faced limits on what they could do and who they could work for. Their limited commuting range determined their opportunities. For those who live far from cities, they faced a very conscribed set of labor opportunities. In contrast, in our new WFH economy these individuals have a much broader menu of potential firms they can work for and do different tasks. This creates new opportunity and excitement for such individuals if internet platforms can help to match them with potential employers. Firms such as Upwork have stepped in to try to make these matches, and Upwork only gets paid if a successful match is made.

The Rising Demand for Flexibility in an Increasingly Uncertain World

During the 1950s and 1960s, many US manufacturing cities featured a dominant industry such as car manufacturing in Detroit or steel production in Pittsburgh. Such cities boomed as the industry boomed but the city's prosperity was tied to the continued success of these industries. These cities suffered when Detroit experienced a reduction in car demand in the 1970s as Japan increased exports to the United States. Pittsburgh's steel factories faced competition from mini-mills distributed across the nation. As these cities declined, workers in these core industries who owned local homes faced the double shock of less labor income and reduced asset values.

Going forward, areas that are home to more WFH workers will face less income risk due to local "boom/bust" cycles. During a boom, footloose workers move into an area experiencing a rising demand for workers. The recent fracking boom in North Dakota highlighted this dynamic as the area's count of young men earning relatively high incomes surged.[34] During a local recession, those with roots have strong incentives to remain and they could suffer a large loss in income in an economy that does not feature WFH. The ability to engage in WFH allows a qualified individual to remain in a place where she has roots while enjoying access to viable employment. The ability to find "gig work" reduces worker unemployment risk. This in turn reduces reliance on government redistribution programs such as unemployment insurance. Economists have coined the term "self-protection" to reflect actions an individual can take to reduce her risk of suffering a negative outcome. Access to "gig work" reduces one's risk of being unemployed (i.e., looking for work but not having a job). Economists have emphasized that unemployment is costly for society (because unemployment insurance is funded from tax revenue) and it is costly for an individual because the time one spends unemployed can be debilitating as one is more likely to engage in destructive behavior. The rise of WFH creates new employment prospects that reduce these risks.

At the same time that workers have a larger menu of employment choices in a WFH economy, each worker also faces more competition with other workers from around the world. In the past, a person who lives in a town of 50,000 people did not have that many job opportunities in a thirty-minute drive from where he lives but he also did not face that much competition for new jobs in the area.

In our globalized economy featuring tough competition between firms in different nations, US workers face rising job risk. Few of us spend our careers at a single firm. Economists have grappled with how to protect worker incomes from rising job loss risk. Nobel laureate Robert Shiller has called for new markets providing labor market insurance against unemployment.[35] Shiller has suggested a new type of insurance to protect people's consumption when their local economy suffers from a recession:

> I proposed a different idea, which I called "livelihood insurance."
> As the name implies, livelihood insurance is...aimed at dealing
> with long-term changes in the labor market, rather than assuring
> temporary wage levels. It would also rely on the market rather than
> a government program. With livelihood insurance, a private insurer would pay a stream of income to a policyholder if an index of
> average income in the insured person's occupation and region de-

clines substantially. Moreover, this income stream would continue for as long as the index stays down, not just for a couple of years.[36]

For those who are WFH eligible, remote work represents a type of implicit insurance because such workers can moonlight using platforms such as Upwork. This smooths their incomes during times when the local labor market offers few opportunities and this means that they will not be forced to quickly move to another area. In the past, unemployed people often had to reduce the asking price for their home in order to be able to quickly move to another location to secure employment. When workers can smooth their incomes by engaging in WFH, this adjustment can be more leisurely and this will reduce stress and wealth loss.

The ability to use the internet to access work during bad times in one's local labor market matters more than ever because Americans are increasingly less likely to migrate across local labor markets.[37] Middle-aged workers who have planted roots in a specific area do not want to move away from their comfort zone. Over the course of our life we are less and less willing to migrate because the long-run benefits of migrating to a better local labor market decline with age since we have fewer working years to recoup the migration costs. Young people have strong incentives to seek out the right geographic area to move to early in life.[38] People want to move to one area and plant roots there.

Workers who are tied to a place and do not have the WFH option face downward earnings risk if there are few local employers. This puts such workers at risk of being exploited by the few major employers in a location. When large firms such as Walmart enter local smaller cities, they compete and undercut existing retailers through pricing competition. Through this competition, smaller retailers go bankrupt and Walmart emerges as the big local retailer. In this case, Walmart emerges as a local monopolist in the labor market and can try to exploit local workers by not paying them because the middle-aged workers do not want to move and do not have good local alternatives. Some labor scholars have argued that this dynamic explains why the share of income going to capital over labor has increased over time.[39] In such a setting where workers face the possibility of being exploited by the big employers in town, the ability to telecommute protects their earnings because this represents their alternative option. The ability to telecommute puts a lower bound on what local employers can pay you because you hold the option of telecommuting.

Coping with Family Responsibilities

The United States is a large nation, and people have family and friends scattered across it. A company's physical location on the map ties down the firm's workers to a vicinity of its headquarters, which raises both the transport cost and the psychic cost of having ties to all the other people in one's life.

Many people have strong ties to the place where they are born. They may have family and friends living there and they have positive memories of their early days. A *New York Times* article from 2014 reports that 71 percent of people born in Alabama live there as adults while 64 percent of people born in Colorado live in Colorado as adults.[40] The 36 percent of people born in Colorado but not living there now may have reasons to return. In the past, before WFH, this option to reconnect with one's past and social ties would have been more economically costly.

The possibility of having the option to telecommute offers eligible workers freedom and flexibility for meeting our life goals and responsibilities. In an increasingly risky world, the option to sometimes engage in remote work will be increasingly valuable.

Over the course of a forty-year career, workers will find themselves in unexpected situations. A worker may have a husband who has a surprise health problem. A worker may have a widowed mother who needs to be taken care of. In such cases, telecommuting allows the worker to remain committed both to the firm and to take care of family needs during a stressful, anxious time. In the short term, a working parent with a young sick child will benefit from having the flexibility to attend to a sick child or a happy occasion such as attending a school play or a sporting event.

Anticipating the demographic arc of our lives helps us to plan for our future. Young people anticipate that in a few decades they will be middle aged and at that point their parents will be old. A person who grew up in St. Louis and has moved to Seattle will have trouble tending to the needs of aging parents who continue to live in St. Louis. The ability to engage in remote work helps workers to tend to their intergenerational family responsibilities without shirking on their job.[41]

College graduates are more likely to move farther distances away from where they grew up relative to less educated people. Given that those with more education are more likely to be WFH eligible, this means that the rise of WFH allows the more educated to have the "best of both worlds": accessing the amenities and the career opportunities offered by geographic opportunities while still being connected to their aging parents. Recent research has documented that among couples who both have college degrees, roughly 50 percent live more than thirty miles from both of their mothers and only 18 percent live within thirty miles of both mothers.[42]

During a time of rising longevity, the demands on the middle aged to take care of their aging parents rise. The misery caused by the COVID crisis at nursing homes serves to underscore this issue of who invests their time to take care of the aging. The ability for workers to be able to tend to their parents for extended periods of time allows families to make the best of a challenging situation.

The opportunity to engage in working from home caught us by surprise in early 2020. When we have little time to react to a sudden new opportunity, this limits how we reconfigure our lives to make the most of an opportunity. In this chapter, I explored how eligible workers' quality of life can change when they are afforded more flexibility in choosing when they go to work and where to work (for example, engaging in WFH while caring for a sick child or parent).

Going forward, workers will anticipate that they could have the option to engage in WFH. This expectation influences their investment choices concerning their career path and their educational investments. These synergistic investments help individuals to unlock the full potential of WFH.

2 *Medium-Term Gains for Workers*

The University of Chicago Booth School of Business is one of the nation's top business schools. The graduate students at this elite program have outstanding undergraduate academic credentials and impressive work resumes. By their mid-thirties, there is a large and growing gender gap in the average pay for women versus men for this subset of elite young people.[1] "Three proximate factors account for the large and rising gender gap in earnings: differences in training prior to MBA graduation, differences in career interruptions, and differences in weekly hours. The greater career discontinuity and shorter work hours for female MBAs are largely associated with motherhood."[2]

This chapter explores how WFH will create new opportunities for women who both want to have families and to have fulfilling careers. I argue that the rise of WFH will help to close the gender earnings gap. There are other key groups in our society who will also gain due to the rise of WFH. Minorities, environmentalists, and those with strong roots to their hometowns will all gain from the new freedoms afforded by WFH.[3]

Work from home (or a coffee shop near one's home) increases our menu of choices over where we work, live, and play. Each worker who is WFH eligible will face tradeoffs about how to allocate one's time. Such workers commute less but lose out on face-to-face interaction at work.

Access to information technology such as our cell phones and computers makes it possible to decentralize and be productive while located far from work colleagues. In the modern economy, there is no "free lunch." WFH workers will face increased competition from qualified global workers who compete for the same jobs in the emerging global marketplace for online talent. By anticipating the opportunities and challenges of the "new rules of the WFH game," workers are better able to adapt and compete.

Spreading Out and Migrating to Areas Featuring Cheaper and Newer Homes

Land farther from city centers is cheaper. Consider the property at 845 Stonehaven Rd. SW, Atlanta, GA 30331. In October 2020, this 2,912-square-foot home featuring five bedrooms and three bathrooms sells for $299,900 or roughly $100 per square foot. This home is eighteen miles from downtown Atlanta. There is brand-new construction such as 212 Stone Creek Ct. in Temple, Georgia, selling for $196,000. This home has four bedrooms and three bathrooms and 1,600 square feet. This area is forty-five miles from downtown Atlanta. A family that can make a down payment of 25 percent would be able to purchase this house by obtaining a thirty-year fixed mortgage of $709 a month at a 3.92 percent interest rate. A rule of thumb is that one should spend no more than 30 percent of one's pre-tax income on housing. This suggests that a family whose total household annual income equals roughly $50,000 per year could afford to buy this house. This example shows how the combination of suburban living and access to cheap housing finance allows more of the American middle class to access new housing.

New survey research highlights that WFH-eligible workers desire such affordable, larger housing. In a recent report based on a survey of over 20,000 Americans, Upwork's economists conclude that the shift to remote work will sharply increase near-term migration in the United States as many WFH-eligible workers seek to move to less expensive housing markets. Over half of the respondents who say that they will move plan to move over two hours away from their current location.[4]

Transportation speeds play a key role in determining where people live. Hundreds of years ago when we only had access to walking (about a three-mile-per-hour commuting speed), we chose to live within five miles of where we worked. Over time as we have had access to horses, trolley cars, private cars, and subways and trains, we have had a greater ability to spread out, but given the realities of commuting, most of us have chosen to live close to our employer.

In England, high-speed trains provide access connecting the suburbs to London. China, Japan, and South Korea rely on bullet trains to connect fringe areas to their superstar cities.[5] Such transport infrastructure allows workers to live far from these highly productive and highly expensive city centers. Highway construction in the United States has created new opportunities for the middle class to live far from cities.[6] When commuters can access a fast transportation mode, each now faces a lower commuting cost per mile of commuting. Some will choose to move farther out.

Engaging in remote work a few days a week is similar to accessing a faster transportation technology. A person who works in downtown Atlanta will take a new look at housing in the distant suburbs if she can engage in WFH, because if she only goes to work two times a week, her total commute time declines by 60 percent. Suppose that the average commute from a distant suburb to a city work location is one hour each way. In the pre-WFH economy, this required ten hours of total commuting per week. A WFH worker would commute for four hours a week from this location.

This reduction in hours commuting each week actually encourages workers to move farther out. In energy economics, this is known as the "rebound effect." The rebound effect posits that when one buys an energy-efficient product, one may increase one's energy consumption. This seemingly counterintuitive claim depends on the law of demand. A Toyota Prius is a highly fuel efficient vehicle that achieves roughly 50 miles per gallon. If one always drives 10,000 miles a year, then a person who switches from a light truck to a Prius will reduce her gasoline consumption, as she now only consumes 200 gallons per year. But, note that the Prius driver faces a lower price per mile of driving. If the price of gasoline is $2 a gallon, then to drive a mile costs this driver just $200*1/50 = 4$ cents. Facing this low price, the Prius driver may choose to drive more miles. If this mileage demand response is price-sensitive enough, then the purchase of a fuel-efficient vehicle may cause the driver to consume more gasoline!

This same "rebound" logic applies in the case of WFH. WFH lowers the total hours of commuting for any given distance from where one works and this price effect encourages people to move farther out. At the fringe of cities, there is farmland. Suburbanites will start to bid for this farmland and for it to be converted into new housing.[7]

As some WFH-eligible workers choose to spread out and live

at the fringe of metropolitan areas or move to other areas, this reduces the aggregate demand housing in the center city and in the nearby suburbs. This in turn increases housing affordability for everyone including those who are not WFH eligible. This dynamic highlights how factors that affect one group (the WFH-eligible workers) impact everyone else in the economy. In my own recent empirical research, I have used Zillow data and document that this dynamic is already playing out.[8]

The ability to move to cheaper, better housing without suffering a huge increase in commuting times will offer the greatest benefits to immigrants and minorities who have not accumulated much wealth from their parents. Studies of racial inequality have noted the huge wealth gap between whites and blacks. In 2013, the median white household had a wealth level thirteen times higher than the median black household.[9] When a household seeks to buy a home but does not have access to wealth, the potential buyer will need to obtain a larger loan to finance a more expensive home. The alternative is to live in less desirable areas where housing is cheaper but crime is higher and the local schools are worse, or to choose to live farther from the productive city core and face longer commutes.

In a recent National Bureau of Economic Research (NBER) working paper, I document that black families are less likely than white, Hispanic, and Asian families to purchase homes in expensive housing markets such as California and Seattle and Boston.[10] In expensive housing markets where homes may cost $1 million, banks will often require a 20 percent down payment. If black households do not have $200,000 in cash, they will not be able to buy such a home. This matters because America's most productive cities feature the highest home prices. If minorities cannot afford to purchase housing in such areas, then they will live and work in less productive places.

Given these access challenges, African American workers who are eligible for WFH are likely to greatly gain from this option as they will be able to access the quality of housing that they have not had equal access to before. In areas such as distant suburban areas in Atlanta and Houston, there is relatively cheaper housing that also features access to shopping and jobs.[11] In recent decades, blacks have disproportionately lived in center city neighborhoods featuring aging housing that is often in low-quality condition. In my own recent research set in Baltimore, I document that such living conditions raise the likelihood that black children are exposed to elevated lead levels because lead exposure comes from living in old housing and living close to densely populated road networks.

The rise of WFH creates new freedoms that were not possible during a time of daily commuting. Such exurban families do not have to lose access to center city life. With the rise of Airbnb, such families have the option to rent someone else's urban housing unit, which allows the family to visit the city during off-peak times to enjoy the city's culture and amenities.

When commuters are not tied down to choosing a home close to where they work, they have the freedom to choose from a much larger menu of affordable housing options. WFH allows each person to pursue her own vision of "the good life." When people have access to cheaper housing, some respond by having larger families.[12] People who want to have a large family move to places where housing is cheaper and they can afford a home with more bedrooms. Over the course of one's life, this vision may change as young people and older people are attracted to the big center cities while many people with young children seek out more space.

An ongoing debate among urbanists asks whether the rise of information technology (IT such as cell phones and the internet) reduces the demand to live in cities. In an influential article, Jess Gaspar and Edward Glaeser argue that information technology increases the demand for urban living because email and access to social media such as Facebook allows one with specific interests to meet the "right people" and discover the best places in the city given one's individual passions. They argue that technology improves the urban quality-of-life experience.[13] In a similar sense, the rise of WFH offers the possibility of quality versus quantity tradeoff. Many WFH-eligible workers may reduce the quantity of their trips to work but configure their work schedule such that they maximize the quality of those fewer interactions when they do commute to work.

Environmentalists Migrate to Areas Featuring Natural Beauty

In 1900, 27.6 percent of Americans lived in the Northeast and 34.6 percent in the Midwest. In 2019, 17.1 percent of Americans lived in the Northeast and 20.8 percent in the Midwest.[14] The American people are moving to the Sun Belt as they seek out warmer winters. The declining price and improved quality of air conditioners over time accelerated this trend as summer humidity in the Southeast became more tolerable.

People pay more for the same home if it is located in a place with a great climate. Such workers also often earn less in such places because they pay both through lower earnings and higher home prices for local amenities. In my research with Dora Costa, we document that in recent decades people are paying a higher real estate premium to live in places such as California that have a great climate.[15] In geographic areas that are desirable, such as the California beach areas that feature great beauty and mild climate, home prices are higher than in places featuring more challenging extreme weather in winter and summer. In the case of real estate markets, there is no "free lunch." Home prices act as the great equalizer as they represent a type of entry fee for living in paradise.

More educated people are willing to pay more to live a "green" lifestyle.[16] Given that US college graduation rates continue to rise, this means that there will be a rising demand for living in and visiting places in America that offer this opportunity. The United States features great beauty as there are multiple national parks and many places to ski, fish, and hike. Many Americans have a desire to live near water to enjoy the benefits of boating and exercising along rivers, lakes, and streams.

Before the WFH opportunity arose, one might be viewed as a surfer, hippie, or ski bum if one chose to forsake a lucrative job in a big city to live in an environmental paradise. Remote work allows more people to choose where to live based on lifestyle considerations. Golfers will choose to live in different places than those who love to fish or hike. People differ with respect to how they rank different locations in terms of quality of life. Skiers will rank areas differently than specialty wine growers and golfers. Leisure time is more enjoyable when one can enjoy it with friends and have access to a menu of activities that one values.

Footloose WFH workers who have similar tastes for environmental passions will tend to choose the same locations. As more nature lovers now have the freedom to move where they want to go and are less tied down by their work location, they will cluster together close to beautiful places such as national parks and skiing areas and surfing areas. Communities of like-minded people will form and enact rules and regulations that preserve the area's quality of life. Tourist websites will convey the environmental experience offered by such a location, perhaps in the foothills of a national park, and more people will visit it.

The concentration of educated, well-paid WFH workers will bring enough local purchasing power to create sufficient local demand for niche variety products and stores such that a green "consumer city" will take root nearby. For example, in an oceanside surfing community vegetarian restaurants will open and so will bike-sharing firms. Such synergies between the private sector and the area's natural beauty will make the area even more desirable for like-minded people to move there. Young people will anticipate other young people moving there. In the late 1960s, young hippies moved to Haight-Ashbury in San Francisco to join the counterculture scene. Environmentalists anticipate that they will meet like-minded people and have access to stores and consumer experiences that they value when they move to environmental paradise places such as Boulder, Colorado, or Santa Monica, California. Such beautiful locations solve a coordination problem. Environmentalists who do not know each other want to live in close proximity to each other but cannot communicate with each other to agree about where to go. Beautiful places draw them in because of their direct beauty and the anticipation that other like-minded people will move there and this reinforces the area's appeal.

Elected officials in these naturalist areas can build on this momentum by introducing legislation that creates "green lifestyle infrastructure" such as bike lanes, electric vehicle charging stations, and other rules to further enhance the quality of life for environmentalists. Such communities serve a social value as they represent a type of "demonstration" project, showing the rest of the nation what life could be like in such a community. The rise of Airbnb allows more people to visit the area to experience it for themselves without having the tourist experience of staying at a hotel.

Each of these environmentalist hubs will need to make a decision concerning its zoning. A NIMBY issue has arisen across the United States such that beautiful places choose not to build much housing. This effect is especially pronounced in progressive cities such as Berkeley, California.[17] When a high-demand area does not build new housing, home prices soar and the middle-class and poorer people are not able to afford to live there. In the US today, local land use policies are determined locally by the incumbent residents, and they can choose to effectively lock out outsiders. Such individuals often rationalize their "slow growth" strategies by saying that they want to preserve the character of their area. While there is certainly some truth to this statement, by limiting local growth this limits the ability of outsiders to move to paradise.

The insiders would counter that their home area will not continue to be paradise if more growth takes place. Such a prediction is based on a simple extrapolation notion that more people translate into more resource consumption and more congestion of local services. A key idea in economics is to allow prices to reflect scarcity. If a jurisdiction's water, energy, and traffic space are in high demand, then allow their prices to rise to reflect this scarcity. Such price adjustments will allow a growing town to not run out of water or electricity or feature congested roads. Quality-of-life degradation takes place in cases where growth proceeds and these resource prices are priced artificially low by local governments. If the new entrants to the area are richer than the incumbents, then allowing in-migration to the "green paradise" will raise the average tax base and fund better local public services.

Migration as a Strategy to Adapt to Emerging Climate Change Risk

During an age of rising climate change risk, some areas such as Northern California face elevated fire risk while other areas such as Miami face greater sea level rise risk. During the 2020 COVID challenge, the American West faced many serious forest fires that heavily polluted the air. These shocks portend even worse future shocks because global greenhouse gas emissions concentrations continue to rise.

There is a certain predictability to which geographic areas are vulnerable to what types of climate shocks. Some parts of the country face greater hurricane risk than others while some areas face more wildfire risk and other areas face greater risk of significant sea level rise. Geographic areas that prove to be better equipped to handle these challenges, either due to their topographical features or to wise local governance, will become increasingly attractive. The ability to "vote with our feet" and migrate to safer areas provides new safety opportunities and peace of mind for such migrants but also has a second beneficial effect. Areas that lose migrants because they fail to be climate resilient will suffer a loss of the local tax base and this competition for people and jobs gives lagging places an incentive to "wake up."

In the 2020 presidential election, Joe Biden raised the issue of the climate change challenge and Donald Trump tended to dismiss this issue. Even Republican counties will be more likely to invest in safety precautions if their area experiences accelerated population loss. States and areas that lose population lose their tax base and lose political clout as their count of congressional representatives shrinks. This fact encourages elected officials to invest in climate resilience. The rise of WFH increases the ability of people who seek such climate safety to move to new areas. In the past, such individuals might choose to remain in a region such as Northern California because of the area's productivity advantages despite the fear of rising climate risks. WFH offers our diverse population the flexibility such that those among us who are deeply concerned about climate resilience can make their locational choices by prioritizing the avoidance of such risk while suffering less of an income loss.

Does One Suffer a Career Cost from Locating Far from "The Action"?

By moving physically farther away from one's office, one raises the price of going to the office in terms of commute time and this reduces face-to-face interaction. The cost to the individual and the firm will vary on a case-by-case basis. Will the worker feel out of the loop? Will the worker learn less and make fewer valuable career connections? Will the boss give you worse assignments because you are not one of his pets? Will you be taken less seriously?

Consider a company where some ambitious workers go to the headquarters on a daily basis while others seeking flexibility only go in two days a week. The latter group may worry that they are sending a signal that they are not committed to the cause. If WFH workers actually do face an "out of sight, out of mind" issue with their bosses, then a strategic game will emerge. Suppose that

Matthew is an ambitious worker who seeks to be promoted at a firm and he knows that his rivals are WFH workers who only go to work one day a week. Matthew might say to himself, "As Woody Allen put it, 90 percent of life is just showing up. If I go to the office three days a week, this extra facetime will allow me to impress the bosses and I'm more likely to get the promotion." The bosses should anticipate this strategic thinking and pass a rule saying, "All workers can only come to the office two days a week." Such a rule levels the playing field and limits the inefficient competition to be the "boss's pet."

During the COVID crisis firms had to allow workers to engage in WFH to reduce their exposure to the virus. Going forward, each firm has strong incentives to experiment with different configurations of how it arranges its workforce. As the company learns about worker and overall productivity, the firm has strong incentives to reoptimize as it learns. If remote WFH workers feel out of the loop, then this creates an incentive for companies that hire such workers to open smaller headquarters similar to Amazon HQ2 and spread them out across the nation. Such satellite offices allow spread-out WFH workers to go to the nearest one to connect to headquarters. Over time, workers learn about whether they face hidden costs of engaging in WFH (i.e., being "out of the loop"). The firm retains the option to encourage such workers to commute more often to these regional headquarters.

Artificial Intelligence as the "Matchmaker"

In the recent past, a worker located "close to the action" to raise the chances of receiving plum work assignments. My mother has learned this point in the New York City legal system. She is a lawyer who receives cases assigned to her by a city clerk. The city clerk can decide which lawyer is assigned to handle a case. This city clerk has the power here to choose someone he likes. If he is more favorably disposed to people whom he has met more often face to face, then lawyers who engage in WFH and rarely visit this clerk are at a disadvantage when it comes to being assigned new cases and their earnings will suffer. While there are several special features related to this specific case of the city clerk handing out assignments, one worth noting is that the city clerk works for a nonprofit entity.

This is a very different task assignment setting than a for-profit firm. The rise of reliance on artificial intelligence (AI) and algorithms for assigning workers to tasks may diminish the costs of physically "being out of the loop." In the movie *Caddyshack*, the young caddies gathered around the leader each morning to find out which caddy would be assigned to which golfer. Some golfers had heavier clubs and were worse tippers. Thus, the person assigning caddies to golfers had substantial discretionary power in deciding who would receive the best jobs. In our market economy, this scenario plays out in many settings. If one does not want to pay kickbacks (i.e., bribes), one must put in facetime with the boss to be more likely to earn a plum assignment due to favoritism.

In the emerging WFH economy, algorithms are playing a larger role in assigning workers to tasks. At firms such as Upwork, an algorithm matches remote workers to tasks. This means that the "allocator" (i.e., the guy in *Caddyshack* who assigned the caddies) has been replaced by a formula that is continually refined as new information about past assignments of workers to tasks are evaluated by both parties. After an Uber ride, both the rider and the driver rate the other party. Such information is used by Uber to continuously update its allocation mechanism.

AI matching WFH workers with firms who seek to hire such workers reduces concerns about being physically out of the loop. Firms such as Upwork only get paid when they successfully match a gig WFH worker with an employer. This creates strong incentives for such a firm to invest in the software to create good matches. If a firm is disappointed with the quality of work by a worker with whom Upwork matched them, then the firm may not use this "middleman" again. Upwork gets paid 30 percent of the earnings paid in each case and this provides the incentive to invest in a software that matches the right workers to the job in question.

In the pre-WFH economy, it seems that many people were badly matched with their jobs. Pessimistic anthropology research has claimed that many Americans do not like their jobs and are merely going through the motions to be paid. In his book with the provocative title *Bullshit Jobs*, David Graeber claims that millions of American workers waste their adult years working at jobs that they hate because they do not challenge them and they are not emotionally rewarding and do not create lasting value.[18] Such a claim is both important and highly cynical about modern working life. It hints at huge inefficiency as people sit at a desk and wish that they were somewhere else pursuing their true passion. If Graeber is correct, then American capitalism has brought about a huge misallocation of our scarce time as people are not doing the work they are actually passionate about. Graeber's book was written about our pre-zoom world (i.e., 2019 and earlier). For people to spend decades of their lives trapped in employment misery suggests that our system is not optimized to match the right worker to the right job. A "good match" should be one that is mutually beneficial to the firm and the worker and where the worker gains more than just a paycheck.

Suburbanites are likely to gain more from the rise of internet-matched remote work. A suburban resident only has a limited set of job alternatives that are a close commute to where she lives. In contrast, on the internet a platform such as Upwork features many different jobs offering a menu of different opportunities. This raises the likelihood that a worker with specific passions and talents can be better matched to the "right" job.

The Gender Earnings Gap

Based on Census Bureau data from 2018, women of all races earned, on average, just 82 cents for every $1 earned by men of all races. This ratio is determined by comparing the median annual earnings for women working full-time, year-round, to those of their male counterparts.[19]

Labor economists have offered several interconnected explanations for this ugly fact. Some make an "apples and oranges" point that the average man has more market skill than the average woman. This is not a statement about innate ability. Instead, one's skill in young adulthood depends on a series of life choices such as training in STEM fields and knowledge of valued skills such as computer programming and statistical analysis. A second explanation is that women continue to bear the majority of the family responsibilities for rearing children and this cuts into their marketplace ambitions and limits their opportunities. Economists have studied the earnings penalty for becoming a parent. Men face no such penalty while women do face a significant earnings penalty that varies across nations. This earnings penalty is 11 percent in Spain, 20 percent in Denmark, 30 percent in the United States, and 60 percent in Germany. The child's school day and summer schedule require a flexibility that interferes with many typical workplace schedules.[20] Men and women of the same age differ in labor market experience because young women's work spells are interrupted by childcare responsibilities and seeking jobs offering hour flexibility.[21]

There are additional explanations for the earnings gap, including that male bosses discriminate against women, which leads to differential mentoring and pay. If men and women have differential access to capital, then women will face greater challenges in launching their own businesses. Many women also move to cities that promote their spouse's career but offer them fewer opportunities. Recent economics research has documented that socialization at work tends to help men as they get to know their bosses over drinks and participating in hobbies such as golf.[22]

Will WFH Increase Married Women's Labor Force Participation?

The majority of Americans live in the suburbs of metropolitan areas. Many married women live in suburbia with a spouse and young children. In the past, these individuals, many of whom are college educated, chose not to work. Many upper-middle-class families with young children live in the suburbs because the suburbs offer more affordable, larger homes with backyards.

A spouse, often the wife, who stays home has limited labor market opportunities in close vicinity to her suburban home. Many mothers with young children might consider part-time work but they face commuting costs. The greatest variety of job opportunities are located in the city center, but it does not make sense to commute to the city center and then work a half day. Mothers with young children and school-age children often value being close to home where their children go to school. Urban economists have documented that when confronted with these tradeoffs, many suburban female adults chose not to work in an economy where WFH has not been an option.[23] Commuting costs create an important inefficiency in our labor market. There are talented women who want to work at least part of the day but the realities of the commute limit their ability to do so. WFH solves this problem for them.

New empirical research documents that women are willing to sacrifice earnings in return for shorter commutes to work. The French labor market has certain institutional features that allow researchers to quantify this tradeoff. French job seekers must declare to the Public Employment Service (PES) the minimum wage and the maximum commute they are willing to accept. As their statements matter for the job search services provided by the PES, they have an incentive to be attentive and to answer truthfully.[24] Due to these policy features, the economists observe where each unemployed person lives and where they take a job and the wage they earn when they take a job. Relative to men, women take jobs at lower wages closer to where they live. This distaste for commuting explains the 15 percent male/female wage gap in France.

This case study from France has key implications for American women. Most American married women live in the suburbs, in low-density areas featuring few employers, and this reduces the likelihood that each woman can find an interesting part-time job close by. Without such good local matches, each woman has less of an incentive to work and this means that with each passing year a divergence takes place between her and her full-time working (often male) contemporaries who she went to school with. The scarcity of good jobs offering part-time work in the suburbs, a location that she and her spouse chose, diminishes her career prospects. Before the rise of WFH, educated women were closing down their career prospects by choosing to prioritize the well-being of their children and their family. This interplay between a family's demographics and the cold realities of the urban economics of commuting is crucial here for understanding how earnings gaps emerge.

The rise of WFH offers a new employment option for stay-at-home mothers. Women who have previously worked for an employer can choose to work part-time from home rather than quit working. This arrangement preserves the match-specific worker/firm relationship capital that has been developed. The anticipation by the woman that she can continue to work part-time with the firm and have the option later in life, such as when the children are grown, to increase her hours creates strong incentives to continue the relationship.[25] Women who continue to work for their original employer have greater continuity in their careers and greater life balance.

Stay-at-home parents have new employment options in our internet economy. Over the last few decades many women have been self-employed.[26] Such an arrangement gives them greater flexibility over their hours and days of work. The rise of remote work could further increase opportunities for them. Internet platforms such as Upwork are two-sided platforms as workers seeking employment post their resumes and employers seeking workers post their tasks. Artificial intelligence (AI) algorithms play a key matchmaking role here by curating the set of job opportunities a person sees. I set up my profile on Upwork and was impressed with the alternative tasks that I was offered by the AI. As with any two-sided matching platform, the more job offerings an applicant sees, the more likely that person will find value in the platform. In this sense, as remote work grows as a socially high-status activity, this process will gain its own momentum.

As stay-at-home spouses earn more income, this boosts the family's finances and helps to reduce variability of household consumption because the family is no longer solely reliant on the one "breadwinner." This should reduce family stress and increase the quality of life of the stay-at-home spouse.[27]

Balancing Work and Family

Many women, seeking workplace flexibility, are drawn to such fields as veterinary medicine, pharmacy, and optometry. In the 1970s, 10 percent of new veterinarians were female while today it has jumped to 80 percent! "What are the reasons for women's enormous inroads in this field? Compelling evidence suggests that the increasing ability of many veterinarians to schedule their hours and reduce or eliminate on-call, night, and weekend hours has been a contributory factor."[28] Such occupational choices are driven both by personnel preferences and by seeking to minimize anticipating challenges in balancing various responsibilities.

In other occupations such as the law or investment banking, an ugly self-fulfilling prophecy can emerge. If the firm's best guess is that a young woman is likely to quit soon, such as to raise a family, then this creates an incentive for the firm to reduce its costly training and mentoring of the worker, which in turn makes it more likely that the young worker will quit because the firm has failed to put in the time and effort to mentor her and she does not feel valued. Economists label this differential treatment of workers by gender "statistical discrimination." Statistical discrimination refers to the case when a decision maker imputes the group average—in this case the quit rate for women of a given age—to predict an individual's propensity to leave. Firms often engage in statistical discrimination when they are missing data. The "missing data" in this case pertains to whether a specific worker will quit to raise her child. Given that this key data is not known, a firm then relies on its historical data to calculate what percentage of women of the same age have quit in the recent past. This is the firm's best guess of the likelihood that a given worker will quit.

To appreciate this sensitive point, suppose that 50 percent of thirty-three-year-old women working as associates at a law firm quit the firm to start a family. The partners at such a firm can calculate this fact based on their data over the past decade. This fact actually creates an incentive for the firm to engage in more mentoring of young male associates at the firm because they are less likely to quit.

In the pre-WFH world, a mother of young children would be unlikely to work part-time if she lived in the suburbs. The commuting alone and the responsibilities involved with a young child would eat up too much of the day to make this a worthwhile investment. The good news here is that the rise of WFH helps to escape this ugly equilibrium. A female worker who seeks to raise children can signal to the bosses that she will work from home and perhaps work 40 percent fewer hours than her male counterparts during the child's early life but that she aspires to ratchet up her hours in the medium term. The firm will want to retain talented individuals and will be more likely to mentor her along the way to accommodate her work/life balance.[29] More men might be willing to be the primary childcare provider in the family if they can engage in some work from home. This dynamic would also contribute to an increase in a mother's labor force participation.

Earnings penalties for job interruptions differ greatly by type of advanced degree. Researchers have sought to estimate this penalty using data from the Harvard and Beyond (H&B) survey data. The H&B surveyed members of Harvard College's graduating classes from 1969 to 1992. "A large fraction of the women (and men) in these classes—around 60 to 65 percent—pursued one of the four advanced degrees: MBA, JD, MD, and PhD. The penalty incurred from taking time off is largest proportionately for MBAs. Translated into the fraction of earnings forgone, MBAs give up 41 percent, PhDs and JDs 29 percent, and MDs just 16 percent for a job interruption equivalent to 18 months during the 15 years after receiving their BA...At 10 to 16 years out, 23 percent of Booth School MBA women who are in the labor force work part time."[30]

Goldin and Katz, professors of economics at Harvard, conclude that women's balancing of family and career causes these earnings gaps to emerge between men and women. Going forward, as young women anticipate that they will face this same challenge, those who seek to have such "work/life" balance will make investments to prepare for WFH. The expectation that young women will be able to engage in WFH helps them to better balance careers and family. Such young women will have greater incentives to invest in their skills because they will anticipate that they will have greater workforce attachment and more choices over who to work for if they have WFH-eligible skills.[31]

The historical fact that the gender gap increases with age does not need to be a future fact. As women engage in WFH this will signal their commitment to remain in the workforce. Their firms have an incentive to anticipate this dynamic and will respond by investing more in mentoring and developing the skills of these workers. A key point here is that the profit motive encourages such firms to cultivate the talent of their workers. If this dynamic game plays out, then the synergies between the investments made by the worker and by her firm help to raise her productivity and her lifetime earnings. In this case, the rise of WFH helps to close the gender gap.[32]

A key unknown relates to whether eligible women will engage in more WFH on average than men and what are the consequences of such differential engagement in WFH. Suppose at a given company that the average man goes to the office four days a week, while the average woman with children goes to the office two days a week. Each person knows his/her own personal priorities concerning their career ambitions and their personal goals and responsibilities at home. A valid concern here is that this work arrangement will lower the probability that women are promoted in the organization because on average the men are putting in more "face time." Economic analysis offers two insights here. First, economists often embrace the view that decision makers know what they are doing and that we (the observers) should respect workers' decisions as they assess short-run personal gains versus medium-term career success. Second, competitive forces actually work to help women in this case. In the modern economy, attracting and retaining skilled workers is a key for a firm to succeed. Those firms that successfully integrate young mothers into their workforce will be more likely to succeed. As more women achieve leadership positions in companies, this will only reinforce the efforts by firms to figure out ways to achieve the "best of both worlds." If young women are concerned that they are facing career costs by working at home four days a week, then bosses will have an incentive to reconfigure how work is evaluated and how women are mentored to reduce this differential promotion gap. In this "Big Data" age, firms can engage in such self-diagnostics so that a problem does not fester.

Power Couple Formation and Locational Choice

Demographers have documented that people are more likely to marry a spouse with the same level of education. I met my wife at the University of Chicago's PhD in Economics program. When we graduated, she took a job as an assistant professor at MIT in Cambridge, Massachusetts, and I took a job at Columbia University in New York City. We knew that this arrangement was not a long-run solution for us because we wanted to live together in the same city. Both of us are highly educated and ambitious about our respective careers. At the same time, we also sought to live together.

Before the rise of WFH, educated married women often faced the "tied mover problem." Consider a couple who is thinking of marrying but both are determined to pursue their careers. They work in narrow niche fields. She is a patent attorney and he is a physicist specializing in string theory. If his only job offer is in Cornell in Ithaca, New York, they have a big problem. He will be asking her to sacrifice her career to live with him in this small city. She faces an ugly choice: face a grueling commute from a big city or find a less satisfying job as a trailing spouse in the small town. Their marriage could suffer because of the bundling between where they live and where she has to work. WFH unbundles this problem and improves their quality of life.

In the past, such power couples had a strong incentive to move to big cities to solve this colocation problem. When couples move to a major local labor market such as New York City or Chicago, they have a wide variety of local firms that each of them can work for. This means that neither spouse will need to sacrifice their own career in living with their partner. In the year 2000, my wife and I published a paper on the economic geography of power couples. Such couples feature two spouses who have at least a college degree. Over the years 1960 to 2000, more of these couples were forming as education attainment increased and more of them were locating in major cities.[33] This evidence supported our core hypothesis that big cities solve the colocation problem. But rents are higher in such cities and not all ambitious, educated couples want to have such limited geographic choices.

For highly educated power couples the ability of one or both of the spouses to engage in WFH will increase the family's total labor supply and the anticipation that WFH is feasible will encourage some women to invest in more workplace human capital. Together these two forces will increase the incomes of highly educated households. In this sense, the rise of WFH will increase income inequality across married couples.[34] In our new economy, such couples can configure their lives in many different ways. Consider a couple where one works for a firm in Washington, DC, and the other works for a firm in Baltimore. In the past, they may have chosen to live between these cities, about twenty miles from each. In a WFH economy, they can choose to live in the city where they prefer to live and one of the spouses will make the longer trip a few times a week to the other city. The key point to note is the increase in menu for such couples as they have so many new options for how they configure their lives.

Does the Rise of WFH Strengthen or Weaken Marriage?

Nobel laureate Gary Becker pioneered research on the economics of marriage.[35] He studied why marriages form and continue. In his research conducted in the 1970s, couples enter a marriage contract as a type of commitment to each other. Knowing that they will spend decades together creates incentives for each to make relationship-specific investments with an aim toward a more productive family unit. For example, one spouse may learn how to cook his spouse's favorite meal even if nobody else enjoys eating it. Such relationship-specific investments would be less likely to take place in an economy featuring no marriage. In this case, relationships can easily dissolve; anticipating this risk, partners will invest in general skills rather than relationship-specific skills. Becker posited that the gains to marriage are due to creating incentives to specialize. In a traditional 1950s setting, a woman specialized in the home sector while the man specialized in going to work. Becker argued that a couple would remain married if their total output from working as a team (including raising children) exceeded what they could achieve as two individuals on their own.

In recent work, economists have further refined key hypotheses related to understanding the determinants of divorce. One recent theory argues that if women earn more than half of the household's income, this raises the risk of divorce because it threatens many men's self-esteem as they lose their place as the primary breadwinner.[36] If WFH raises women's income such that they earn a majority of the household's income, then the rise of WFH will offer a new test of this theory.

In the modern economy featuring a greater share of women working, there is less specialization between the spouses. For example, many economists (including myself) are married to other economists. My wife and I have similar leisure preferences and we like to go to the same places and restaurants. I enjoy these experiences more when she is around (and I hope she feels the same way!).[37] The rise of WFH will strengthen marriages if women take advantage of this opportunity and increase their income, and through such rising household income, reduce stress and allow the couple to focus on what they enjoy doing together.

In an increasingly risky labor market, risk-averse men will want to marry a spouse whose income offers a diversified source of funds for the family. Remote work is not tied to the local labor market conditions. This means that a family with a WFH-eligible spouse faces less local labor market risk. Middle-class couples have less consumption volatility if the wife is an equal earnings partner.[38]

In the WFH economy, there are more possibilities for where such couples live and work. In our new economy, they can live in Baltimore and one spouse can commute to Washington, DC, two days a week. This example shows how remote work increases the menu of possibilities for married couples. They can live closer to one of the spouses' family, or they can choose to live in a cheaper housing market, or they can make their own idiosyncratic locational choice such as moving closer to nature.[39] Couples who have similar geographic and leisure tastes will be better able to enjoy experiences together and this will strengthen their bond.

New Labor Market Opportunities for African Americans and Hispanics

Back in the 1950s and 1960s, many African Americans in Northeast cities worked in manufacturing. Over several decades these cities have deindustrialized due to a combination of factors including international trade and regional competition. As these cities lost this employment, unemployment rose in center city communities and job growth took place in the suburbs. Few black people owned cars and thus they had trouble accessing these suburban jobs. Back in 1968, my friend, the economist John Kain, introduced the spatial mismatch hypothesis to urban economics. Kain sought to explain why black unemployment was high. He argued that blacks disproportionately lived in the center cities and the jobs were suburbanizing. Since their incomes tended to be low, few black people owned cars. Given that public transit is slow and often unreliable, this lack of transport access contributed to the high black unemployment rate.[40] Kain's hypothesis is still relevant today. His hypothesis is actually highly optimistic as it argues that black unemployment would be much lower if this group had better job access. He focused on reducing transportation costs as a policy lever for addressing this issue. Faster transportation helps to bring people from their home to a job. WFH reverses this logic as the job is brought to a person's home!

The sociologist William Julius Wilson has argued that black communities have suffered from a paucity of working role models.[41] The rise of remote work creates the possibility that minority workers will live in cities where they already have social ties. This dynamic expands the set of "role models" living in the cities. Sociologists have stressed that black community norms among young people were harmed by the loss of employment opportunities for black men as factories closed. Young men did not know successful adults in their community and this impacted their early life investments. A growth of professionals in such neighborhoods who engage in remote work could reverse this dynamic. In this sense, geographically spreading the employment base out of the elite coastal cities can offer several benefits. For shrinking cities such as Baltimore and Cleveland this can boost the tax base, create a local multiplier effect by creating local service jobs, and slow down the falling prices of durable housing in such cities.

Today, the leading productive places in the US economy are majority white, expensive cities such as Boston, Seattle, Portland, and San Francisco. In Seattle, less than 2 percent of residents in neighborhoods such as Capitol Hill are black.[42] Qualified African Americans may not want to live in these cities and may not have the savings to live well in these cities.

Before 2020, African American residents of Baltimore moving to Seattle meant both sacrificing their social network and arriving in a city where they were part of a very small minority. African Americans seeking jobs in tech face specific challenges. The tech cities feature expensive housing and few minority communities. The major tech firms do not have many minority employees to act as role models and peers.

At the same time that San Francisco and Seattle are home to few African Americans, hundreds of thousands of African Americans live in cities such as Baltimore, Detroit, Cleveland, and St. Louis. These cities do not have the full gamut of high-paying tech and finance jobs that Boston, San Francisco, and Seattle feature. This fact arises because industries tend to cluster in specific cities (i.e., finance in New York City, tech in Silicon Valley) versus being uniformly spread across the nation's cities. A data scientist who wants to live in Baltimore will not find many jobs there. This reduces the incentive for those who want to live their lives in Baltimore to train in these skills.

Before the rise of WFH, firms such as Amazon faced a challenge in hiring African Americans as data scientists to work in Seattle. Seattle features few African Americans living there and few African Americans are trained in data science. These two facts are interconnected. If a young black student anticipates that she can only find good work in data science if she moves to Seattle, she may not invest in these skills because she does not want to live there and she has no role models who have already taken this path. If this logic is correct, then an optimistic prediction going forward is that the count of minority data scientists will increase as they engage in WFH and have the opportunity to work for great companies while living in the places where they are more comfortable.[43]

Companies have increasingly expressed their desire to diversify their workforce. In their public statements, major companies recognize that the downside of locating in tech elite cities is that this hinders their ability to hire a more diverse workforce. To provide one example of how firms are rethinking their own economic geography, consider Pinterest. Pinterest, Inc., announced that it has terminated its lease for approximately 490,000 square feet of office space to be constructed near its current headquarters campus in San Francisco, California. This action is intended to support a more diverse and geographically distributed workforce at Pinterest. "As we analyze how our workplace will change in a post-COVID world, we are specifically rethinking where future employees could be based," said Todd Morgenfeld, CFO and Head of Business Operations of Pinterest. "A more distributed workforce will give us the opportunity to hire people from a wider range of backgrounds and experiences."[44]

The leading tech companies are well aware that they face a diversity gap. During a time when more companies are thinking through what they can do to contribute to social justice, expanding career outreach opportunities through WFH would appear to be low-hanging fruit. Amazon's HQ2 in Crystal City, Virginia, is a very attractive headquarters for WFH workers who live in the city of Baltimore. Improvements in train service between Baltimore and Washington, DC, would further enhance regional integration and economic opportunity. If more WFH-employed minorities are matched with the nation's leading employers, then a dynamic process unfolds that helps them and helps their communities in places such as Baltimore. As these young people move up the economic ladder, they become role models in their communities and young people look up to them for their success.

In the past, if one sought to live in a majority black city, then this limited the labor market opportunities available. This in turn had dynamic effects. A young person who expects to live his life in Baltimore and to work in Baltimore will be less likely to obtain the skills to be a data scientist if there are few data science jobs in Baltimore and the option to engage in WFH is not available. The anticipation that remote work opens up the possibility of achieving this "best of both worlds" creates an incentive for young people to invest in their skills.

The fact that qualified black employees prefer to live in cities with high percentages of black residents poses challenges both for tech companies and for the many universities located far from these places. Every American university seeks to recruit a more diverse set of students and faculty. This creates another spatial mismatch in the academic labor market.[45] Across the United States, there are many universities located in suburban and rural places. These schools seek to diversify their faculty to hire excellent scholars from a broad range of backgrounds. Many of these nonurban campuses have great trouble recruiting minority faculty. Recognizing this challenge, an innovative solution that has been proposed is to allow some of the faculty to be based remotely (for instance, in Baltimore) and to zoom in for classes and sometimes visit the campus. This arrangement would work well for senior faculty but it would pose some social capital and networking challenges for junior faculty.

How Will the Rise of Remote Work Affect the Quality of Life for Those Not Eligible?

Not everyone can engage in remote work. If 35 percent of the workforce is engaged in remote work at least a few days a week, this will have at least three effects on other workers. First, service jobs demand will rise in the residential areas where remote workers move to. As remote workers move farther from city centers, this will create exurban demand for service workers at the Starbucks and other stores where they shop. Land prices are cheap at the suburban fringe and the purchasing power of such local service providers will be higher than if they sought jobs in the center city.

While service workers cannot work remotely, they can move to remote locations where rents are cheaper if more people work from home. If 35 percent of the workforce begins to work from home three days a week and thus are home five days a week, there is a demand for a service sector in areas where they live. This creates new jobs for less educated workers in such areas. In these areas, housing is cheap. This increases the quality of life for such service providers. There will also be new construction jobs as new homes are built farther from the employment centers. Families who spend more time at home will invest money to upgrade the home.[46] This creates new opportunities for those who supply home improvement services. Some people may add a new office to their home or other features to customize it to their needs.

While there are significant opportunities for less skilled workers to live and work far from the cities in the cheaper parts of metropolitan areas, one countervailing force is the rising minimum wage. In cities, the minimum wage is usually not binding as workers must be paid higher nominal wages to attract them. In contrast, in more suburban and exurban areas, being required to pay service workers $15 or more per hour may reduce demand for workers. If workers can find very cheap housing far from the cities, then many would be willing to work for less than $15 an hour. While most people think that a high minimum wage is "good" for low-skill workers, economists emphasize the likely unintended consequence. When employers are required by law to pay a higher than competitive market wage to people, they create fewer jobs. For example, such firms can substitute and rely on robots or other pieces of capital. Economists argue that a higher minimum wage increases unemployment for less skilled workers. In places where housing is cheaper, the minimum wage will more likely be a binding constraint on employers. The net result here is perhaps counterintuitive. Less skilled workers will gain more from the rise of WFH when they live and work in states with less generous minimum wages.

Throughout this chapter, I have focused on how the WFH eligible reconfigure their lives to make the most of this new opportunity. Here it is important to note that those who are currently not WFH eligible are not locked into this category. Younger workers can retrain in fields to open up this possibility for themselves. Parents of younger children can make investments in their children to raise their probability of being WFH eligible in the future.

Those who work in the service industry and thus earn a living from face-to-face interaction still gain from the rise of WFH because they gain from a larger menu of options of where to live their lives. If a wealthy environmentalist community forms in Bozeman, Montana, then this creates new opportunities for those in the service sector to live and work there. While this option may not be attractive to everyone, the key is to increase the menu of possibilities. Non-WFH-eligible workers know themselves and their life goals, and they will make the right choices for themselves and gain from having a larger menu of alternatives.

As more people have the opportunity to live and work where they want to be, this increases not only their physical and mental health but also the accountability of our institutions. If there are places whose governments are failing to meet the desires of local residents, then people will be more likely to move away. In this setting, real estate prices will more quickly reflect changes in local quality of life. If an area features a rising crime rate, in the new WFH economy people will "vote with their feet" and real estate prices will decline in that area. This demands that local officials be more responsive in addressing emerging quality-of-life challenges because if they fail to do so, the tax base will shrink.

While this has been an optimistic chapter, I must add a few cautionary notes about concentrated urban poverty. WFH creates an incentive for the American people to spread out. This chapter has sketched out the benefits from this emerging trend. At the same time, such suburbanization may contribute to the further isolation of the urban poor. Poor people live in center cities in areas such as Baltimore and Detroit because there is old, cheap housing and there is good public transit.[47] If the poor remain in these center city areas and richer people are suburbanizing, then there is greater geographic isolation of the poor and this may reduce political support for programs that redistribute to them because there is an "out of sight, out of mind" effect and the physical distance between the groups acts as a type of moat. Past research in urban economics has documented that college graduates are more likely to suburbanize when violent crime increases in the center city.[48] This propensity to engage in "flight from blight" is likely to increase in a WFH economy because educated people no longer commute to center city jobs five times a week.

II *Firms*

3   *How Will Firms Adapt?*

Before 2020, some of America's greatest companies made huge bets as they invested billions in new corporate campuses. Apple's headquarters opened to employees in April 2017. It has 2.8 million square feet of space and at least 12,000 employees work at the building. It cost at least $5 billion to build. It features seven cafes, a thousand-seat auditorium, and a wellness center, as well as an integrated bus station and several miles of bike trails on the campus. Apple made this enormous investment because it anticipated that its future is in Silicon Valley and it wanted a workplace environment to attract ambitious workers and to provide a setting where they can be happy and productive.

Firms may have underestimated how much their workers value working from home. The shutdown of face-to-face work in early 2020 acted like a major social experiment as workers and firms experienced daily WFH. A "silver lining" of the crisis is that workers and firms learned about the firm's productivity and worker quality of life and well-being when workers have fewer face-to-face interactions with each other and the firm's leadership. In the past, there may have been a type of stigma associated with remote work such that those who sought it out were viewed as less dedicated to the firm and less serious about their careers. Going forward, the possibility of engaging in remote work now seems normal.

If the COVID crisis had struck in 1980, there would have been a much greater disruption of firm productivity. In 1980, we did not have cell phones, or distributed cloud computing where workers could access company records without going to the office. We did not have high-speed internet or software such as Microsoft Teams and Zoom for connecting us to meet face to face over the internet.

The previous two chapters explored the new opportunities offered by WFH and possible ramifications depending on how workers responded. In this chapter, I focus on how firms will adapt to the new opportunities and challenges posed by engaging in at least part-time WFH. How will profit-maximizing firms configure their work arrangements to continue to be profitable while experimenting with new ways of organizing their workplaces?

Will the Demand for Downtown Commercial Real Estate Decline?

In choosing how much real estate to rent or buy and the location of such real estate, for-profit firms confront a classic urban trade-off: rents are higher in more productive, more beautiful areas, but being close to where the "action is" raises a firm's profile and helps it to recruit talent, be aware of emerging developments, and interact with local banks, lawyers, and marketing teams. Whether these traditional face-to-face interactions can be done remotely remains an open question.[1] Firms that believe they can be as productive through virtual online interactions as with face-to-face meetings will be the most likely to decide that they need much less commercial space in major cities.

Economic geographers have documented that key industries are spatially concentrated. High tech has clustered in the Silicon Valley region while finance has tended to cluster in New York City and entertainment industries in the Hollywood region.[2] Once an industrial cluster has formed, this past momentum feeds on itself as ambitious startup firms are more likely to locate there to be close to the action. If industries such as finance continue to rely on face-to-face interactions, then the demand for commercial real estate in a city that specializes in finance (such as New York City) will remain high. Alternatively, in a connected economy featuring fast trains across cities and easy regional flights (e.g., Southwest Airlines), some firms may calculate that they do not need to be in superstar cities because they can substitute quality trips (i.e., flying in for a week of meetings) for quantity of interactions (renting commercial space for years at a time). These decisions will be made on a company-by-company basis but will hinge on the fundamental issue of whether face-to-face interaction raises productivity.

In recent years many shopping malls have suffered vacancies as the rise of Amazon has reduced the demand to shop face to face. Does this portend a decline in demand for commercial office space?[3] In major commercial markets such as Manhattan, a few major financial firms utilize a huge amount of space. Barclays, JP Morgan Chase, and Morgan Stanley are part of a banking industry that has long been a pillar of the city's economy, with more than 20,000 employees. Collectively, they lease more than 10 million square feet in New York—roughly all the office space in downtown Nashville.[4]

Companies such as Facebook, Amazon, Apple, and Google have all recently built very expensive new corporate campuses.

These investments were made because they expected that face-to-face meetings would continue to be a key part of their day-to-day operations.

Facebook added a new building, called MPK 21, to its headquarters in Menlo Park, California. MPK 21 opened in late 2018. It was designed by Frank Gehry and built by Level 10 construction in less than eighteen months. MPK 21 cost about $300 million to build, as part of a roughly $1 billion investment in the headquarters. MPK 21 features a 3.6-acre rooftop garden with over two hundred trees and a half-mile-long pathway, along with five dining options and fifteen art installations.

Amazon began construction on its HQ2 in Crystal City, Virginia, in 2021. However, its main presence remains in Seattle, where it maintains over forty buildings as part of its headquarters there. Although the company has spent $4 billion on its headquarters there, the company's approach to its offices differs from other major tech companies like Apple and Facebook, as it tries to blend into the surrounding community as opposed to creating an enclave.

Microsoft's headquarters are in Redmond, Washington. Over 47,000 people work at the Redmond location. Microsoft commenced a massive renovation of its campus in 2018, adding "17 new buildings, 6.7 million square feet of renovated workspace, $150 million in transportation infrastructure improvements, public spaces, sports fields and green space." These renovations will allow the company to employ up to 8,000 additional employees at its headquarters. Microsoft claims the new buildings "will be more open and less formal, divided into a series of 'team neighborhoods' while capturing more natural light and fostering the type of creativity that will lead to ongoing innovation to advance the industry and benefit our customers." The renovation focuses on creating open, flexible workspace with ample open space.[5]

One notable feature of these new office buildings is their emphasis on worker health and quality of life. Apple's headquarters celebrates that the office does not need air conditioning because of its natural ventilation system. In an era of pollution spikes caused by wildfires in the West and extreme heat, the ability of commercial buildings to "take a punch" is valuable for highly productive workers. In recent work, Pei Li and I documented how high local pollution levels in China affect the cognitive ability of indoor workers. Specifically, we studied the time it takes judges to make a ruling at trial. Merging data on air pollution by city and year and month and day, we found that when it is more polluted outside, judicial cases take longer to be completed. This effect is even larger for older judges.[6] Research on how outdoor environmental conditions affect indoor worker productivity helps for-profit firms optimize how they configure their offices.

Workers at major firms such as Twitter are revealing how much they value WFH. "Nearly 70 percent of Twitter employees said in the survey that they want to continue working from home at least three days a week. Still, single and younger employees showed a preference for coming back to the office, while parents and older workers said they prefer to work from home."[7]

Established firms that seek to retain and recruit talent at a reasonable salary have strong incentives to think about the amenity features of the jobs they seek to fill. If workers have more freedom to configure their lives and live where they want to live and commute to the main office less often, then this increases job satisfaction.[8] Google provides one prominent example as it pursues a mixed strategy. Alphabet's chief executive, Sundar Pichai, envisions that 20 percent of the employees will be full-time WFH workers and a large share of the workforce will have access to more flexible WFH schedules for a few days a week.[9]

When established firms that have roots to a particular area, such as Amazon in Seattle, choose to allow their workers to engage in more WFH, this has important implications for the center cities because a type of negative multiplier effect may play out. If Amazon's Seattle workforce who commute to work on a daily basis declines, then this reduces local service-sector demand. Lunch places near Amazon and nearby Starbucks may have fewer customers on weekdays. The major firms have little incentive to factor these multiplier effects into their own WFH decisions.

In contrast, nonprofits such as major universities often embrace a "double bottom line" mentality. The leadership of Johns Hopkins University is trying to figure out how to balance engaging in WFH versus its responsibilities to the city of Baltimore. Given that this university is tied to the physical place (Baltimore), the entity has strong incentives to be a "good community citizen."

This issue has been openly discussed and is addressed on the Johns Hopkins University webpage, where the following question is posed: "Haven't we just proven that we can carry out the university's mission while working remotely?"

The official university response is revealing:

We have been amazed by the resilience of our staff during the pandemic and their ability to quickly adapt to challenging new circumstances. However, we do not yet know what the effects of large-scale remote work will be on productivity, culture, and innovation over the long term. In particular, we have little experience in hybrid work environments in which some team members are on site and others are working remotely.

We also consider the university's role as an anchor institution in Baltimore to be central to its mission, and the physical presence of thousands of our faculty and staff on our campuses every day contributes meaningfully to the city's economic and cultural vitality.[10]

This quote highlights that the nonprofit university (Johns Hopkins) views itself as having a "double bottom line" objective: to take actions that make both the university and its host city stronger. Going forward, each institution will wrestle with this same issue. In recent decades, Baltimore has struggled, both due to losing population and due to a remaining population that features many who have incomes below the poverty line. In contrast, a major private firm located in prosperous Silicon Valley would be less likely to be concerned that its medium-term WFH decisions for its workforce could significantly injure its host city.

The Rise of Decentralized Employment

Every major firm will consider the costs and benefits of keeping its workforce located at expensive center city buildings. The firm has strong incentives to recognize the synergies among workers.[11] The firm benefits from the new ideas generated by face-to-face interaction among its own workers. At the same time, the firm employs many people who are doing "back office" activities. These individuals play an important role at the firm but they are paid middle-class salaries and they would prefer to have a shorter commute from their suburban homes. These workers will often gain from the firm's choice to engage in fragmentating its activities. Improvements in information technology facilitate this push to fragment the firm.

In recent decades, as information technology has improved, people have suburbanized, and downtown real estate rents have risen, firms have moved some workers to the suburban fringe. Many credit card offices such as Visa have moved their back offices to North Dakota. Such firms are able to identify those pieces of the business that do not gain from being located in the center city and the workers in these divisions are often willing to work for a lower nominal salary if they have a shorter commute and can live in nice areas with more affordable housing prices.

Firms have suburbanized as the nation's highway infrastructure has been built up. The construction of the federal highways encouraged population suburbanization in the 1950s, 1960s, and 1970s.[12] As the population suburbanized, many jobs suburbanized. If remote work encourages a new round of suburbanization, offices may also suburbanize to facilitate face-to-face weekly or monthly meetings. The ability of center cities to retain people and jobs will hinge on the unique amenities and culture they supply and their ongoing productivity advantage for the entities that choose to continue to be headquartered there.

Firms will anticipate that they can decentralize and locate in a city with cheaper real estate but still have access to direct flights and fast trains to visit superstar cities for face-to-face meetings. Some firms will find this to be an attractive arrangement. Improvements in cross-city travel allows people to move away from big cities and continue to be productive as they use cross-city trains and airplanes to connect and have face-to-face meetings. In recent decades, low-cost airlines such as Southwest have popped up to serve regional routes with regular convenient flights. Southwest's efforts facilitate firm fragmentation because workers can spread out but remain connected. One creative economics study documented that researchers were more likely to write research papers together when Southwest Airlines connected their respective cities with a direct flight.[13] A direct flight lowers the time cost of face-to-face communication and this leads to more interaction and more breakthroughs. After reading this paper, I worked with my co-authors in China and we found a similar result for scientists across China's universities located in different cities. When high-speed rail connects their cities, the interaction between scientists increases and they write more papers together. We also found that scientists are more likely to move to secondary cities that have newly connected bullet train access to the superstar cities of Beijing and Shanghai. Housing is extremely expensive in these cities, and by moving to second-tier cities that are connected by high-speed rail, scientists pay less for housing and still have access to the superstars.[14]

Even before 2020, Amazon was building up smaller offices in cities such as New York City, Phoenix, San Diego, Denver, Detroit, and Dallas. In Manhattan, the firm has opened up a 2,000-employee cluster at the historic building that once housed the Lord & Taylor flagship department store on 5th Avenue.[15] This strategy of creating regional hubs creates the possibility of hybrid arrangements as workers are based there but hold the option to work from home in a vicinity of these new employment centers. This dispersion of activity out of Seattle gives geographically dispersed WFH workers an increased ability to engage in face-to-face meetings with bosses and coworkers without flying across the nation. There are important synergies between opening satellite campuses and allowing workers at these campuses to engage in WFH. This will further help such firms to diversify their workforce as they accommodate a wider variety of worker lifestyles.

Startup Demand for Office Space

Over the last thirty years, Silicon Valley has been home to many highly productive new firms; it has great weather, easy access to San Francisco, and great local universities. Flash-forward to 2022 and the area still has the great weather and the geographic access to great universities but it has fewer of these star firms as their workers engage in WFH. Does this fundamentally make locating in Silicon Valley much less desirable to smaller firms?

The new generation of startup firms continues to be attracted to cities. The leaders of such firms are attracted to the buzz and lifestyle of urban life. The firms need to find financing and to attract early customers. Such firms need to develop a reputation with mentors to benefit from word of mouth among potential venture capitalist investors. Some of these firms are working on their prototypes and they need to hire ambitious employees (many of whom are young).

One urban economics theory for why startups tend to locate in areas that are known to specialize in that industry is known as "labor pooling." If a tech startup locates in Nebraska, it will benefit from cheap rents but it will have trouble finding the right workers with the necessary skills. Qualified workers may be afraid of joining an unproven startup located in Nebraska because if that firm fails, the newly unemployed worker will need to uproot his family and move again. In contrast, a startup that locates in an established city will have a thick local talent pool and workers will know that they face less unemployment risk if their new firm fails.

In our emerging WFH economy, startups will be able to hire workers from around the world. This means that access to local talent is no longer such an important feature that draws new firms to established industrial geographic clusters. If cities adopt road pricing and if WFH-eligible workers spread out, a startup can locate at the fringe of Silicon Valley and have the best of both worlds of cheaper rents and access to the center of the action to have some quality face-to-face interactions.

Even in a WFH economy some startups will seek space in dense center cities. The demand for such space hinges on what a startup gains from locating in a center city like Seattle or San Francisco. Each new firm's leadership will need to predict how the firm's profits and productivity will be affected by locating "close to the action" versus going remote. Such firms can experiment to see how they are performing and can later reverse course if they learn that the organization is underperforming.

Many empirical studies have documented that young firm productivity is higher when they locate in cities featuring more college graduates. While urban economists cannot run randomized experiments, we can choose where a firm locates and then study its productivity; this correlation between productivity and local human capital suggests that learning and networking are key factors in raising the probability that a firm succeeds. Talented workers are also attracted to the consumer city where they can live well and can have new experiences and meet like-minded people. In this sense, high human capital cities solve a coordination problem.

Young, ambitious people want to meet face to face to find their niche. In a larger city, there are more possible matches to find the right friends and romantic partners for any one individual.

The Gains from Going Remote

There are significant possible cost savings for firms that engage in active WFH. Firms such as First Base are standardizing the package of furniture and software and computing so that each home worker can be comfortable and productive. In its survey of the firms that it works with, First Base Survey reports that most companies keep office space, but at 50 percent of the square footage they formerly had, allowing all workers to be in the office for one to two days a week. Thirty percent of companies are getting rid of offices entirely. Workers at these companies are leaving expensive cities to be closer to family. First Base estimates that it costs $20,000 per worker/year for office space and that this cost declines to $2,000 per worker/year for an excellent remote setup.

One claim is that office space will become a type of consumer product. As the WeWork model of renting space at high frequency highlights, more firms may seek out arrangements similar to renting out a hotel suite to engage in brainstorming sessions, client presentations, and employee training. Such flexible arrangements would reduce a firm's fixed costs and allow it to upgrade into higher-quality space when it needs it versus renting out more space during times when larger groups are being brought together. I can imagine that some firms may almost become "nomadic" as they feature face-to-face meetings of different subsets of workers in a given space in a given city.

Because the growth in WFH has been so recent, we know little about how the productivity of small startup firms will be affected by the rise of WFH for more mature firms. Suppose that Jeff Bezos and his top executives at Amazon rarely go to the main office any more. Does this reduce the attractiveness for startups to locate near Amazon in Seattle? The market test will be if commercial rents decline and if fewer startups locate in such places going forward.[16]

In my own recent research set in China, I have studied the productivity of new industrial parks.[17] Mayors of Chinese cities acquire farmland from farmers and then prepare these large vacant parcels located at the suburban fringe of cities to welcome in new firms to locate close to each other. My colleagues and I have documented that these parks generate greater geographical productivity gains for nearby firms when the parks attract firms with a higher degree of human capital and that are for-profit (not state-owned) enterprises. China's mayors have a strong public finance incentive to create a local ecosystem of firms that gain from being close to each other. The city collects more money from the land auction when firms anticipate that they will be really productive by locating close to other productive firms.

Unlike the case of the strong hand of the Chinese state directing businesses to specific locations where the state wants development, US startups must choose where they will locate without full information about the spillover gains they potentially will enjoy. Such freedom leads to some successes and some bad choices. This trial-and-error issue becomes even more important as the major firms engage in more WFH because this affects the extent of the local productivity spillover effects.

Some startups are choosing not to have a central location at all. There are fully distributed remote startups that include @deel, @doist, @Gitlab, @zapier, @github, @Modulz, @Remote, @Commsor, @Parabolco, @linear_app, @GraphyHQ, @CircuitApp, @getstarkco, @Automattic, @MySwimPro, @hop inofficial, @teamguilded, and @FirstbaseHQ.

For example, consider Remote. This company helps firms that seek to hire remote workers in a specific nation by ensuring compliance with that nation's labor laws and completing the necessary paperwork to hire such a worker, thus reducing the transaction costs of hiring in a nation that the company has never hired from before. Another startup is MySwimPro, which provides an app that is now used by more than a million swimmers to help them train to achieve their goals. Those startups that go remote chose to remain low cost and nimble.

Over time more startups are choosing to be remote. One is Filmhub (@filmhubhq on Twitter), an online film distribution company, which currently has fifteen employees. Its CEO claims that the firm saves at least $5,000 a month in rent. In January 2021, Kim-Mai Cutler reported results based on her survey of ninety startups that have received venture capital funding from Initialized Capital.[18] She finds that their preferred geographic location has changed over time. In 2014, 75 percent of the startups in her fund were based in the San Francisco Bay Area. Her team recently surveyed their current startups and the economic geography has shifted. Thirty-seven percent of the startups expect that they will operate in a hub-and-spoke system with many decentralized smaller offices, while 36 percent will be completely decentralized and only 27 percent will be at one physical office. In the new emerging economy, only 28 percent of the firms who responded expect to be in the San Francisco area.

A strategy question arises. If your rivals have a physical presence, what is your firm's best response? Should you continue to be 100 percent remote? The answer to this riddle depends on the classic tradeoff. A remote firm has lower costs and this allows it to price its product more aggressively without losing profit. Such a firm is geographically flexible and can send its sales team to places where new opportunities arise. Such a firm can also hire workers already based in a hotbed for the industry and simply ask them to work remotely. As more startup firms become 100 percent remote, there may be strength in numbers as the venture capital suppliers take them more seriously. Imagine an alternative economy where there are few 100-percent-remote firms. They may appear to be "weird" to venture capitalists rather than being well managed and cost cutting.

There are other startups that do seek to have a physical presence without locking in to long-term rental contracts. Such startups can rent space in an incubator that offers proximity to a major city and network opportunities with other firms colocated in the same building. Such a flexible real estate contract design revisits the success of the WeWork business model.

The WeWork's strategy has been predicated that such startups actually want to cram into a type of work dormitory arrangement. WeWork offers a customized service package that is differentiated from the traditional office product. Much has also already been written about the environment which includes open community spaces, entertainment areas, baristas and free beer on Friday afternoons (although this may be disappearing), in addition to the usual corporate services such as Wi-Fi, copy machines, conference rooms, etc. Part of Neumann's genius was that he tapped into the significant unmet demand particularly on the part of SMEs (small medium enterprises). He recognized SMEs needed more flexible lease terms with respect to the duration of the lease as well as corporate amenities that were more "current" than the typical bland office product. WeWork spaces are "cool" and have a "hip" tech feel analogous to that of incubator spaces. SMEs and Enterprises are willing to pay for flexibility and the environment. Indeed, they love it. SMEs can expand or contract on almost a real time basis without being locked into comparatively long term leases of three to 10 years.[19]

Will WFH Employers Reduce Worker Pay?

If employers move more of their activity away from high-cost cities and allow more workers to engage in WFH, how will this affect worker compensation? Economists have noted that those workers who are paid the most money tend to work at firms based in the most expensive cities such as San Francisco.[20] The fact that workers earn high nominal salaries in cities featuring very high home prices means that their real earnings are not as high as they seem to be. This suggests that firms located in expensive cities could still attract and retain valued workers if they give these workers the right to engage in WFH on a weekly or permanent basis.

Firms recognize that working from home is a valued job attribute. Firms will offer this perk to attract new workers and reward strong performers. Given that this job benefit is not taxed, there are gains to trade between the firm and the worker. The same logic applies to job attributes such as good health insurance. The nontaxed feature of this job attribute provides firms with an incentive to offer it.

Labor economists emphasize that a job's total compensation has many features beyond merely the annual pay and job benefits such as health insurance. Workers care about their expected hours worked, promotion probabilities, and work responsibilities and they will take into account the cost of housing in the vicinity of their employer.

Labor economists continue to debate why some workers are paid more than others. One school of thought argues that workers are paid per unit of skill. In this case, there is a competitive market for skill (determined by aggregate supply and demand) and a worker with more of this skill gets paid more. An alternative theory for why some workers are paid well emphasizes "efficiency wages" such that firms "overpay" workers to buy their loyalty and to encourage such loyal workers to exert extra effort. An executive who has worked closely with a loyal executive assistant for decades may choose to pay this employee quite well.

Workers always have some discretion in determining their workplace effort. If a worker feels that she has been treated unfairly or if she does not feel loyalty to her firm or boss, she may shirk and try less hard. WFH workers may feel disconnected from the firm and may thus shirk on tasks that are hard to monitor. At the same time, if WFH workers rarely go to work, their bosses may not have a personal connection with them and these bosses may feel less loyalty to the workers.[21]

A profit-maximizing firm faces a tradeoff. It can motivate its WFH workers to work hard by using either carrots or sticks. A "carrot" is to pay high wages relative to the worker's alternative offers. A "stick" is to introduce a strict "Big Brother Orwell style" computer monitoring system so that the worker knows that the firm can closely monitor her effort and output and use Machine Learning to calculate the hourly revenue she generates for her firm and benchmark her performance relative to other workers. This internal tournament provides incentives for the WFH worker to work hard, but it may not build up loyalty and could create resentment. A for-profit firm has strong incentives to consider these tradeoffs. If this is a job that features little training and where there are many potential qualified workers, then the firm hiring the WFH workers may not care if any one worker is "not happy" because such a worker can be easily replaced. When workers have rare skills and have firm-specific knowledge that is costly to rebuild, then the for-profit firm (even without altruistic bosses) has strong incentives to compensate the worker so that she remains at the firm. The WFH discussion matters in this case because such a worker is less likely to be loyal to the firm—she has not had the same amount of face-to-face interaction with the firm and its leadership than she would have had if she went to work five days a week.

In determining its compensation policy for WFH workers, each firm will anticipate that how it treats its current employees determines its reputation, and its reputation affects its ability to recruit high-quality workers in the future. Firms that earn a reputation for being a "family friendly" good job can pay less as workers are willing to work at such firms without being paid "combat pay." In the competition for recruiting and retaining talent, some firms such as the Brattle Group, an economic consulting company, have sought to establish a niche as a family friendly firm.[22] Workers there know that their workdays will not run into the night. The firm pays lower total compensation than rival firms but the hours are better. Such a firm may be more likely to offer the work from home option to further distinguish itself as a family friendly firm. Firms know their core niche and can compete on this margin in the talent market.

Firms that are inflexible and do not allow workers to engage in WFH will have a recruitment challenge as they will have to pay higher wages and will experience more employee turnover. Such turnover means that the firm incurs higher costs searching for new workers and higher costs training these new workers. In industries where firms are in tight product market competition, those inflexible firms will have a higher cost structure and they will be more likely to go bankrupt. This logic suggests that competition in both the output market and the labor market will nudge firms into encouraging workers to engage in remote work unless this significantly undermines the firm's creative productivity and corporate culture.

The Urban Economics of WFH Worker Mentoring and Retention

All growing firms face the challenge that incumbent workers are aging and thus new workers must be recruited, trained, and mentored. The rise of WFH could pose a mentoring challenge for growing firms because middle-aged upper management workers will be the most likely to desire working from home and thus will not be in the office on a regular basis to mentor the young new employees. The shrewd firm will anticipate this challenge and will reward some charismatic middle managers to be active "coaches" for younger employees.

Young workers learn more quickly through face-to-face interaction. Thus, the rise of WFH poses new challenges for organizations that seek both to build corporate loyalty and to build up the next generation of the firm's leaders. The rise of WFH could reduce firm loyalty toward workers. Widespread WFH could lead to a type of "out of sight, out of mind" mentality among management. If the new generation of WFH workers are anonymous employees, then this will have several implications for firms. Firms that used to have a tight loyal corporate culture may now attract workers with a different personality. In an extreme case, such firms may attract loners who do not mind not having much interaction with management. The managers of a firm always face competitive pressure to focus on maximizing profit. In setting compensation for workers, such firms may be aggressive in solely offering workers the minimum compensation to recruit such workers. In an increasingly competitive labor market, the introduction of WFH may lead to slower earnings growth in part because bosses feel less altruism toward workers who they do not really know. Again, the key question here is whether face-to-face communication is essential for building up friendship and altruism within an organization. The answer will vary by corporation.

In some corporations, the quantity and quality of output from a given worker can more easily be determined. The quality of a computer code can be checked once it is written to see how effective it is to do the task at hand. In a team production setting, such that a group of workers work together to produce group output, it will be more difficult to tease out any one worker's contribution to the final output. In this case, the boss has more discretion in determining who to credit.

Firms that recognize that WFH is posing organizational challenges have strong incentives to experiment with different strategies to build up the organization. Such firms will invest in hosting quality face-to-face interactions so that WFH workers are invited to the campus to spend a few intensive days together. This approach would mirror what weekend MBA programs seek to achieve. In such programs, full-time workers spend their weekends in class bonding with their professor and their classmates. Such an intense experience conserves on transportation costs and helps to build up real bonds between people.

If WFH workers feel that they are "out of the loop," then firms will have trouble retaining them. The firm's human resources office has the data and the incentives to experiment with what strategies work best for the firm. A firm can open several smaller headquarters around the nation to facilitate monthly meetings with WFH workers spread out across the nation. These firms can interview workers who leave the firm and incumbent workers and workers who turn down the firm's job offers to learn about how the firm can do a better job in competing for and retaining talent.

How Does WFH Affect a Firm's Productivity?

If most workers are happier while engaging in WFH and their productivity does not suffer, then why in the recent past were people going to work five days a week? Was it to signal loyalty? Was it to show strength and resolve? Did the bosses enjoy the attention they received from obsequious workers? The answers of course will vary on a case-by-case basis.

In a competitive industry where firms seek to maximize their profits, such firms will consider how engaging in WFH affects their revenue structure, their ability to attract and retain talent, and their cost structure. Firms recognize that a cost of fewer daily face-to-face interactions is that there will not be as many brainstorming impromptu meetings. This calls for new strategies for collecting and storing information. In 2020, much has been discussed about the importance of asynchronous communication and good writing. In the past, meetings were elitist in terms of who was and was not at the meeting. The new WFH firm can be more democratic by making documents that can be edited and seen by all. When workers engage in work from home, they are likely to have fewer interactions with each other. A recent literature in economics has explored the spillover effects concerning how having productive peers influences one's work. Imagine if you had the NBA star Michael Jordan as a teammate. Does his presence help you to "raise your game"? This literature has found that having productive peers does raise a face-to-face worker's productivity. Whether these effects will vanish in a WFH economy remains to be seen. In the past, part of the productivity gain of going to the office was the access to central records. Recall—if you are of a certain age—the days when offices had file cabinets full of records. With such data now computerized and sitting on the cloud, there is no reason to go to a physical library or the archives to look up information. In this sense, the geography of tapping into information has changed as the process has become decentralized. It is now easier to be in the loop even if you are physically far away.

In fully remote work, the very idea of "what is this firm?" arises. One answer is that such a firm is a decentralized rolodex such that each member of the team knows her role, does her job, and anticipates that her work will be assessed by someone higher up in the organization. The bosses are essentially assembling a jigsaw puzzle as they think through how these spread-out pieces actually fit together and produce a coherent whole that the market values. This process generates revenue for the firm that is then distributed to the workers and owners of the firm.

In this age of Big Data, firms have the tools to see such emerging trends in real time. For the new generation of WFH workers, there will be many benchmarks of worker productivity, happiness, and stress levels to track how workers are performing. In 2020, some researchers have uncovered very surprising results. One research team documents the declining performance among elite chess players competing from home during the COVID pandemic.[23]

If workers are unhappy with the new work arrangements, then the firm's profits will fall because productivity will suffer and turnover at such firms will rise as workers quit. This will raise the search costs for such firms. Firms that develop a reputation for having excellent work conditions can attract great workers without resorting to "combat pay." This provides a strong incentive for firms to consider the well-being of their workers.

In recent years, different companies have been experimenting with allowing workers to engage in remote work. One Chinese firm randomly assigned workers to engage in WFH. The firm then gave those workers who had been working from home the option to return to work. More than 50 percent of those who had been randomly assigned to work from home chose to go back to the office. This experiment highlights that people know themselves and know their own goals. When given a menu of how much WFH they can engage in, workers will choose the right option for them, weighing the tradeoff between having an easier commute versus the challenge of engaging in self-control while at home and potentially feeling "out of the loop."[24] Firms with good computer databases that track the performance of individual workers over time can keep up on these dynamics and reconfigure the interactions between workers to maximize their performance and meet the firm's goals.

In the case of WFH, the same approach can be used by companies to learn about how to achieve the benefits of WFH while minimizing the costs. Companies need to figure out how to make WFH workers feel valued and how they can ask the "dumb" questions that help new workers learn the ropes and be more productive. The firm has strong incentives to experiment with creating intense two-day huddles that bring workers together to have long periods of face-to-face interactions. Some companies are already using artificial intelligence to match different WFH workers to facilitate new friendships and workplace collaborations that might not have taken place in a firm with siloed WFH workers who are all strangers. Such "community collisions" build up new workplace social ties.

In the past, companies such as General Motors had a chief economist whose job responsibilities included creating and digesting macroeconomic forecasts to anticipate emerging challenges and opportunities for the company. In our new economy, a firm's chief economist can access the firm's administrative data and search for clues about performance dynamics and emerging human resource challenges. Firms whose leadership "know that they do not know" how WFH is affecting the organization will be more likely to identify emerging challenges and to adapt to them through an iterative experimental approach. Real-time productivity indicators and workforce retention and hiring data provide the analyst with the raw ingredients for engaging in a real-time diagnosis of whether the firm is unlocking the full potential of WFH. If a firm fails to productively use WFH, it holds the option to revert back to office work. The chief economist's research will inform this key decision. Those firms that are more successful in achieving the full benefits of WFH will have a competitive edge against rival firms in their industry as they will attract and retain talent.

Such market competition raises the likelihood that firms will figure out how to optimize WFH in their human resources strategies.

The Rising Risk Posed by Offshoring

Competitive pressure in product markets such as the competition that US firms face from rival Chinese firms nudges US firms to seek out cost-minimizing strategies. For every firm, labor costs is the firm's major expenditure category. Each firm has strong incentives to carefully think through their approach: How many workers does it need? What are the costs and benefits of keeping these workers in the US versus engaging in offshoring? Should these workers be based in the expensive downtown or can activity be decentralized?

Ongoing improvements in computers and information technology software help foreign-based workers compete for US jobs.[25] Suppose that a future virtual reality zoom experience feels identical to meeting face to face. Such an innovation would accentuate the offshoring threat and this would lead to US workers facing downward wage pressure unless they upgrade their skills to better compete with foreign rivals.[26]

The offshoring of service jobs, particularly call centers and computer software in India, has grabbed recent media attention. In his bestseller *The World Is Flat*, Thomas Friedman wrote of how he had "interviewed Indian entrepreneurs who wanted to prepare my taxes from Bangalore, read my X-rays from Bangalore, trace my lost luggage from Bangalore and write my new software from Bangalore."[27] Such international competition with cheaper rivals puts downward pressure on American wages.

While no worker is happy about an earnings cut, such workers may prefer the bundle of having the right to engage in WFH and their new reduced salary.[28] The rise of domestic working from home creates a type of happy "middle ground" for US companies. Since these workers can spread out and live where they want, they can be paid nominally less. While these workers are paid less, they will be happier workers with less life stress. Over the next few years, if we observe that WFH worker salaries in nominal terms are rising slowly but these workers are staying with these firms and are being productive, then this is strong evidence that worker quality of life is improving. Such workers would be more likely to quit if they viewed their quality of life as bad.

Some US workers will suffer economic dislocation due to employment offshoring.[29] Routine tasks that a firm needs done such as proofreading of a document can be done by any trained, language-competent person around the world. For those US workers who face increased foreign competition, they have several adaptation strategies. First, they could move to a cheaper location so that their rents are lower. This would allow them to accept a pay cut that would make them more competitive with their international rivals. Second, they could invest in new skills that allow them to stand out relative to their competition. An example from international trade is relevant. When China joined the World Trade Organization, its exports to Europe sharply increased and firms in Italy and other EU nations lost sales as they were in head-to-head competition with Chinese imports. Researchers have documented that Italian firms adapted by moving up the quality ladder and producing higher-quality products.[30] The general economics question this raises is one of adjustment costs. What did it cost these Italian firms to make this quality change? How many incumbent firms were not able to adapt? What became of the workers who lost their jobs at the sluggish factories that could not compete with Chinese imports?

At the start of chapter 1, I quoted Warren Buffett, who expressed great optimism about our ability to adapt to new work conditions. In truth, there are large differences across people in our ability to adapt and these distributional effects have key implications for our politics, as those who face adaptation challenges often seek to elect leaders who will protect them against change. In recent years, we have seen populist support for politicians who promise to build walls at our borders to keep rival workers out. In the case of WFH, the open questions include: How will different workers adapt to new labor market competition? How many will respond by investing in strategies to increase their own competitiveness versus how many will rely on elected officials to protect them through increasingly generous transfer programs and through blocking competition?

III *Locations*

4 The Rise of Remote Work and Superstar Cities

In recent decades cities such as Boston, New York City, San Francisco, and Seattle have prospered due to the boom in specific industries such as entertainment, finance, and technology. In a more footloose WFH economy, these cities will face more spatial competition as new potential destinations such as areas in Austin, Texas, or Miami, Florida, compete for talent. Economists emphasize that such jurisdictional competition for attracting and retaining talent pushes incumbent elected officials to "raise their game" in terms of offering higher quality of life per tax dollar charged. The rise of WFH means that more workers have greater freedom to "get up and go" if they are unhappy with their current quality of life and the market real estate prices they face.

The fortunes of cities change over time. Back in the 1960s, Boeing was one of Seattle's major companies. Between 1968 and 1971, this company's total employment in Seattle shrank from 108,000 to 38,000.[1] In recent decades, Seattle's economy has soared due in large part to the rise of Microsoft and later the rise of Amazon, creating a booming local tech cluster. During this period of growth, local home prices rose and this increased local public revenue. Amazon's King County in Washington has experienced 7 percent annual home price growth from 2000 to 2020.[2] Since 2011, the City of Seattle's tax revenue has grown by an average of 6 percent a year.[3] When a city enjoys a tech boom, local tax revenue soars and this creates middle-class jobs and funds a variety of local government investment programs and pro-poor policies. Seattle pays its public-sector workers quite well. For the year 2019, the City of Seattle posted data on public-sector worker pay. The data set indicates hourly pay for 12,223 employees. The average worker in the city earned $44.70 per hour and 50 percent of workers earned at least $44.54. The top 25 percent of workers earned more than $55.40 an hour. This pay exceeds what similar public-sector workers earn in New York City. The Seattle police were paid even more. Based on 1,980 Seattle workers for the police agency, the average hourly pay in the police department was $52.20 and the top 25 percent in the police department earned at least $60.60 per hour.

This case study of Seattle highlights how a city's prospects are tied to the rise of superstar firms. Could commercial and residential rents fall sharply if fewer Amazon employees live and work in downtown Seattle? The Columbia Center is a seventy-six-story commercial skyscraper located at 701 5th Avenue in Seattle, close to Amazon's office complex. Such a building represents a durable piece of urban infrastructure.

In the midst of the COVID crisis, researchers have documented rising real estate prices and increased daily activity at the suburban fringe of metropolitan areas.[4] Whether these trends persist going forward hinges on the productivity and the unique "consumer city" opportunities offered by superstar center cities.

Recent Gentrification Concerns in Superstar Cities

Before 2020, house prices were growing sharply in America's most productive cities. In superstar cities such as Boston, San Francisco, Seattle, and other coastal cities, very little new housing is built. This means that any increase in demand for housing raises both home prices and local rents. This impacts the local renters who are at an increasing risk of being priced out of the neighborhood where they have planted roots.

When a city experiences a boom, and when new supply cannot be built, the iron laws of supply and demand predict that local rents will rise. The open question is how local renters respond to these changes. It is notable that US cities do not feature long-run residential rental contracts. In contrast to commercial real estate leases that often last ten years, residential rental agreements are often one-year agreements. Renters could sign multiyear rental agreements to limit their risk of being priced out by rising rents.

Since such medium-term rental contracts do not exist in cities such as San Francisco and Seattle, renters are exposed to rent hike risk. Some of these residents have responded with protests, and sometimes violently, as seen by morning and evening attacks on commuter buses transporting workers to and from Apple's Silicon Valley headquarters in 2018, which resulted in smashed windows. An earlier attack in 2013 on a bus carrying Google employees had also resulted in smashed windows, and protests followed, decrying how the well-paid tech sector had pushed up house prices in the San Francisco Bay Area.[5]

While productive firms do pay high salaries to their workers and these workers bid aggressively for local housing, many economists believe that supply-side constraints are the main cause of soaring real estate prices in superstar cities. These cities have not introduced traffic road pricing and they have chosen to build very little new housing. A coalition of environmentalists and incumbent property owners have skillfully used the zoning code to not allow new housing to be built. During December 2019, the City of Seattle issued new housing permits for 910 new housing units to be built.[6] In a booming city of 745,000 people this is a tiny amount of new construction.

In cities such as San Francisco and Seattle, there has recently been a contentious relationship between progressive city leaders and the tech companies. Tech companies have been accused of not sharing their wealth and not being good local citizens as they drive up real estate prices and gentrify the area, driving out small businesses and changing the character of the city.

On May 14, 2018, Seattle's city council unanimously passed an annual head tax of $275 per employee on businesses with gross revenues over $20 million. The tax, which would have affected the city's 600 largest employers, was repealed by a 7–2 city council vote less than a month later, far in advance of when it would have gone into effect. A combination of construction labor unions, large employers, and economic development agencies effectively lobbied to have the head tax repealed and won support from the seven city council members and mayor who were up for reelection in that year. Intended to fund efforts to address the city's ongoing homelessness crisis, the passage of the head tax and its subsequent repeal highlight the complicated relationship between city leadership and its largest employers, including Amazon and Starbucks.

Some residents have blamed Amazon for stressing the city's

transit and education systems and driving up home and goods prices, exacerbating inequality in the city. They questioned whether Amazon was paying its fair share.[7] Part of the proposed solution was to force the city's largest employers to pay more to address these issues.

As Seattle progressives have sought to tax Amazon's success in the city, the company has become increasingly involved in local politics. The company has made significant campaign contributions to Seattle politicians and the super PACs that support them in recent years, beginning with a $350,000 donation to Mayor Durkan's reelection campaign in 2017, a year before she passed the head tax.[8] Amazon spent a record $1.45 million on pro-business political campaigns in 2019, more than any other company in the city.[9] The increased spending follows the election of Socialist Alternative party member Kshama Sawant to the city council and the council member's criticism of Amazon and other large employers for not doing enough to address civic issues. Mayor Durkan, who was never enthusiastic about the head tax, may have viewed it as an attempt to placate both sides, which instead had the reverse effect.[10] The increasing involvement of Amazon in Seattle's civic affairs is both a response to criticism and a recognition that the growing company that employs over 50,000 people in almost fifty buildings in the city could not stay out of civic issues forever.[11]

In July 2020, Seattle city council member Teresa Mosqueda introduced a proposal that passed 7 to 2.[12] Called the "JumpStart" tax, companies with annual payrolls of more than $7 million would be taxed on their pay to employees making more than $150,000 per year. As amended in the budget committee, the tax rate would range from 0.7 to 2.4 percent, with tiers for various payroll and salary amounts. For example, a company with a payroll of more than $7 million and one employee making $200,000 would pay a tax of 0.7 percent on $200,000—or $1,400.[13] This tax is expected to generate more than $200 million a year for the City of Seattle, with Amazon paying a large share of this total.[14]

Going forward, the rise of WFH is likely to give major firms a credible threat to migrate away from their origin cities. The leadership of major companies are wrestling with how to achieve their multiple goals of being profitable and contributing to society as a whole. Major companies like Facebook and Google have no desire to receive negative publicity about the local consequences of their success. These companies feature younger leaders who embrace a double bottom-line mentality, and these firms must continue to hire young talent. If young potential employees view these companies in a negative way, then this affects the quality of the talent these firms hire going forward and the wages they must pay.

Facebook has established a billion-dollar fund to create affordable housing near its campuses.[15] Facebook's $1 billion will be spent over the next decade on a variety of initiatives. The company plans to spend $250 million in partnership with the State of California to build mixed-income housing on state-owned land in communities without enough supply. Another $150 million will go to the Bay's Future Fund for the construction of affordable housing in San Francisco. Facebook is donating $225 million in previously purchased land near its headquarters in Menlo Park, California, to produce more than 1,500 units of mixed-income housing. Some $25 million will go toward the construction of housing on county-owned land for teachers and "other essential workers" in partnership with Santa Clara County.[16]

Superstar Firms as "Good Neighbors" in Their Origin Cities

The recent adversarial relationship between modern superstar companies and their home cities stands in contrast to how past US major companies interacted with their home cities. Consider Ford, Chrysler, and General Motors—the three major carmakers headquartered in Detroit. The relationship between the Big Three domestic carmakers and the city of Detroit offers a valuable historical case study. Following the 1967 Detroit riots, the city formed the New Detroit Committee, a coalition of community leaders, politicians, philanthropists, and business leaders in Detroit that included James Roche, president of General Motors; Virgil Boyd, president of Chrysler; and Allen Merrell, vice president of Ford Motor, as founding members. The biracial committee that included the head of the NAACP was formed to address the conditions that led to the riot of 1967 and provide funding and technical expertise to grassroots organizations working on these issues. A main focus of the group was providing jobs to unemployed African Americans, which was believed to be one of the causes of the unrest. The committee also promoted housing integration, affordable housing construction, and improvement of the city's school system.

They advocated for federal funding and private business to address these issues, calling for "federal involvement in terms of great sums of money and leadership.... The job cannot be done without the fullest participation of private and local interests." The full-time staff of the New Detroit Committee was "drawn largely from local business, labor, governmental and civic groups.... [Chairman] Hudson asked from the very beginning that cooperating businesses and other organizations send to the Committee only their most talented, irreplaceable personnel." Michigan Bell Telephone Company and the Chrysler Corporation partnered with city high schools "to put business resources and talents to work solving inner city problems."

Local businesses also focused on hiring chronically unemployed people: "Companies like Ford, General Motors, Chrysler, J. L. Hudson and Michigan Bell have all become involved in special programs of inner city hiring. Most recent reports…indicate that an estimated 12,000 of the so-called 'hard-core unemployed' have been hired by Detroit area firms. This has been coupled with an encouragingly high rate of retention, which, in the experience of several firms, more than matches retention rates through their regular channels of employment." While the impact and effectiveness of the New Detroit Committee is debatable, it is clear that the major employers of Detroit were highly engaged in addressing what they saw as the city's issues in the late 1960s and early 1970s.[17]

Kodak in Rochester provides another example. While Kodak's founder George Eastman is not as well known as his contemporaries Andrew Carnegie, Murry Guggenheim, and John D. Rockefeller, his philanthropic endeavors and commitment to Rochester, New York, where Kodak was born, were no less impressive. Over the course of his career, Eastman gave generously to educational institutions, hospitals, and youth organizations. His largest commitment was to the University of Rochester, to which he donated $50 million, and endowed schools of music, medicine, and dentistry. He established six dentistry programs for poor children in Rochester and declared that Rochester was "the town I am interested in above all others." He and his friend Dr. Durand purchased hundreds of acres of property along Lake Ontario and donated them to the City of Rochester for a public park, Durand-Eastman Park, in the early 1900s. He established the Eastman Theatre in Rochester in the 1920s as a center for music and silent movies.[18]

Going forward, the rise of WFH may reduce the incentive of major firms to be a local civic booster. Major firms must be aware that the Biden administration is considering whether to enact new antitrust rules and to more heavily regulate these firms. Amazon is investing in helping the urban poor and middle class in the major cities where it employs tens of thousands of people. In early 2021, Amazon announced a series of pro-poor housing initiatives in Seattle, Arlington, Virginia, and Nashville, Tennessee: "Amazon's new Housing Equity Fund is a more than $2 billion commitment to preserve existing housing and create inclusive housing developments through below-market loans and grants to housing partners, traditional and non-traditional public agencies, and minority-led organizations. The fund will support Amazon's commitment to affordable housing and will help ensure moderate- to low-income families can afford housing in communities with easy access to neighborhood services, amenities, and jobs."[19]

Macroeconomic Productivity Losses from a Dispersed Workforce?

Silicon Valley has thrived during a time when highly skilled workers at different firms live and work in close physical proximity to each other. If tech cities experience a loss of skilled workers due to the rise of WFH, will tech firms experience less economic growth? Will the local economy grow at a slower rate? Since we have never run this experiment before, it is difficult to answer this question using standard urban economics data.

In her analysis of the success of New York City's economy in the 1950s, Jane Jacobs emphasized the learning taking place when different types of firms are located in close physical proximity. Empirical economists have built on her work by documenting that more-educated workers are more productive when they work in high human capital cities. The ideal way to rigorously test this claim would be to randomly assign different people to live in different cities that differ with respect to their share of college graduates. Urban economics predicts that a worker's wages are higher in a city where more-skilled people live and work. This can be measured as the share of adults who are college educated or the count of college-educated adults per square mile.[20]

While researchers document such effects, we do not really understand "why" workers benefit more from working in geographic areas with other skilled people physically nearby. A plausible explanation is that such proximity facilitates more face-to-face interactions with other skilled and ambitious people:

> It has often been assumed that knowledge is like love in the famous 1977 John Paul Young disco hit: "in the air, everywhere I look around." This assumption has its origins in the work of Alfred Marshall, who stated in his 1890 book *The Principles of Economics* that "the mysteries of the trade become no mysteries; but are as it were in the air, and children learn many of them unconsciously."[21]

Urban economists have emphasized that such "knowledge in the air" in educated cities represents a positive externality. When Amazon hires 1,000 computer scientists to work in Seattle, it hires them in order to raise the firm's profits. Such a firm is likely to over-look how its actions impact the overall Seattle economy. Local real estate property owners win from this move because housing supply is limited in Seattle and the new hires have the purchasing power to purchase nice homes. Their migration to Seattle attracts startups who want to be close to this major company and this creates a domino effect.

Could WFH reverse this effect? The answer depends on who moves in and who moves out of Seattle in our new WFH economy. Imagine if the least ambitious seek to be full-time remote workers and they move away to the distant suburbs and other smaller and cheaper cities. Suppose their housing units are filled by young "go-getters." In this case, the emerging game of "musical chairs" could actually strengthen a city such as Seattle because the "average" local worker/resident has more skill and ambition. People are not physically changing here. Instead, there is a composition shift of who is and is not living and working in such a city.

Firms such as Amazon have a strong incentive to measure their own productivity effects due to allowing their workforce to spread out. They have the option in the future to bring workers back to headquarters if the WFH experiment has unforeseen negative effects. For example, as Amazon's workforce spreads out away from Seattle, will the firm lose significant productivity gains? The answer hinges on how effectively zoom sessions substitute for face-to-face communication. For teams of Amazon workers who already know each other, the productivity losses from zoom sessions will be small. For new workers who work remotely, Amazon has strong incentives to monitor whether their productivity is lagging and to experiment with strategies (such as bringing them more often to a HQ or HQ2 to "huddle"). I predict that there is a quantity versus quality tradeoff. While there will be fewer face-to-face meetings in a WFH economy, they will be of higher average quality when they occur.

While Amazon has an incentive to configure its WFH to maximize its own profit, it does not have a strong incentive to internalize the forces that Jane Jacobs emphasized. If Amazon allows many of its workers to engage in WFH and they both work from home and spread out across the United States, this could reduce the productivity of other firms in Seattle because their workers learn less and gain less from being there. If this is the case, then Amazon's embrace of WFH would actually lower Seattle's economic growth by more than its direct impact because of a multiplier effect.

If this dynamic actually takes place, urban economists will quickly document this effect. By the year 2030, we will know much more about whether a tech city such as Seattle has experienced a productivity slowdown as more local tech workers either exit to engage in remote work or commute to Seattle offices less often. One possibility is that as skilled workers spread out across locations, there will be a type of convergence across geographic areas as other geographic areas catch up in productivity to the star areas. Given commuting costs, landowners in superstar cities enjoyed an asset value windfall as tech workers were willing to bid up prices in order to have shorter commutes. In this sense, the extremely productive geographic clusters enriched those lucky individuals who own the nearby land. In a recent study, I document that black people are less likely to have bought such property in highly productive cities such as Boston, San Francisco, and Seattle.[22] This fact highlights that our geographic clusters of productivity that are home to few African Americans also have few African American homeowners. These facts highlight how our past non-WFH economy actually contributed to income inequality across geographic groups. It remains an open question whether a type of efficiency versus equity tradeoff arises as the rise of WFH leads to a greater geographic spread of economic opportunity but also reduces some of the productivity spikes that we achieved in the past in our superstar cities.

Past Recoveries from Major Shocks

In late 2020, news stories often reported that major companies who have been headquartered in superstar cities are relocating and are allowing more of their workers to engage in WFH. This could pose risks to these host cities that have prospered for decades.

Urban economists study how cities recover from past shocks. Unlike other scientists who can run controlled experiments, urban economists must rely on natural experiments. We cannot run a controlled experiment such that one city is randomly assigned to suffer from a terrible shock while another city is assigned to the control group and then observe the urban dynamics in both cities. Given that we cannot engage in such experimentation, we look for events in the past when cities have faced great duress.

Over the centuries, cities have displayed amazing resilience. Consider New York City. It has been punched hard by the 1918 Spanish flu, the Great Depression, the deindustrialization of the 1960s, the 1970s financial crisis, and the 2001 terrorist attacks. "Each time, people proclaimed the city would forever change— after 9/11, who would want to work or live in Lower Manhattan?— but each time the prognostications fizzled."[23]

Major disasters often have a "silver lining." In the aftermath of the 1872 fire in Boston, the city's economic growth accelerated because the fire allowed for a rearrangement of economic activity and this encouraged a repositioning of businesses throughout the city to maximize the gains to trade.[24] This coordinated migration is unlikely to have occurred if the fire had not taken place. The potential for a "silver lining" of a major shock is also seen in the aftermath of the 1906 fire in San Francisco and the Chicago fire.[25]

Natural disasters can wreak havoc on cities by killing and injuring people, dislocating residents, destroying businesses and homes, and damaging infrastructure. However, a possible silver lining of natural disasters is that they provide the opportunity to reorganize and redesign large areas of a city to better fit current economic realities that would otherwise be very difficult or impossible due to a large amount of durable capital being owned by a variety of stakeholders. The Great Fires of Baltimore, Boston, and Chicago all prompted demands from residents for their cities to be rebuilt with improvements in traffic flow, water infrastructure, and electricity.[26] The 1906 San Francisco earthquake and resulting fire, one such event, destroyed 28,000 buildings in the city. The reconstruction that followed responded to a continued rise in demand for housing in the city. Developers were uninhibited by city building regulations, which they effectively resisted, and a zoning code, which was not enacted by the city until 1921. By comparing neighborhoods that were razed by the fire to those that were not across several time periods, one study found that residential areas that were destroyed by the fire increased their density by 60 percent eight years after the fire relative to unaffected areas, with a treatment effect of twenty-nine additional units per acre. While the impact subsided over time, small differences were still present in 1950 and 2011.[27] Other studies found similar medium-term beneficial effects from the Great Boston Fire of 1872, as outdated buildings were destroyed and land was redeveloped, resulting in increased land value.[28] These examples highlight how a "silver lining" can emerge when a shock occurs.

Since 2000, New York City has experienced two major shocks—the terrorist attacks of 9/11 (2001) and Hurricane Sandy (2012). In the latter case, while the hurricane caused significant damage to housing along the coast, the macro-productivity of the regional economy was minimally affected. NYC likewise proved to be amazingly resilient in the aftermath of the 9/11 attacks. Research on the medium-term effects of wartime bombings has documented a remarkable resilience of affected areas such that they quickly recover from the shock.[29] Wall Street firms were already engaging in firm fragmentation before the attack and the attack probably accelerated this trend, but the southern Manhattan area enjoyed a great decade in the 2000s as the residential community boomed and Manhattan thrived as a green "consumer city."[30]

In the case of a terrorist attack, it can cause enormous localized damage, but after the event there is a rebuilding phase if people believe that life will go back to normal. Economic researchers have studied the urban real estate implications of the 9/11 terrorist attacks with a focus on whether these shocks accelerated the trend of job suburbanization.[31] Following the 9/11 terrorist attacks, real estate vacancies in high-quality buildings located in Chicago (one of the largest economic centers in the United States) increased greatly. Professors of economics Alberto Abadie and Sofia Dermisi hypothesized that this increase in vacancies was a result of the increased perceived fear of terrorist attacks. These fears are often more greatly associated with taller and more influential buildings, which was represented in the data where buildings in the "shadow" (0.3 mile radius) of Chicago's largest buildings suffered the greatest increase in vacancies.[32]

A California Exodus?

In December 2020, Elon Musk announced that he was selling his California real estate and moving to Texas. Is his decision a leading indicator of an emerging migration trend away from this sunny state? In recent decades, San Francisco, San Jose, Los Angeles, and San Diego have enjoyed a real estate boom due to their great quality of life, international investors' willingness to live there, and booming tech, media, and biotech industries.

California features productivity advantages because of its unique climate, topography, and beach amenities. No other part of the nation is so beautiful, and it is no accident that despite its high taxes the state is home to a large share of the nation's billionaires even on a per-person basis (165 of the nation's 614 billionaires live in California). California features 27 percent of the nation's billionaires despite being home to only 11 percent of the nation's population.

California taxes high-income earners at 14 percent of their annual income, which is easily the highest state-income-tax rate in the nation (Hawaii is next at 11 percent, then New Jersey at 10.75 percent). California has enjoyed a long period of economic success, partly due to its Mediterranean climate, excellent universities, connections to the global economy, high quality of life, and large skilled labor force. Many people and businesses have been willing to relocate to the state despite its relatively high cost of living.

California is famous for its great beauty and for the difficulty that developers have in building new housing in the state. These two facts are related. Many advocates of slow growth argue that new development must be blocked in order to protect the state's natural capital. In recent decades, the state has built very little new housing and home prices reflect aggregate supply and demand. According to Zillow February 2021 data, the median home price in the state equals $624,000, while for the nation as a whole it equals $269,000, and in San Francisco County it is $1.6 million.

Facing these prices, it is not surprising that in recent years, large numbers of people and businesses have been leaving the state for places like Texas and Utah. In 2016, an estimated 1,800 businesses left California, with 299 of them relocating to Texas.[33] In 2017, 661,000 people left California while only 523,000 moved to the state. Of those 661,000 leaving the state, 63,200 moved to Texas and 59,200 moved to Arizona.[34] There are signs that the state, famous for high-wage tech jobs in Silicon Valley, is falling behind the rest of the nation.

In recent years, California has ranked at the bottom for creating new jobs that pay above average wages and ranked at the top in creating low-wage jobs.[35] The Tax Foundation ranked California second worst in the nation for its state business tax climate.[36] A 2018 survey by the Pacific Research Institute found that high real estate costs, housing affordability, public education, and regulatory and tax burdens ranked high on a list of concerns driving business executive decisions on whether to locate in California.[37] There are increasing concerns that the state's public education system is not providing students with the skills required to succeed in a modern workforce, as three out of five high school students are not college or workforce ready.[38]

The rise of WFH creates new opportunities for those firms

and workers who do not greatly gain from living and locating in California to choose other locations. Companies with the option to relocate or grow their presence in other states may take that opportunity in a future with increased work from home possibilities. Business and venture capital leaders are increasingly considering leaving California due to concerns over property and nuisance crime, restrictive zoning, and local government responsiveness for alternatives like Texas.[39] States like Texas, Utah, Colorado, and Washington present attractive, relatively low-cost options with talented labor markets and growing industry clusters. A recent survey of Bay Area tech workers found that over 40 percent expressed interest in moving to a less expensive city if their employer allowed them to work from home full-time.[40] Companies can respond to this demand by exiting the expensive Golden State and relocating to a cheaper alternative if being close to tech talent is no longer a requirement. If people and firms continue to flow out of California and relocate to emerging tech and business hubs, the state may lose its edge as the center of action as viable alternatives in places such as Austin, Denver, and Salt Lake City continue to grow.

History versus Expectations Revisited

In explaining a city's population and economic growth over time, Nobel laureate Paul Krugman emphasizes the importance of history versus expectations. Early in America's history, New York City became a trading port with Europe. People settled in Manhattan to work and to trade. This historical development created momentum as more people moved there.

The expectations of people and firms also play a key role in determining a city's future. The expectation that New York City will continue to have a bright future leads more young people to move there.[41] Perhaps surprisingly, leading tech firms are investing more in urban space in superstar cities. Major tech firms are making large investments in remote purchasing space in Manhattan. Amazon has several Midtown office properties including the Lord & Taylor Building. This redeployment of a department store highlights how buildings can be repositioned in the new economy. "We know that talent attracts talent, and we believe that the creative energy of cities like New York will continue to attract diverse professionals from around the world," said Ardine Williams, Amazon's vice president of workforce development.[42]

New York City continues to have several rare features that young people value very much. Young people continue to value face-to-face interaction and New York City brims with energy every hour of the day. The city's access to water and the ability to walk the city offer unique synergies between natural beauty and the consumer city.

Even if America's superstar cities lose some of their productivity advantage due to their exporting middle-class WFH workers, they will continue to be very attractive "consumer city" and tourist destinations that offer new experiences that the suburbs cannot offer.[43] Declining center city crime and investments in "greening" such areas by having walking and biking trails in cities ranging from Chicago to Boston increase the attractiveness of living downtown.[44] If such cities lose employees to WFH, they will have the capacity to pivot to building up their consumer city features and attracting young people and older people to live a type of European city lifestyle in these center cities.

Cities that continue to have good quality-of-life fundamentals (such as California cities with great weather) hold the option to auction off development rights to developers to build more housing. By reducing development red tape and encouraging more development, such cities become more affordable and attractive to young people seeking the urban experience.[45] By increasing housing supply such cities can raise tax revenue and create a new more affordable urban experience. This increases the quality of life for the young and minorities who often do not have the access to capital to finance investing in expensive real estate.

City leaders and local property owners have strong incentives to keep an eye on whether their city's count of college graduates is rising or falling. This easy-to-observe metric indicates whether the footloose skilled are "voting with their feet" to enter or exit the place. The healthy local economy both grows its own set of young college graduates who choose to continue to live in the city and attracts other educated people to move there.[46]

Commercial Buildings Conversion into New Housing

In many major US cities, there are iconic commercial office buildings such as 30 Rockefeller Center in New York City, the Transamerica Pyramid Building in San Francisco, the Prudential Center in Boston, and the John Hancock Tower in Chicago. What will become of these properties? Can they be converted into residential housing?

Commercial property owners may choose to incur costs to convert their property into residential real estate. If commercial real estate rents are high because a given building is located in a productive part of the city close to other commercial towers, then the conversion of those buildings into residential real estate can lower the value of other commercial rents because they lose access to productive partners. Individual owners of commercial properties, who tend to focus on their own profits, have little incentive to recognize whether their actions convey benefits or harms to nearby building owners.

If high-cost cities experience a sharp decline in commercial rents, some owners may be reluctant to sell at a much lower price. Real estate research based on data from Boston condos in the 1990s found that owners do not sell for a price below what they originally paid for the asset.[47] In a bust, however, homes tend to sit on the market for long periods of time with asking prices well above expected selling prices, and many sellers eventually withdraw their properties without sale. Behavioral economists have advanced an explanation called "prospect theory," which argues that asset owners keep in mind the asset's purchase price and this price anchors their current decisions as they do not want to sell an asset for a loss. If the value of commercial buildings in superstar cities declines and if the asset owners engage in such behavioral logic, then they will be slow to sell their buildings to residential housing developers. Such individual behavior can have macroeconomic consequences for the city as the conversion of buildings from outdated commercial uses to demanded residential uses would be slowed due to price negotiations.

Regulations such as zoning laws can also slow down the transition. A misallocation of space will occur if there are vacant commercial properties adjacent to residential buildings with high rents and the commercial property cannot be rezoned for residential property. In Manhattan's recent past, industrial space existed because Manhattan was a center of manufacturing in the 1950s. As these firms closed, this space was illegally used as residential space. If the land use code were more flexible, this transition of using buildings for their highest and best value would occur more quickly.

The Urban Vision of Jane Jacobs Revisited

Urban scholars celebrate the writing and activism of Jane Jacobs. Throughout her life she championed the preservation of historic neighborhoods such as Greenwich Village in New York City and battled with modernists such as Robert Moses who sought to build highways connecting cities to suburbs but paved over older "slum" neighborhoods in the name of progress. She opposed high-rise buildings that destroyed the walking organic nature of neighborhoods. She wrote:

> How can the city tie in its old buildings with its new ones, so that each complements the other and reinforces the quality of continuity the city should have? Can the new projects be tied into downtown streets? The best available sites may be outside downtown—but how far outside of downtown? Does the choice of site anticipate normal growth, or is the site so far away that it will gain no support from downtown, and give it none? Does new building exploit the strong qualities of the street—or virtually obliterate the street? Will the new project mix all kinds of activities together, or does it mistakenly segregate them? In short, will the city be any fun? The citizen can be the ultimate expert on this; what is needed is an observant eye, curiosity about people, and a willingness to walk. He should walk not only the streets of his own city, but those of every city he visits.[48]

In the 1960s, Jacobs sought to preserve a Manhattan neighborhood featuring low-rise buildings and sidewalks that encouraged walking. This urban vision embraced "limits to growth." The laws of supply and demand teach us that when the supply of housing is limited by not building upward on scarce land and demand is high because of both local job growth and great quality of life, real estate prices will soar and the middle class will be priced out. It appears that Jacobs wanted to limit entry to her beloved city. She worried that irreversible damage would be done and the old city would lose its charm as slums were cleared in the "name of progress."

The rise of WFH actually helps to alleviate the concerns raised by preservationists such as Jacobs because it reduces the aggregate demand by commuters to live in these areas. People with an aesthetic taste for such areas will be attracted to live there.[49] In the most desirable areas, home prices will be quite high. At the same time, the exodus of firms who do not greatly benefit from locating in the dense center city and the workers who work for these firms will together reduce demand for local land and this should help to make such areas more affordable so that the next generation of urbanists can enjoy living in more affordable areas.

5   *New Opportunities for Other Areas*

In the early 1970s, the Rolling Stones recorded *Exile on Main Street* in southern France. The British band moved to France to record this album partially due to the differential in national taxes. In the mid-1960s, George Harrison of the Beatles recorded the song "Taxman." The lyrics of the song do not follow the usual rock and roll formula of singing about love and having fun. Instead, Harrison expresses his displeasure at facing a 95 percent marginal tax rate in England.

Musicians can record their music anywhere where there is a music studio. Such studios are not a very expensive piece of capital equipment. In this sense, music recording is an early example of WFH. These artists were considering their tax exposure as they chose where to work. In more recent research, it has been documented that superstar European football players tend to migrate to European nations with lower tax rates.[1] Both the Rolling Stones and football players have something in common with remote workers—they can locate anywhere and still be productive.[2]

Many professional golfers live in Florida as they travel to tournaments and play and then move on. Florida does not have a state income tax. If golfers such as Tiger Woods lived in California they would be paying 13.5 percent and would face a total tax rate of over 50 percent per year. Similar to footloose golfers, WFH workers can live anywhere. Zero-income tax states include Alaska, Florida, Nevada, South Dakota, Texas, Washington, and Wyoming.[3] In December 2020, Goldman Sachs announced that it was weighing the move of its asset management arm to Florida.[4] Now that more firms are considering engaging more WFH, they are becoming more responsive to differential tax incentives across states. Low tax areas that are close to very productive cities gain from their geography. For example, New Hampshire does not have a state income tax but it does tax interest and dividends. It tries to lure tech companies to locate on its border with access to Boston.

California features high taxes but it is home to more than 40 million people including many billionaires. Geographic differences in taxes alone do not determine where people locate. If an area has exceptional quality of life, then a person may want to live there despite the high taxes. If the high taxes help to create a paradise, then a person will be more willing to pay the taxes and to enjoy the exceptional local services.

Areas differ with respect to their quality of life. Los Angeles offers consistently enjoyable weather and proximity to both mountains and oceans, whereas Bozeman, Montana, has widely variable weather and is more than a thousand miles from either ocean. Such different places compete to attract increasingly footloose people. The United States is a huge nation that offers WFH workers many opportunities for choosing where to live. And each of these WFH-eligible workers may have his own unique approach when deciding where he wants to go.

As each individual has greater freedom to go where she wants to go and spend her scarce time, our national well-being increases.

This chapter sketches out how our nation's economic geography is likely to change as more WFH-eligible workers spread out. Key issues arise concerning what localities seek to experience population growth versus which areas will enact policies to limit economic growth. Which American areas seek to remain small and not be "the Next Nashville"? A theme throughout this chapter is the central importance of quality of life. Those areas with great quality of life will experience rising demand among WFH workers to live there.

The New Scarsdale: The Rise of Exurban Sprawl

I grew up in Scarsdale in the 1970s and 1980s as my father commuted by public transit to New York City. Scarsdale is roughly twenty-five miles from New York City and is known for its excellent public schools. Scarsdale's housing is now expensive and this will pose a budget challenge for many WFH workers. Many WFH workers in the future will seek out suburban living in areas known to have great local amenities. And as the middle class can now live farther from a work location, their menu of local residential communities increases.

Incumbent homeowners are not eager to welcome thousands of new WFH workers to build new homes in the area. While there are nearby golf courses and other pieces of unused land that could be converted into new housing, there is a long tradition in the United States of incumbent homeowners using local land use laws to slow new construction.

In this case, the rise of WFH combined with an inability to build more housing will simply lead to higher home prices in suburban areas like Scarsdale, and this benefits the incumbent homeowners who now own a more valuable asset. From the perspective of the footloose WFH who cannot afford these Scarsdale homes, where do they go? The combination of the rise of WFH and the fact that many great suburban communities such as Scarsdale will not welcome new growth creates a growth opportunity for new communities to form that can offer excellent schools and other valued local public goods such as safety and greenery.

The Rise of New Cities?

In 2019, 82.5 percent of Americans lived in a metropolitan area, yet these metropolitan areas include only 18 percent of the land in the United States. The rise of WFH is likely to lead the US population to spread out around the nation. While the US already has many cities, new jurisdictions may form. Paul Romer, the 2018 Nobel Laureate in Economics, has discussed why creating new cities (which he calls charter cities) creates exciting possibilities for creating better governance.

> Moving from bad rules to better ones may be much harder than most economists have allowed....
>
> The key to the project is a charter city, which starts out as a city-sized piece of uninhabited territory and a charter or constitution specifying the rules that will apply there. If the charter specifies good rules (or in our professional jargon, good institutions) millions of people will come together to build a new city.[5]

Can a "new" Scarsdale be built farther from cities that welcome WFH workers and their families? The answer to this question hinges on how a jurisdiction produces great schools and other high-quality local public goods. Given enough tax revenue, it is easy to build beautiful new buildings and to hire a football coach, but a great school also features great teachers and great peers. Great teachers have many choices over where they live. They will be more likely to accept a job at a new school featuring new educational rules if the pay is good and the local lifestyle and quality of life is good and good nearby housing is affordable. In the distant suburbs, all of these features seem achievable. If there are not that many great teachers in the nation, then a "new" Scarsdale would have to pay high salaries to attract such teachers. If the charter city is expected to have a great quality of life, then great teachers would be willing to work there at a lower salary than they would earn in a less desirable location.

A charter city will feature a new school district and will not feature an incumbent public-sector teachers union. While unions offer benefits to their members, union rules often limit the flexibility and experimentation of such an organization. There are often rigid rules about how teachers are compensated (based on seniority) and there are other limits placed on the school's principal in determining how to configure the school. We as a society continue to learn about how children learn. Such uncertainty about this key production function means that school leaders need more flexibility over configuring the curriculum and how teachers versus internet technology are used to educate different children. Union work rules often limit this experimentation.

The charter city creates a new jurisdiction with fresh rules in a geographical area where there are no incumbent interest groups such as public-sector unions blocking new approaches to educating young people or policing. Urban research has highlighted how rare are the cases where new approaches such as charter schools can be introduced.

In a new charter city, the new schools would have more flexibility over how they are run and how their curriculum is set. Such schools will develop a reputation and this will lead the next generation of WFH workers who have "done their homework" to decide if this jurisdiction is right for them. WFH workers may realize that they do not know what their quality of life would be in a new charter city at the fringe of a metro area. Such individuals could rent for a while in such an area to see if the lifestyle delivers on what they expected. Such a "tasting" reduces regret about locking in too early in an unproven new area.

In higher-quality school districts, new migrants will pay higher property taxes but they will recognize that these revenues are used to provide high-quality local public education. In communities such as Scarsdale, there is no rental housing and the area is almost all zoned for single-family homes. These two rules effectively exclude the poor and this guarantees that the bulk of the property tax revenue collected from the local residents is used for educational programs that the typical taxpayer desires. There are few redistributive transfers taking place in Scarsdale because the ratio of the town's poor people to rich people is tiny.

In a newly built exurban "Scarsdale" that caters to WFH families, the average income in the community will rise as more of these workers move to a quasi-rural place. The growth in the count of WFH workers would allow the school's student population to grow to a scale to take advantage of scale economies. If only ten people want to live in an area and pay higher taxes for an elite school, this is not a sufficient scale of demand to open such a school. With the introduction of road pricing and WFH, more people would consider moving to such an exurban new school district and this would benefit everyone who lives there because then the scale economies could be enjoyed. To appreciate this point, suppose it costs $5 million to build a new school and $1 million a year to operate it. If the school only has 100 students, the average cost to operate the school is $6 million divided by 100, which equals $60,000 per student. Such a school would need to charge $60,000 a year per student in tuition to break even. If the school attracts 1,000 students, and the school now hires extra teachers so the operating cost is $2 million per year, the average cost per student would be $7 million divided by 1,000, which equals $7,000. This simple example highlights how the scale of student demand drives down the average cost, and the scale of student demand is determined in large part by their parents being able to engage in WFH.

If more parents are working from home, some of them will want to educate their children from home perhaps for a half day and then send the child to a local school for the rest of the day. While the 2020 COVID experience has been miserable, during normal times a much better balance could be achieved. The parents of a gifted child could rely on advanced Khan Academy videos for a half day each day and then send the child to school to socialize and learn other material. The combination of studying from home and attending "real school" opens up many new menu combinations to meet the needs of different children. In the past, parents commuted to work and their children commuted to a local school. Going forward, there are new possibilities for parents to sometimes work at home and have their children study at home on those days. This arrangement will benefit families whose children have special needs and special talents. A key theme throughout this book is how our market economy accommodates our diversity. I foresee that WFH will greatly help here.

Throughout this section, I have focused on one metric of local public services—school quality. In reality there are many other dimensions of what defines a community, including religious communities, environmentalist communities, and other lifestyle communities. In our internet-connected economy, people will research where they want to live and they will "shop around" before moving to such a place. In the footloose WFH era, communities that create a physical place that is both attractive and inclusive for the people who seek a specific focus will attract WFH workers.

As more of the population has access to an increased menu of residential alternatives, this will raise the well-being of each of them as they will be better matched to the areas where they want to live and the types of people with whom they want to associate. A potential downside of such migration is a type of self-segregation as religious areas arise and environmentalist areas arise. This dynamic will mean that the rise of WFH will increase our ability to "vote with our feet" to live with like-minded people. This will strengthen bonds between like-minded people. Robert Putnam, the author of *Bowling Alone*, would point out that this residential sorting imposes one major downside: after this "Big Sort" there will be a growing set of Americans who do not often interact face to face with people holding a different worldview. During our partisan times, this lack of face-to-face interaction with people who hold very different views from one's own views may have important implications for our democracy. As a concerned citizen, I believe that we should watch out for this potentially socially costly downside from WFH. As an economist, I want to stress that there is a key "what if" here.

Back in 2019 before the rise of WFH, were people really interacting in face-to-face discussions with others who held very different beliefs? With the rise of the internet, social platforms such as Twitter do allow different people to interact. We all know that the implications of such platforms such as Twitter and Facebook for our democracy remain open and very important social questions.

The Environmental Cost of Increased Sprawl

If more people start to live farther from center cities, significant environmental degradation could take place. When we live closer to the city center, we are more likely to use public transit and to live in smaller housing units. These two effects are linked together because land prices are higher closer to the city center. When land prices are high, people consume less land by living in high-rise apartment buildings in smaller housing units. High population density facilitates the introduction of public transit systems. Such compact living shrinks our carbon footprint. This is the reason that people in urban Asian nations such as Japan, China, and Korea have a much smaller carbon footprint than Americans. In dense urban core areas such as Manhattan and Hong Kong, public transit use thrives. The subway and bus network allows individuals to walk to a convenient transit hub and use public transit to reach a destination. When people live in the suburbs and exurbs, they do not use public transit. Public transit is a transport technology that works best in center cities. In Japan, a large share of electricity is generated using nuclear power and this zero-carbon source means that any electricity consumption does not contribute to the climate change challenge.

We produce less pollution when we live at higher density but we are exposed to more pollution when we live at higher density. A pithy observation in environmental economics states: "The solution to pollution is dilution." In other words, if we spread out, we reduce our exposure to air pollution (such as PM2.5) and water pollution disease risk (such as typhoid). As we have learned in 2020 from the fear of COVID contagion risk, there continue to be demons of density associated with living and interacting in close physical proximity. By spreading out, those who greatly value physical proximity can do so while others can live in cleaner, safer, cheaper areas and still have access to the cities.

As the WFH-eligible spread out to live in new places, this has implications for local air quality and the production of greenhouse gas emissions because people drive more when they live at lower population density. The simple algebra for determining how a person's transportation choices impact local air pollution can be expressed as miles driven multiplied by emissions per mile. This algebra reflects the quantity and quality of economic activity. If suburbanites drive more than center city residents but if they drive "green cars," then they do not contribute to local pollution or greenhouse gas emissions. The new generation of vehicles creates much less local air pollution than vehicles built before 1990. While vehicle fuel economy has increased in recent years, the continued reliance on fossil fuels to power vehicles means that transportation's share of overall US greenhouse gas emissions continues to rise.

Although the Biden administration seeks to reduce the nation's greenhouse gas emissions, raising gas taxes is politically very unpopular. Those who live outside of cities tend to oppose such gas taxes because such rules would lower the real incomes of people who have to drive more miles. The recent Yellow Vest protests in rural France highlight this point. The people of Lansargues actively protested increases in gasoline taxes and said that President Macron was being elitist as he lives in Paris—an expensive city with excellent public transport.[6]

In my own research set in the United States, I have documented that suburbanites tend to oppose greenhouse gas emissions policies.[7] This fact is not solely due to the fact that Republicans tend to live in the suburbs. Using standard statistical techniques, I have documented that Republican areas do oppose climate mitigation policies, but controlling for this factor, those who live at lower population density are less likely to support climate policies.

A possible solution to this emerging policy challenge of increased vehicle mileage at the suburban fringe caused by WFH workers is the rise of the electric vehicle. If electric vehicles (EVs such as Tesla and its less pricey rivals) become higher quality and cheaper, and if the power is generated by renewables, then the pollution externality associated with driving diminishes.[8] Recent work in energy economics has argued that electric vehicles can be dirtier than conventional vehicles if they are charged in the Midwest where power comes from coal-fired power plants.[9] In California, the grid is already "green" as this progressive state uses little coal and relies on natural gas and renewables.

As some WFH workers move far from the cities where land is much cheaper, they will live in larger homes. This could also increase their carbon footprint. This unintended consequence will be less likely if these new homes feature solar panels that charge the home and an EV vehicle. The synergies between building "green homes" that are energy efficient and feature sufficient solar panels to power both the home and the EV creates new exciting possibilities of decarbonizing the suburbs. The key engineering innovation here is cheap batteries so that the sun's power generation can be stored and used when the EV owner wants to travel.

The rise of WFH will lead to many new homes being built. If electricity prices are expected to be high and if there are state mandates for zero-energy homes, then major home builders such as KB Home will build homes with solar panels that are large enough to charge the home and to charge the family's electric vehicles. This will create an incentive for WFH workers, even those who are not environmentalists, to buy EVs rather than gasoline vehicles.

The rise of WFH encourages people to move farther out and drive more but they will live in new housing with the built-in technology to foster a zero-carbon lifestyle. Given that people who live far from cities drive more, this usually means that they consume more fossil fuels and thus pay more in taxes if gas taxes and carbon taxes increase. This urban economics logic helps to explain why center city residents are more likely to support carbon mitigation policies. Such center cities attract progressive people, and once they live in a center city, they have a smaller carbon footprint because they can walk and use public transit and live in smaller apartments than their suburban counterparts.

The possibility that WFH workers who live at the fringe live in new zero-energy homes with solar panels that charge their electric vehicles opens up the exciting prospect that WFH work will shift carbon politics. In this case, WFH helps to accelerate this green transition because more of our housing stock will be zero carbon and the transport emissions from WFH workers who own electric vehicles will shrink. If a growing percentage of suburban residents produces few greenhouse gas emissions, then they will pay less out of pocket if the United States enacts a carbon tax. This creates an incentive for them to support such carbon taxes because they would gain the implicit insurance benefits of facing less climate change risk without facing higher prices for energy.

New home construction firms will gain valuable experience and enjoy scale economies due to learning-by-doing effects. Learning by doing means that zero-energy home builders' cost of production is a declining function of cumulative experience. As these firms gain experience by building for WFH families, this lowers the cost of the "green home" for everyone in the economy.[10] Nobel laureates Robert Lucas and Paul Romer have emphasized that once we have a blueprint for producing a technology, the cost for producing another unit of the good is low. In the case of "green homes," the rise of WFH increases the likelihood that for-profit housing developers create a successful blueprint that can be scaled up.

Real estate is a long-lived durable good. In Los Angeles, I live in a home built in 1962. When WFH workers build new homes at the fringe of metropolitan areas, they have strong incentives to think about what the quality of life will be like in that area in the future. Progress in climate science has allowed climate forecast firms to make pinpoint predictions about expected future increases in summer heat and flood risk. Homeowners have strong incentives to build resilient housing that can withstand these expected future trends. In this sense, the expectation of future climate change causes upfront adaptation investment. For example, more powerful air conditioning and more solar panels will be installed in a home located in a place that is expected to become even hotter in future summers. A cost-minimizing family will compare the upfront cost of installing the solar panels and air conditioning now relative to bearing even larger future air conditioning bills to offset the heat.

In the American West, there have been increasingly severe fires caused by drought and heat. In order to reduce ambient PM2.5 levels, there have not been controlled burns to reduce the forest fuel. This has meant that when fires do occur, there is the potential for huge blazes such as what took place in fall 2020 in northern California. The rise of WFH could lead more people to live in the fire zones.

Economics teaches us that both demand and supply factors jointly determine the possibility of building new housing at the periphery of major cities. In early 2021, at the fringe of the Los Angeles metro area, an important lesson is offered about how the risk of climate change and greater fire risk in the heat and drought-plagued American West may increase the regulatory costs of building new housing.

Consider the proposed Tejon Ranch development.[11] Located seventy miles from the city of Los Angeles, planning has been underway to build 20,000 homes on 6,000 acres. In April 2021, a judge's ruling slowed down the project, expressing concerns about the extra greenhouse gas emissions this new development will cause and about the extra fire risk that the new residents will face. While the rise of WFH increases demand to live in new, affordable housing such as this, state and local officials will have to decide what risks and costs are exacerbated by permitting such new housing to be built. The key economics point here is that local supply-side conditions play an important role in determining where the rise of WFH causes local economic growth.

In a 2017 *New York Times* editorial, Enrico Moretti argued that stringent housing zoning in center cities such as San Francisco, Portland, and Seattle has raised local land prices by limiting housing supply and making the local area more desirable and hence increasing demand. Such high home prices at the core pushes people to the exurban fringe.[12] The rise of WFH only accentuates this effect. Recent research documents that subsidized fire-fighting services in these areas only increases the number of people who live there.[13] Improvements in building codes can play a productive role in offsetting some of these risks.[14]

Reducing the Environmental Costs of Farmland Conversion

As WFH workers move farther out into the peripheries of Silicon Valley and New York City and Chicago, they will encounter farmland. Environmentalists are concerned that suburban sprawl paves such farmland and that this poses risks for the United States in terms of lost biodiversity and reduced domestic food supply.

The greater Silicon Valley area offers an informative case study about the effects of land use restrictions meant to preserve farmland. Over 17,000 tech firms operate in the Bay Area, directly employing over 750,000 people; this represents one-fifth of the region's overall workforce. The Bay Area ranks first in the nation in terms of tech-sector job growth, with over 33,000 tech jobs added in 2018 alone. Construction of new housing units in Bay Area cities has lagged population growth. San Francisco's stock of housing units increased by 6 percent from 2010 to 2018 while its population grew by nearly 10 percent. Oakland only increased its stock of housing units by 1.8 percent in the same time frame while also seeing population growth of nearly 10 percent. For the entire nine-county Bay Area, the number of housing units grew by only 4 percent, a growth rate less than half that of its population increase. This low rate of construction of housing has contributed to the Bay

Area having the highest median home value of any metropolitan region in the country.

Silicon Valley is world renowned for being the high-tech home of successful companies such as Apple, Facebook, and Intel, but is less well known for its thousands of acres of farmland. In 2017, the Silicon Valley counties of Alameda, San Mateo, and Santa Clara had 517,338 acres of land in farms, comprising 33 percent of the total land area of the three counties. While this may seem like a large share, it has actually dropped by 11 percent since 2002 from 580,475 acres, mirroring changes at the state level.[15] A similar reduction in the number of farms occurred over the same time period with an increasing share of small farms. The share of farms that were one to nine acres in these three counties grew from 37 to 44 percent from 2002 to 2017, while the share of farms held by all other size classes shrank, except for the largest-size class of farms over 1,000 acres. In Alameda County, the number of farms with over 1,000 acres nearly doubled from eight in 2002 to fifteen in 2017.

Farmland preservation creates a tension between urban interests and environmental interests. The overall San Francisco local economy could be even stronger and more inviting if there was more affordable suburban housing in relatively proximate locations near the area. One study argued that America's overall income level is lower because more housing is not being built in productive places. The transformation of farmland into suburban housing could greatly enhance the macroeconomy's efficiency.[16]

California's farmland does serve a unique role for the state's economy and for America's consumers. Together, the total value of agricultural products in the three Silicon Valley counties was $502 million in 2017, which accounted for less than 1 percent of the total value of agricultural products among California's fifty-three counties ($59 million).[17] At the same time, the three counties accounted for over 2 percent of its acreage in farmland. In 2017, the counties' main products were wine grapes ($18 million) and cattle ($16 million) in Alameda County, floral and nursery crops in San Mateo County ($103 million), and mushrooms ($75 million) in Santa Clara County. Santa Clara County was the only major producer of any product in Silicon Valley, ranking second among all California counties for its production of mushrooms. However, this valuable crop only accounted for around 0.05 percent (150 acres) of the total land acreage of harvested crops in 2017.[18] While there has been a trend over the last two decades of less land being used for farming in these counties, there continue to be opportunities to transfer land-intensive agricultural uses such as livestock production into uses that are more productive.[19]

In allocating scarce land between housing and farmland, economic logic suggests that it should be allocated to the entity that values it the most. An important point here is that with farmland, such farmland offers a flow of profits to the farmer and it offers existence value to environmentalists who value knowing that there continues to be pristine farmland in the nation. This "existence value" is especially valuable if the farmland helps to protect valuable biodiversity.

As WFH workers seek new places to live farther from work centers, an interdisciplinary team of urban planners and ecologists should work together to identify adjacent parcels of land featuring high versus low biodiversity levels. The high biodiversity level places can be protected by being designated a state park or protected by a land trust that purchases the land and protects it from development. For land deemed to have relatively low biodiversity value, real estate developers could be allowed to build new housing for WFH workers in these areas. This approach achieves two goals: it expands the set of affordable land for development in the beautiful state of California and it prioritizes protection for the most valuable land in terms of biodiversity.[20]

As farmland close to productive cities is converted into WFH housing, food prices could rise. But it is important to note that the United States participates in global agricultural markets. If the US grows less farm output, we can import farm products from the rest of the world and this will boost incomes for those poor farmers. If prices for oranges and almonds significantly rise, then this creates an economic incentive for farmers to keep farming and not sell their land to real estate developers seeking to build homes for WHF workers. In this sense, capitalism's invisible hand signals scarcity and guides these land allocation decisions.

One often overlooked benefit from converting farmland into housing is to reduce drought concerns in the American West. Many climate scientists have noted that the American West faces greater drought conditions going forward. The farming sector is a major consumer of water, with farmers consuming roughly 90 percent of the water in the American West.[21] Current water laws give such farmers the right to very cheap water that they are not allowed to sell to urbanites. This creates disincentives to conserve water, and so profit-maximizing farmers choose to grow very water-intensive crops such as alfalfa. Given that farmer water consumption is highly subsidized, the transfer of land from farming to residential housing actually increases the sustainability of the region in the midst of ongoing drought. To repeat this surprising point, climate change raises drought risk in California. Farmers have little incentive to conserve on water consumption. Facing these realities, one way to balance aggregate demand with shrinking aggregate supply of water is to transfer land out of farming and allow the WFH workers to use such land for their own housing desires. This suggests that the rise of WFH, by encouraging workers to live farther from cities, will help the American West to adapt to climate change! If farmers were originally charged a higher price for water, then this logic would not hold.

The Rising Demand to Live in Warm-Winter and Climate-Resilient Cities

For decades, the American people have been moving to the Sun Belt.[22] The US population is aging as the large Baby Boomer cohort grows old and the count of children declines. Millions of upper-middle-class people want to live in warm places such as Florida, Phoenix, and Las Vegas.

These migrants seek access to leisure activities and good hospitals. This creates local service-sector jobs for the less skilled. These cities are affordable because they encourage real estate developers to build. As the US population ages, older successful people seek out warmer areas with good medical care and transport accessibility. This suggests that cities such as Phoenix and other Sun Belt cities could enjoy an additional boom because housing is affordable in the cities where real estate developers face lighter regulations on building new housing.[23]

The rise of WFH could actually make cold winter places such as Bozeman, Montana, more desirable over the course of the year as WFH-eligible workers can live there during more pleasant seasons and then move away during the cold winters. In a sense, this forms a portfolio for mobile people. When investing in the market, one seeks out stocks and bonds that create a balanced portfolio to align with one's individual circumstances. In terms of accessing great weather, a flexible renter can be a type of nomad living in a certain area depending on what season it is. A place such as Bozeman could experience an influx of people during its best seasons and during cold winters mainly attract those who love winter recreation.

Going forward, more of such amenity seekers will also be attracted to climate-resilient places. While there are many known unknowns about emerging climate change risks, all people seek to be safe and comfortable. Places that have been repeatedly hit with natural disasters such as tornados, hurricanes, wildfires, and drought will be less attractive. In one of my recent studies, we document that counties struck with major natural disaster shocks lose population and the remaining population's poverty rate increases. Our explanation for the second fact is that the richer, more footloose people who lived there are able to leave, and other richer, more footloose people are less likely to move into such a place.[24] Areas that face fewer of these risks will be more likely to attract footloose WFH people.

In the age of Big Data, new companies are being formed that specialize in assessing place-based risk, such as 427, Jupiter, Coastal Risk Consulting, and the First Street Foundation. Those WFH workers who care about climate resilience will be more likely to move to the areas that these climate-risk-assessment firms deem to be safer. Such companies play a role similar to Moodys and Standard and Poor's role in evaluating Wall Street risks. On Wall Street, firms that have been deemed as risky by the rating agencies face a higher interest rate when they seek to borrow. In a similar sense, geographic areas that are deemed as risky by the climate rating entities will feature cheaper real estate to compensate buyers for taking on this new risk.

In a world facing greater climate change risk because of rising global greenhouse gas levels, those places that prove to be climate resilient will attract more WFH migrants and will enjoy local economic growth. The United States is a large nation featuring hundreds of cities that offer urbanites many choices concerning where they live and work, and this menu of cities creates the possibility of "voting with your feet" and moving to the right location that balances a person's life goals.

The rise of WFH allows those who are concerned about emerging climate risks to avoid living in an increasingly risky place because their job is headquartered there. This ability to unbundle place of residence from place of work promotes adaptation. Rival locations will compete against each other to attract these WFH climate migrants. This competition among places to attract these successful migrants creates the right incentives for areas to experiment and try new adaptation strategies to enhance their climate resilience. This competition benefits all residents (not just WFH workers) as their area becomes safer than it would have been if the area had not sought to attract WFH workers.

An open question is whether climate-resilient places achieve this status because of "God-given" topography conditions or due to wise local public policies such as planting trees to reduce the urban heat island effect and taking proactive steps to reduce flood risk such as erecting well-designed sea walls. The US Army Corps of Engineers continues to implement new projects to protect geographic areas. One example is investments to protect Charleston, South Carolina, from flood risk by installing infrastructure such as a surge wall and pumping stations.[25]

Jackson Hole: The Rise of Beautiful Places

The United States features many beautiful locations ranging from Jackson Hole in Wyoming to Sedona in Arizona to Carlsbad and Santa Barbara in California. Enterprising real estate developers can simply Google "America's favorite beautiful tourist destinations" and use that geographic list to plan ahead for WFH worker arrival. In the past, few would dare to live in such locations full-time because of limited work opportunities. WFH eliminates this concern.[26]

If Jackson Hole, Wyoming, is an increasingly attractive destination for WFH workers, will real estate developers face the same local NIMBYism that housing developers have faced in Manhattan, San Francisco, and the greater Silicon Valley area? This same dynamic could play out in these high-amenity places. Don't forget that Joni Mitchell lyric: "They paved paradise, put up a parking lot"! Which beautiful areas will be "pro-growth" and allow ample real estate development?

If WFH fuels growing demand to live in beautiful places and if incumbent residents in these places engage in NIMBY behavior, then local real estate prices will soar and this will mean that only the incumbents who become rich from real estate price growth and the super-rich who can afford these asset prices will be able to access these "gated" communities. In this case the rise of WFH contributes to elitism and inequality as only the wealthy can live in paradise.

When opposition to new growth arises, is it due to a genuine concern about destroying paradise or are such concerns mainly a justification for keeping outsiders out? A troubling feature of American land use regulations is that the local incumbents set the policy. Outsiders such as those who live in New Jersey but are thinking of moving to Jackson Hole have no way to express their desire for Jackson Hole to accommodate more residents since outsiders do not vote on local issues. Such outsiders can "buy their way in" by purchasing one of the existing homes. This creates a scarcity of such slots and enriches the incumbent property owners.

Consider an alternative set of land use laws such that real estate developers can purchase the right to build new housing from the local incumbents. Real estate developers, as profit maximizers, would be more likely to take this action if they anticipate that there is a market for selling new homes in beautiful places to WFH workers who want to migrate to the beautiful place.

Beautiful places will attract environmentalists who want to live there. However, the environmentalists who already live there often raise genuine concerns about paving paradise and this justifies their opposition to local growth. The introduction of market price incentives and Big Data analysis can be used here to reach the sweet spot of allowing for new construction while protecting the environment. Road pricing can be used to reduce local traffic congestion. Land can be rezoned to encourage a new urbanism on plots of land in the beautiful place to have compact development and encourage ride sharing, biking, and walking. Energy and water pricing can be introduced to encourage conservation and green construction of real estate that conserves on resource consumption. The net effect of this suite of policies is to permit growth without suffering environmental degradation. Local real estate developers can be encouraged to protect natural capital if they expect that the likelihood that they will receive future development permits hinges on demonstrating that the current set of new housing projects does not degrade the local environment. Such credible threats give developers an incentive to contribute to the region's environmental health.

If developers anticipate that local residents will monitor how their incremental projects are affecting local quality of life, then those developers who seek to continue to build in the area have strong incentives to develop a reputation for protecting and fortifying the community's assets. This set of market incentives reduces the likelihood that common local property will be degraded. Real estate developers have a profit incentive to protect the environment. A beautiful area commands a price premium for recently constructed real estate. Developers will anticipate that they will be blocked from building future real estate if their current projects cause local harm.

Even before 2020, Bozeman, Montana, was experiencing an economic boom as more people grew to appreciate the area's unique quality of life. The rise of WFH only accelerates this effect as more people can now live and work there (while working remotely) for more months. The area's planners now face a "Goldilocks effect" of how to achieve the win-win of enjoying economic growth without degrading local quality of life.

An urban planner in Bozeman wrote about the tradeoffs her area faces: "Our wide-open spaces, abundant outdoor recreation, safe communities, top-notch schools and thriving economy make this a phenomenal place to visit and live, pandemic or not. Nearly all of our local and regional planning documents articulate goals that emphasize new growth near developed areas and conservation of agricultural land and wildlife habitat."[27]

Beautiful areas such as Bozeman will need to make decisions about how much growth they will allow. Local residents will vote on local land use laws and these laws determine the opportunities for people considering moving there. In this internet age, it is easy for prospective migrants to find news and videos about a place such as Bozeman or Malibu or Boise. Such information helps to shape one's imagination such that one has a sense of what it would be like to live there. Improvements in air travel through Southwest and other cheap airlines and the rise of renting other's homes through internet platforms allows people to visit such places to see if it is "as good" as it looks on the internet.

While great places will attract web traffic organically, local boosters continue to seek strategies to advertise their place to enhance its attractiveness relative to traditional destinations such as New York City and San Francisco. Consider the new owner of the National Basketball Association's Utah Jazz. Ryan Smith paid over $1 billion for the team and he is using it as a platform to market the greater Utah experience: "Utah's given me everything. We were told we couldn't build a tech company out of Utah, that we had to go to Silicon Valley. When I was taking venture capital in 2011, half the venture capitalists wanted us to move out of Utah. We've shown that we can win in Utah. That's pretty exciting."[28]

In an economy featuring much more WFH and where major companies are choosing where to locate regional hubs, nontraditional areas such as Bozeman are now in a better position to compete for such footloose high-income individuals. Elected officials of such areas face a choice concerning how much time they spend marketing the benefits of moving to their area and what facets of local quality of life they emphasize. A type of "Goldilocks effect" will emerge as these areas will seek to attract high-income people while limiting the possibility of extreme gentrification that displaces longtime middle-class renters.

As beautiful places attract more full-year residents, this will create the local purchasing power to provide new opportunities for niche restaurants and stores to cater to these restaurants, and this rise of the consumer city creates synergies with the area's natural beauty. These service-sector jobs in turn create new opportunities for lower-skilled workers and a construction boom will take place.[29]

As a wealthy, educated WFH population moves to such areas, the high-level service industry will colocate nearby, including legal firms, dentists, hairdressers, and fancy restaurants. Together this creates new job opportunities and raises the quality of the consumer city.[30] In recent decades, Las Vegas has become an increasingly sophisticated city in terms of restaurants and culture. Superstar chefs have demonstrated that they can open restaurants in multiple locations by writing out their recipes and food preparation methods. Such blueprints allow high-amenity areas to embrace the "consumer city" mentality and this creates synergies that will attract even more WFH workers and tourists to the area.

Examples of Cities Actively Seeking to Recruit WFH Workers

While everyone knows what cities such as Los Angeles, Miami, and New York City have to offer, there are other much smaller cities that are "hidden gems."[31] According to the US Census Bureau, as of 2019, there were at least 780 cities with a population of 50,000 people or more in the country, and many more above 10,000. Santa Fe has a population of 83,000 people. If there are 40 million WFH-eligible workers in the United States, and if one in a thousand of them chose to move to Santa Fe, this would be 40,000 people and would increase the city's population by 50 percent. This example is meant to highlight how very small increases in probabilities translate into huge population growth for smaller cities.

Across the United States, some cities build very little new housing. In California, 43 percent of the housing stock was built before 1970, while in Berkeley, 83 percent of the housing stock was built before 1970.[32] Berkeley is a highly desirable area, and the only explanation for why so little housing is being built is regulations and zoning rules that limit the ability to purchase older homes, demolish them, and build new homes or build taller multifamily apartment buildings. This highly educated, progressive city has chosen to be slow growth, and this restriction of housing supply raises rents and lowers the purchasing power of the middle class and the poor.[33]

Other cities are actively working with new economy firms to lure WFH workers to move there.[34] One of these firms, called Common, has sought out host cities that want to be "remote work hubs." Common hosts joint living space in cities (think of college dorms), and it foresees the synergies in partnering with cities that want to attract more such WFH workers. The five early participants in this program include New Orleans, Bentonville in Arkansas, Ogden in Utah, Rocky Mount in North Carolina, and Rochester in New York. In upper New York State, Rochester is taking steps to position itself to attract WFH workers by leveraging the green features along the Genesee River that flows through the city. "The goal is to create a downtown hub that will attract entrepreneurs, artisans, and other workers and offer them a variety of choices for living and working together."[35]

Each of these cities features cheap housing and seeks to diversify its employment mix and raise its profile as it competes against larger cities. One example is New Orleans. It seeks to diversify its economy from a heavy reliance on tourism and bring in some tech workers. Another example is Rocky Mount. It is a former tobacco town that seeks to attract talent so that it can better compete with Raleigh. Each of these ambitious cities recognizes the key role of great quality of life in luring footloose talent.

The Comeback of Postindustrial Cities

The rise of WFH creates new opportunities for postindustrial cities such as Baltimore, Cleveland, Detroit, and St. Louis. In recent decades, these cities have experienced large outflows of population. Baltimore's population has shrunk from a peak of 900,000 in 1970 to 600,000 today. These outflows have led to very low home prices and a decline in morale and civic leadership, and although such cities feature a high-quality, highly affordable housing stock, they offer few vibrant jobs. With the rise of WFH, some workers will take a second look at these cities.[36]

Starting in the 1960s major US cities ranging from New York to Los Angeles to Pittsburgh began to deindustrialize as manufacturing jobs moved to the US South and abroad. While some post-manufacturing cities such as Pittsburgh have now transitioned to new economic growth engines that revolve around the area's universities and natural beauty, there are other cities such as Baltimore that have faced greater challenges in transitioning to become home to a robust set of growing industries.

Many Rust Belt manufacturing cities have become poverty magnets in recent decades as the major industry (such as car making in Detroit) declined as the region deindustrialized. In recent decades, manufacturing cities such as Baltimore, Cleveland,

Detroit, and Philadelphia have suffered as these middle-class jobs vanished. When a city features a durable housing stock and a shrinking jobs base and a shrinking population, home prices decline and this creates a poverty magnet effect as the average poverty rate increases.

Housing prices in these cities are well below peer cities. Among the 200 largest US cities, Cleveland (197th), St. Louis (180th), Baltimore (169th), Pittsburgh (152nd), and Philadelphia (149th) rank at or near the bottom quartile of housing price rankings. Detroit has the cheapest housing prices as of August 2020, with a Zillow Home Value Index of just $38,721, compared to over $650,000 in New York City (16th highest). Remote workers who still want to live in a major US city, but also seek to avoid paying the high housing prices of San Francisco and New York City, can save a lot of money by relocating to such inexpensive places.

Washington, DC, and Baltimore are forty miles apart, but the same house in Baltimore can be valued at more than 50 percent less. At a time when many worry about the housing affordability challenge, the migration of people to medium-sized cities with a high-quality and affordable housing stock can help the new migrants and strengthen these destination areas. Going forward, those who work in Washington, DC, and have the option to engage in WFH can live in Baltimore. This dynamic makes Baltimore a type of urban suburb.[37]

In cities such as Baltimore and Detroit, homes are selling for $30,000. Such depressed market conditions mean that real estate investors are not buying homes and upgrading them to prepare to sell them to others. In this case, older homes just keep depreciating in quality. Baltimore faces quality-of-life challenges ranging from garbage and a large rat population to a high murder rate. Baltimore has not enjoyed the same progress in recent years that nearby cities such as Philadelphia and Washington, DC, have enjoyed.

Does investing in real estate in cities such as Baltimore now offer a profitable investment opportunity? Expectations play a crucial role here. If potential Baltimore real estate investors are pessimistic about the city's prospects because the local murder rate remains stubbornly high, the local schools are not well ranked, and there are few major employers in town, then these investors will choose not to invest and the capital stock will continue to deteriorate.

If real estate investors are more optimistic about the medium-term demand for such housing, then they will be more likely to purchase them and repair them because this could yield a good rate of return over the next five to ten years. As the WFH economy grows and more African Americans with good WFH jobs seek out the opportunity to live in an affordable major city such as Baltimore, this increase in local demand for such housing would give developers an incentive to begin the upgrading process because it then becomes a more profitable activity.

By attracting more upper-middle-class people to live in the city, other investors will be more likely to reconsider investing in the city. In this sense a type of virtuous chain reaction could be triggered to create new synergistic investments to upgrade the city's physical capital and human capital.[38]

From the perspective of the urban poor in cities such as Baltimore, will WFH improve their quality of life? On one hand, their rents would rise. On the other hand, if postindustrial cities could recruit more college graduates to live in their cities, then this would have several beneficial impacts. If more upper middle-class people choose to live in a Baltimore or Detroit, this creates service-industry demand.[39] As old homes are upgraded, neighborhoods improve and the city benefits from increased tax revenue being collected and neighborhoods gain from an influx of role models.

These new stakeholders in the city would be more active in holding elected officials accountable for the quality of public services. As cities such as Baltimore and Detroit attract more WFH-eligible workers, this could begin to shift the governance of these cities. In these cities, a surprisingly small percentage of people vote and this is likely to affect local governance because there is less accountability of elected officials. Telecommuters tend to be more educated, and more educated people tend to be more likely to vote and to be civically engaged. If enough WFH workers move to these cities, this dynamic would contribute to better local urban governance.

An influx of WFH workers to these postindustrial cities would increase the local public finance capacity to finance costly early education programs. In 2020, the State of Maryland has been debating the implementation of the Kirwan Commission's recommendations for investing in the human capital of children.[40] The recommendations are costly to implement and require significant new expenditure. The payoff of these investments is that they would likely help to close key racial gaps in early life outcomes.

Minority children who grow up in postindustrial cities such as Baltimore and Cleveland have a low probability of earning more as adults than their parents. Raj Chetty and co-authors have used Internal Revenue Service data for children and parents to study the probability that children grow up to be richer than their parents.[41] Minority cities such as Baltimore feature very low rates of income upward mobility, lessening the "American Dream" probabilities of the children earning more than their parents. This fact highlights that new efforts must be taken to reduce the cycle of poverty in these postindustrial cities. When children grow up in poverty, they suffer and are more likely to engage in crime and other activities that cost society as a whole. Nobel laureate James Heckman has argued that enhancing the early education of disadvantaged children and helping mothers be better parents are cost-effective strategies for reducing poverty.[42] Recruiting WFH workers represents a feasible antipoverty strategy for postindustrial cities.

Could Remote Work Revive Parts of Rural America?

Rural America, home to 20 percent of the nation's population, has fallen behind the urban nation in terms of per capita income and quality of life. Deaths from despair (drug overdoses, suicides) are higher in this part of the nation. Whites aged forty-five to fifty-five in rural counties have been the most likely to die prematurely.[43]

For decades, farming areas have lost young people as mechanization has replaced farm jobs. Rural areas are slow-paced places without much to do in terms of jobs or consumption and fun. Young people have responded by moving to the cities and the farming areas are aging and feature little to do relative to the exciting cities. In rural natural resource extraction areas, scars remain from decades of environmental degradation.

Remote work offers new opportunities for people who want a rural lifestyle and can engage in WFH. WFH-eligible workers who want to live in low density can access inexpensive housing and peace and quiet. If enough of these individuals choose to move to these areas, then this brings role models to such areas and more educated, ambitious people who will change the culture of the places where they move.[44] Such a dispersion of talent could reduce the nation's political polarization as some progressive urbanites might move to red-state rural areas. This migration process could reverse the "Big Sort" that has emerged in the United States such that educated progressives cluster in big cities.[45] We tend to socialize with people who live close to us. In a "sorted" setting where rural people never meet urban people, and vice versa, suspicions and misunderstanding and a lack of trust and respect can emerge. If WFH's expansion significantly shifts residential patterns, then more of such bridging social capital may be created.

A growth in richer, more educated people in rural areas will attract more doctors and other professionals to live in such areas and this will improve local service quality as rural areas start to offer some of the same market services that urbanites take for granted. Urban economists have documented positive externalities associated with higher levels of neighbor education. This education effect has been measured in cities. If more rural areas attracted more educated people, would a similar education spillover be observed? The pathways can be debated, but rural schools would have better peers in the classroom. By raising the quality of the local students, such schools will have an easier time recruiting higher-quality teachers.

For rural areas to truly gain from WFH, broadband expansion will need to occur.[46] Approximately one in three rural households reported either facing serious difficulties with internet connectivity or lacking access to high-speed internet entirely.[47]

The Federal Communication Commission's (FCC) definition of "broadband internet"—which does not exactly set a high bar—includes a minimum download speed of 25 megabits per second

(Mbps) and an upload speed of 3 Mbps. According to the FCC's Broadband Progress Report, 19 million Americans—roughly 6% of the population — do not have broadband access. The vast majority of those, roughly 14.5 million, are based in rural areas. In fact, one-quarter of rural Americans and one-third of those living in tribal areas lack internet access that meets the agency's minimum requirements.[48]

In an experiment set in China, researchers examined the impact of the first nationwide e-commerce expansion program on rural households by analyzing a program that connected over 40,000 Chinese villages to e-commerce from 2014 to 2018.[49] They found that greater internet access can affect well-being and income growth in rural areas.

Rural quality of life has suffered for decades because such areas lack the urban amenities that urbanites take for granted. There are too few doctors in such places. Their migration to rural places and their revenue from working there can be enhanced by telemedicine.[50] The rise of Amazon Prime and drone delivery opens up the possibility of next-day delivery and this helps to close the "consumer gap" between rural and urban areas as Amazon opens up its retail menu to rural people.[51]

If enough WFH workers choose to locate in rural places, then their aggregate purchasing power and contributions to local culture represent a more organic alternative to a recent push in public policy directed to place-based subsidies. Economists typically do not support such spatial subsidies of underperforming areas because this encourages people to remain in a place with weak fundamentals.[52] It would be more beneficial for the macroeconomy as a whole for these individuals to migrate to more productive places.

In recent years, economists have recognized that the weakness in this logic chain is to ignore migration costs. Some people are truly tied to their origin location and do not want to move. For those who are tied to an unproductive place, they will suffer from poverty if new economic opportunities cannot be directed to their area.

In areas such as West Virginia, scholars and policy makers have wrestled with identifying infrastructure and human capital investments that can boost such places. The track record for these well-intentioned policies is mixed. Elected officials will designate a geographic area as an opportunity zone and grant it special tax incentives, but it is very difficult to determine whether such incentives stimulate new economic activity or simply reshuffle activity (i.e., the zero-sum game) that would have taken place elsewhere, perhaps in the same state. For example, boosters of professional sports teams argue that attracting a professional team to a city will stimulate local economic growth. They point to the number of people who eat dinner and go to bars close to the stadium on game nights. Such boosters add up the money spent at these restaurants and bars and credit the sports team for creating this new local revenue. Urban economists counter by asking: "Would these attendees have gone to another restaurant or bar in the same city and spent the same amount of money if there had not been a game?" If the answer is "yes," then the sports team created no marginal increase in local revenue. Instead, the game reshuffles money that would have been spent locally anyway.

If rural places can compete and attract some WFH workers to live there, this represents an alternative, more organic strategy of bringing economic growth to an underperforming region. WFH workers will demand local services and this creates jobs for the local service economy and in housing construction. Such "trailblazers" would also act as role models for the local youth. Rural people would now have a greater incentive to invest in skill formation because they can live in the rural area and work in nonfarming and non-resource-extraction jobs.

The early movers to a beautiful place will bear some risk. In underdeveloped places, there are not good local public services. Nearby public schools may be of low quality and fire and police protection may be thin. The first movers to such an area would be making a bet that others will follow them, and as local purchasing power and tax revenue increases, local public services will improve. Parents of school-aged children would have to rely on Khan Academy and other internet-based strategies to upgrade their children's education. This example highlights a potential coordination failure. Scattered WFH workers who want to move to a beautiful rural location face coordination costs in moving to the same place. Since they do not know each other, they cannot coordinate their migration. Recall the "New Scarsdale" example I gave earlier: when there are fixed costs to building new institutions, the average cost per family declines when more of such people who value good schools all independently choose to move to the same place. The good news here is that local real estate developers can coordinate this activity. The developer of new homes has a profit incentive to bundle in good schools if WFH potential buyers value nice new housing in areas with good schools. Just as Donald Bren became rich building planned communities in Orange County, California, similar opportunities will arise in beautiful rural areas with some access to cities and regional hubs.

America is home to countless beautiful, scenic rural towns that people visit for vacations and breaks from the city. While work from home offers the opportunity to live in some of these places, some may not be able to absorb a large increase in population due to constraints such as broadband internet infrastructure, local school systems, and limited housing development opportunities. This begs the question of what are some possible examples of places that are both beautiful and could accommodate an increased population due to remote work?

Mount Vernon, Washington, is home to the often-photographed Skagit Valley tulip farms, which draw visitors from around the world during its annual tulip festival. The small city of 30,000 is located sixty miles north of Seattle and ninety miles south of Vancouver, while being just thirty-three miles from Bellingham International Airport and just off Interstate 5. The city has a fiber-optic backbone internet infrastructure with an eye toward economic development. While home prices in the city have almost doubled since 2012, at $400,000 they remain almost half of Seattle's home prices. Although the public school district ranks behind the state average in math and reading scores, the area is home to several high-ranked private schools. In 1998, the city was ranked #1 on a list of best small cities in the US and its population has more than doubled since 1990, demonstrating the potential for rapid expansion.

The coastal town of Rockport, Maine, is home to just over 3,000 residents and the Maine Coast Heritage Trust's Aldermere Farm Preserve, one of the many nature preserves in the area. The town also features nearby access to great hiking and skiing with a multitude of lakes, ponds, and streams. The town is 80 miles northeast of Portland, Maine, and the Bangor International Airport and 180 miles northeast of Boston. Almost all homes in Rockport have access to fixed-line internet service. Housing costs are around the national average and the town has some of the best public schools in the state. The small town, whose population has remained relatively unchanged in the past two decades, recently approved a $1.63 million infrastructure bond to upgrade public facilities and infrastructure in the town.

Not all rural areas are likely to equally benefit. Rural towns such as Minden, West Virginia, that have been harvested for natural resources face lingering environmental damage from past natural resource extraction.[53] Because WFH workers would tend to seek out desirable areas, pollution-scarred rural places are less likely to enjoy a WFH-induced comeback.

Brad Humphreys is a native West Virginian and a graduate of West Virginia University, where he now serves as a professor of economics. He predicts that WFH could increase spatial income inequality within the state as "the rich get richer." The widest broadband access exists in the state's far eastern panhandle, which is basically a bedroom community of the Washington, DC, MSA (metropolitan statistical area); the northern panhandle, which is basically a bedroom community of the Pittsburgh MSA; and the relatively populous corridor between Charleston, the state capital, and Huntington. These places also have the usual high-density consumption amenities like restaurants, grocery stores, and entertainment venues, and better transportation infrastructure, in terms of interstate highways. These areas will be well positioned to benefit from increased WFH.

Humphreys points out that there are other parts of the Appalachian region that feature great natural beauty. There is an open question of whether WFH will boost these areas.

The counties that lie along and near the Allegheny Front mountains, which runs northeast to southwest from roughly Cumberland Maryland to the Greenbrier Resort in Greenbrier County, contain a concentrated mix of attractive tourism-related natural amenities, including ski resorts, hiking and mountain biking trails, National Forests, and scenic mountain views. This part of the state also has good access to the Baltimore/Washington/Richmond conurbation. This part of West Virginia closely resembles the Smoky Mountains between Knoxville TN and Asheville NC that have experienced substantial tourism-driven economic development.[54]

The rise of WFH poses a classic "chicken versus the egg" issue. For decades, urban economists have debated whether people move to areas featuring strong job growth or whether employers move to areas where people want to live. WFH shakes up this debate, as workers will now have much greater flexibility in seeking out where they want to live. Throughout my research career, I have argued that places with great quality of life will boom because skilled people will want to live there. The rise of the opportunity to engage in WFH only increases my belief in this hypothesis. As major firms such as Amazon and Google choose where to locate their respective HQ2s, they have an incentive to locate them in areas such that remote workers who want to live in their own niche areas can easily access them for quality face-to-face interactions.

By decentralizing and opening multiple, spread-out, smaller headquarters, the major firms can hire from a nationwide talent pool and grant their workers personal freedom over how and where they spend their time. A happier workforce will be more likely to commit to the firm and make the investments that are difficult for a firm's leadership to monitor. In the past, bosses stood over a worker's shoulder to monitor their work. If workers feel empowered on the job and are happy about their life/work balance, then this extreme monitoring is no longer needed. In this sense, productive firms want their workers to seek out their favorite geographic niche.

Each location will have to make a strategic decision about whether to unlock the full potential of attracting new WFH workers to their area or to block such potential residents using local environmental and land use laws. Given that the United States is a huge nation, footloose WFH workers will have plenty of choices, and "slow growth" places (say a Berkeley, California) can reserve the option to change their zoning codes later on. The willingness of different areas to build new housing will play a key role in determining the new economic geography of the nation.

Throughout this chapter I have focused on the new geographic residential opportunities for WFH-eligible workers. Such an enhanced menu might suggest that quality-of-life inequality will increase in America as those who are not eligible are left behind. Fortunately, this logical conclusion is not true. As more Americans become WFH eligible and some spread out and head to the fringe of metro areas or move to rural areas or move to small cities such as Bozeman, this creates new demand for service workers to find jobs in these cities. This dispersal of purchasing power across America creates new freedoms for all service workers. Those with a taste for nature can move to a beautiful place that now has more WFH workers living there. Non-WFH workers will now be more likely to find a service-sector job there. As the population spreads out, more people can live and find work in places where housing prices are lower (farther away from the superstar cities). This dynamic increases real incomes and allows people to be better matched to spend their time in a place where they want to live. This optimistic claim merits careful empirical testing in future years.

Conclusion

The New Geography of Jobs

For decades, the actor Harrison Ford, perhaps best known as Han Solo from *Star Wars* and Indiana Jones from the movies of the same name, has owned homes in Los Angeles and Jackson Hole, Wyoming. His wealth has given him the ability to create a type of geographic portfolio that allows him to spend perhaps six months of the year in Wyoming and the rest of his time in Los Angeles. He and other actors and athletes have been able to achieve the ultimate work/life balance. Harrison Ford has been untethered for decades. He owns and flies his own plane. He is free to choose where he goes.

The rise of WFH effectively transforms many of us into (perhaps less wealthy and less dashing) Harrison Fords, as we can now reconfigure our lives to pursue our own conception of "the good life." Harrison Ford's career and wealth have given him the freedom to be in Hollywood for meetings and then jet to Jackson Hole when he wants to go. Similar to a financial investor who invests 50 percent of her money in stocks and 50 percent in bonds, Mr. Ford creates a time portfolio over where he goes and when. Such a portfolio of time allocation allows him to achieve his own life goals. In the recent past, only our superstars had such freedom. WFH expands such opportunity.

The ability to unbundle where we live from where we work creates new opportunities for many of us. These gains could be even larger for women, for minorities, and for those with special tastes for nature.

Remote work accommodates our diversity. At any point in time, workers differ with respect to what we want from our job and the area where we work. Over the course of our life, we grow as individuals and take on new responsibilities such as marriage, parenting, and caring for aging relatives. Ideally, our work provides us with the flexibility to accommodate our own personal goals and our duties at home. The rise of remote work increases our ability to "have it all" and avoid the pain of commuting on a daily basis. The rise of remote work also exposes workers to more competition as they compete in both national and international markets.

In 2020, the nation ran a huge experiment as millions of people worked from home. In the near future perhaps one-third of American workers will engage in working from home on a part-time or full-time basis. This book investigates how this change in the "work rules" affects the economic geography of the United States.[1]

By offering a possible preview of our medium-term future, I seek to help us to unlock the full potential of this new set of work arrangements. In the modern economy, there are few "iron laws" such that there is a deterministic relationship between cause and effect. The net impact of the rise of WFH hinges on how to make the most of the possible synergies that it offers. While I am optimistic about the great potential for WFH to improve our quality of life, I hope that this book's chapters help to highlight the potential challenges that we will face over the next decade. By anticipating these challenges, we are better able to adapt to them. WFH unbundles where we live from where we work and allows for many different permutations concerning how we arrange our days and our life. Going forward, WFH-eligible workers have strong incentives to make investments in skills to be better prepared to gain the most from it.

Since so many American workers will engage in WFH, this new way of working has implications for those who work in jobs that do not offer this opportunity. As more WFH workers move to locations that meet their life goals, this creates new service-sector opportunities for other workers. This will offer new opportunities for them if they have a specific passion such as mountain climbing or living close to family members. As some WFH move farther from their place of work, this will reduce demand for housing and lead to more affordable center cities.

How Will WFH Change Our Cities?

The United States is a huge nation, but for too long the set of productive points on the map have only featured a handful of places. Millions of Americans were "mismatched" as they faced a tension between where they could find "good jobs" versus where they wanted to live to keep their family ties and to be connected to life activities that give them fulfillment.[2] The population will now reshuffle, spread out and explore new places, and rediscover old places.

The rise of WFH helps to address a fundamental "mismatch" challenge. Modern America features a handful of superstar firms in a few cities such as San Francisco and Seattle. Facing high home prices in superstar cities, many chose to suburbanize to live where housing is cheaper, but these individuals were time-poor as they were often stuck in traffic.[3] At the same time, America has hundreds of other cities featuring a built-up housing stock and infrastructure but few vibrant local employers.

Cities such as Baltimore feature an elegant housing stock but there are few vibrant firms there. The durable housing stock is priced low there because there is supply but there is little demand. Before the rise of WFH, San Francisco featured very expensive housing while Baltimore featured a depressed housing market. WFH creates new opportunities for places such as Baltimore to attract more residents who want to live there but want to work for companies located elsewhere.

As employees increasingly have the opportunity to engage in remote work, some will move away from these expensive cities and this reduction in demand will increase housing affordability in some of our greatest cities. In recent decades, while New York City and San Francisco and Seattle have boomed, other cities such as Baltimore have lost population. The rise of WFH creates new opportunities for such postindustrial cities. If more WFH workers move to such cities, this will help to reduce local poverty by stimulating local service-sector job demand and raising local tax revenues. Rural areas, especially those with great beauty, will experience a renewal as millions of Americans will each have the new freedom to plan out where they want to live once they face fewer commuting constraints. Given that WFH-eligible workers tend to be educated and earn good salaries, many of them will seek out high quality-of-life places. People differ with respect to how they rank the best place to live. Surfers will seek out different places than skiers. Each potential destination such as a Bozeman will need to make local decisions concerning whether it will welcome growth. Such places will need to invest in infrastructure, ranging from air travel access to high-speed internet access to scaling up local services such as roads and schools to accommodate growth.

The Rise of Remote Work Has Implications for Cities around the World

The geographic lessons learned from the US WFH experience have implications for the rest of the world. In Europe today, cross-national differences in culture, history, and language continue to create a desire to remain in one's home nation. An Italian will recognize that France may have better job opportunities but he may not want to move there. The rise of WFH creates the possibility of achieving the "best of both worlds." Europe's fast trains and regional jet infrastructure facilitate monthly corporate face-to-face huddles so that WFH workers can live in their home country without losing out too much on face-to-face interaction with co-workers.

Within the European Union, the rise of WFH allows these nations to achieve the economic gains from integration while still allowing individuals to celebrate their own culture and to live with their own.[4] A French worker can engage in working remotely and can live in France while working for a German firm. Europe's high-speed rail network facilitates face-to-face interaction when the in-person connection is called for; one can travel by train from Paris to London in just over two hours.

Around the world, WFH creates new geographic possibilities. In China, many middle-aged people were born during the "one child policy" era. As their parents age, these individuals have special responsibilities for taking care of their parents. The ability to engage in WFH allows these people to simultaneously be good workers and a good child to their beloved parents.

While WFH poses offshoring challenges for US workers, it creates new opportunities for people in developing countries who can speak English. Research based in India demonstrates that rural people invest more in girls' education when parents anticipate that there are greater job opportunities for them. The possibility of being able to live in a rural area and engage in remote work for a national urban employer creates an incentive for rural people to invest more in the education of their children.[5] Such parents may desire for their children to continue to be rural people and to earn more income and to diversify the family's income stream so that it is less reliant on just agriculture. The possibility of diversifying a family's income stream, as children can work as remote workers, helps families to adapt to climate change. Climate change scholars have worried that the farming sector in the developing world is highly sensitive to climate shocks. Farmers who have long specialized in growing a certain crop could suffer large income losses due to extreme heat and drought. Sending a child to a city offers a strategy for diversifying such risk. The ability to engage in WFH using internet access acts as a substitute for costly urban migration.

In South Korea, the combination of high-speed rail and WFH creates the possibility of decongesting the major city of Seoul. Urban economists have noted the social costs of megacity bigness. Cities such as Seoul and Buenos Aires feature a huge share of the nation's urban population. While this offers agglomeration benefits, it contributes to congestion and pollution. The rise of WFH can help to boost second-tier cities as skilled people can live in cheaper cities while working for firms located in the superstar city. Given the high home prices in Seoul, this will raise the real purchasing power of the middle class.[6]

Ireland is actively pursuing this strategy. "The national government recently announced plans to revitalize moribund rural districts by encouraging office workers to relocate from Dublin, with promises of better broadband and financial support to help local authorities create remote working hubs."[7]

Risks We Face in the New WFH Economy

US-born workers face competition from immigrants who move to the United States and now from international workers who compete for offshored jobs. The rise of WFH creates the possibility that more international workers will compete with US workers for US employment without having to move to the United States. As US workers face greater competition for WFH jobs, domestic workers can compete by investing in greater skill or by moving to places with cheaper rents and this will allow them to compete by accepting lower nominal pay.

Another concern about the expansion of WFH is that it really represents an expansion of the "gig economy." Critics argue that Uber and other gig economy jobs overstate the real pay that workers earn and hide from them the costs they pay in terms of wear and tear on their cars. In a similar sense, some have critiqued internet WFH job platforms such as Upwork for destroying "good jobs." This criticism raises an important issue. The traditional American job features forty hours a week of going to work five days a week and the worker is paid and given health insurance. Workers value this bundle in part because they are not taxed on health insurance and they pay a low rate for insurance because the firm averages across the pool of all workers (an implicit subsidy to sicker workers).

Upwork and other internet labor platforms have faced the critique that firms will use its platform to take one good job and break it into two 20-hour-a-week jobs where neither job offers health insurance. In a competitive labor market, the firm will have to pay well enough to attract these gig workers. If millions of Americans begin to engage in WFH gig work and do not have health insurance, this will create a new market as there is aggregate demand to purchase health insurance. Many of these workers will be younger and pose a lower risk for insurers. For-profit insurers seek to sell insurance policies to healthier workers because they become sick less often and thus the actuaries predict that their annual health costs will be lower. Such firms will compete to sell insurance plans to these gig workers. The federal government can play a constructive role here by creating guidelines for how WFH workers can verify their health status so that insurers can use AI to quickly offer them a price quote. The standardization of information creates a thicker market and reduces transaction costs and helps to create the conditions for guaranteeing economic efficiency. If there are a large number of buyers and sellers who can easily transact with each other over the internet, then a fair price will emerge to allow people who want health insurance to find risk-priced fair health insurance and the firms who offer these policies will earn a profit from selling such policies.

Adapting to New Challenges

The US population is aging and this means that many workers will have aging parents living in other locations perhaps far from one's job location. The ability to engage in WFH helps middle-aged workers juggle both work and family responsibilities. Aging workers face their own health shocks. The ability to engage in WFH may help them to manage chronic conditions while still being productive members of the firm. This possibility will reduce worker stress and improve mental health.

In my environmental economics research, I have studied the challenges posed to US residents by emerging climate-change risk. Pinpoint climate science is making progress delineating which parts of the nation face higher and lower risks from heat spikes, pollution spikes, drought, and natural disasters such as fires and floods. As we learn more about the severity of these place-based shocks, we have strong incentives to invest in strategies to protect ourselves and our families. Those firms and places that have an edge in adapting to these risks will thrive and this creates a strong incentive to build up this capacity.

We will be better able to adapt to climate change because of the rise of WFH. Footloose workers will be better able to move to safer areas and this creates an incentive for elected officials of places to compete to become safer through urban planning and strategic investments. For those who are risk averse, the geographic places that are relatively safer will be more attractive and some WFH workers will seek to move there. As we face the climate change challenge, those places that turn out to be relatively more resilient have an incentive to market this point and this "green advertising" will actually help more of the footloose population to move to "higher ground."

How Much Do We Gain from the Rise of WFH?

The rise of WFH poses a challenge for macroeconomists who seek to measure the average person's well-being over time for a given nation and across nations at a point in time. In comparing living standards across nations, economists have compared health, per capita income, and leisure across nations.[8] Until recently, the United States offered its residents a higher per capita earnings and less leisure than France.[9] While much macroeconomic discussion focuses on a nation's per capita gross domestic product (GDP), we have long understood the limitations of this measuring rod.

> In truth, "GDP measures everything," as Senator Robert Kennedy famously said, "except that which makes life worthwhile." The number does not measure health, education, equality of opportunity, the state of the environment or many other indicators of the quality of life.[10]

When I was a student at the University of Chicago, a prominent professor started every lecture by saying to us, "If your head is in the oven and your feet are in the refrigerator then on average you feel good." The point of this painful joke is that the fictitious average person's well-being may not actually reflect anyone in our diverse society. If over one-third of workers engage in WFH and if a growing number of workers who are not eligible to engage in WFH move to cheaper, better-tailored for them places where they can find service-sector work, then the "average American" worker enjoys improvements in her well-being. By commuting less and by commuting when workers want to go to the office, this effectively increases a worker's amount of time. How each worker allocates this time boost will vary across workers and for the same worker will vary on a daily basis. The greater control over one's daily schedule will help eligible workers to feel that they have more control over their daily quality of life. Standard macroeconomic accounts of national well-being miss out on these nuances.

How much a person gains from engaging in WFH hinges on one's "conception of the good life." A young, ambitious workaholic will value this work option less because she wants to be at the heart of the action so that she can network and be in the loop and burnish her reputation as a "go-getter." In contrast, there are other workers who like their job but wish that they could live in another geographic location because of lifestyle preferences or family responsibilities. This set of workers greatly gains from the new freedoms offered by WFH.

In recent years, economists have shown great ingenuity in estimating our willingness to pay for products ranging from high-quality cell phones to Diet Coke and the Impossible Burger. The Impossible Burger offers the taste of a traditional burger but it has no meat. Diet Coke tastes like Coke but without the sugar. Some people greatly value this unbundling such that one can enjoy the flavor of Coke without the sugar. While our enhanced menu of possible foods we can buy is an important indicator of progress, I claim that our ability to reallocate our time to pursue our passions and responsibilities is a much more important innovation.

In the US economy, there are roughly 150 million workers and roughly 50 million of them will have some access to engaging in WFH. This means that a huge number of Americans will have increased flexibility over their weekday work schedules. To appreciate how much this increases our menu of possibilities, consider a simple example. There are 3,000 counties in the United States. In the past, most workers lived and worked in the same county to reduce their commute times. Every worker chose which of the 3,000 to live and work in. Given commuting speeds, these two choices were bundled together. In our emerging WFH economy, it is only a slight exaggeration that one can live in one county and work in another county. This means that each WFH-eligible worker has nine million choices and this understates the size of the menu because within counties there are many different neighborhoods to choose from. This example highlights the huge increase in personal freedom brought about by unbundling where we live and how often we go to work from where our firm is located.

Each of us accumulates regrets during our life. We make choices and then wonder what our life would have been like had we chosen another path. WFH allows for more experimentation concerning one's work field and the geographic place where one lives. WFH offers great flexibility for switching one's schedule as new "good news" (a family reunion!) or "bad news" (a sick family member) arises. I claim that WFH workers will gain from having fewer life regrets because they are better able to allocate their time so that they can be where they want to be and avoid being where they do not want to be. The synergy between how we allocate our time and where we spend our time has been a major theme in this book. WFH offers tremendous gains for those who have niche preferences for how they spend their leisure time (artists, environmentalists) and those with responsibilities for family and relatives. These individuals greatly value the flexibility offered by WFH as they are not tied down to living within daily commuting range of their employer's headquarters.

In the near term, economists will have a new opportunity to quantify the extent to which different workers value their new flexibility. Labor economists study total pay compensation packages. Before 2020, skilled workers received a salary and benefits such as vacation days, health insurance, and on-the-job amenities such as free food. Going forward, the right to engage in WFH will be another job attribute. If labor economists can access data for the same worker over time and observe her salary and her right to engage in WFH, then this information can be used to measure her willingness to pay for this right. For example, suppose that Matthew earned $205,000 a year working at Apple at age thirty-seven in the year 2021 and at age forty he is earning $235,000 and he has the right to engage in WFH. Suppose that Matthew's rival Sarah was also making $205,000 a year at Apple in 2021 and she works at the headquarters full-time in 2024 and makes $350,000 a year. Suppose the economist sees that Matthew continues to work at Apple. The economist would infer that if Matthew had not elected to engage in WFH, he would earn the same compensation as Sarah and be earning $350,000. Given this assumption, the economist infers that Matthew must value his WFH option by at least 350,000 − 235,000 = $115,000 per year. Why? Matthew chose to sacrifice earning an extra $115,000 per year for the right to engage in WFH. A good researcher would not stop there. Once the researcher has estimated each WFH worker's willingness to pay for this right, the economist seeks to explore "why." How much do factors such as caring for aging parents, spending more time with young children, pursuing hobbies, living somewhere more interesting, each play in determining one's personal benefits from engaging in WFH? An ambitious researcher would also explore how the WFH worker's mental and physical health is affected. Is the WFH worker less stressed and in better physical health when they have the WFH option?

Social scientists continue to seek out different consistent measurements of our well-being. We do not have the equivalent of a thermometer. Social scientists have not devised a similar way to measure changes in our quality of life. Biometrics can be used to measure our quality of sleep and our daily stress levels. Breaking out of the grind of daily commuting will save us time and reduce our life stress. A less-stressed American workforce will emerge.[11] National income statistics such as Gross National Product will not capture such real improvements in our standard of living.

Superstar workers already have the privilege of taking breaks to reduce their stress levels. In recent years, NBA all-star Kawhi Leonard has been allowed to engage in "load management" such that he does not play all eighty-two games. He has a working contract that differs from the average American.

Other indicators of national progress with respect to equity and inclusion will be if the male/female earnings gap vanishes.[12] Another indicator will be whether we observe increased demographic diversity of the tech sector fueled by remote work.

Throughout this book, I have presented examples of how non-WFH workers can gain from the rise of WFH. Such service workers will be able to find different work opportunities in more affordable areas in places where they want to live. If such areas provide high-quality education, then their children will be more likely to participate in the future WFH economy when they are adults. There have been times in American history when the middle class have enjoyed sufficient income growth that income inequality declined. Economic historians point to the great compression era of 1945–65, when the US high school graduation rate soared and the middle class gained.[13] Whether my optimistic claims turn out to be correct will determine whether the rise of WFH reduces or increases inequality in our post-COVID economy.

Acknowledgments

I would like to thank The Searle Freedom Trust Foundation for generously funding this project. My first draft of this manuscript was written during 2020 when I served as the Bloomberg Distinguished Professor of Economics and Business at Johns Hopkins University. I would like to thank my colleagues there for valuable discussions.

At Johns Hopkins, Mac McComas played a central role in reading and critiquing early drafts of the manuscript. Sam Oberly, Charlie Nguyen, Riya Rana, and Roma Wang all helped me research different aspects of the project. I would like to thank my mother, Carol Kahn, for reading several drafts of this book and always being on target with her "constructive" criticism.

I am grateful to the University of California Press for working with me. Back in mid-2020, I approached Tim Sullivan in his capacity as the Executive Director of UC Press to pitch my manuscript. Tim had served as the editor on two of my previous books and I always learn from him. As usual, he was funny and direct. Tim introduced me to my editor, Michelle Lipinski. Michelle's input greatly improved this book. Her wise suggestions and edits have helped to sharpen my arguments and to focus on the essentials. Our discussions helped me to carefully explain how the microeconomic perspective informs thinking about how different people will be affected by the rise of remote work. I would also like to thank Enrique Ochoa-Kaup for working with me in finalizing my published book.

Notes

Introduction

1. Jonathan I. Dingel and Brent Neiman, "How Many Jobs Can Be Done at Home?," *Journal of Public Economics* 189 (2020): article 104235.

2. Anita Balakrishnan, "Apple's New Headquarters Will Reflect Steve Jobs's Desire to Replicate the Outdoors," CNBC, May 17, 2017, https://www.cnbc.com/2017/05/17/apples-new-office-will-reflect-jobs-desire-to-replicate-the-outdoors.html.

3. Jerry Useem, "When Working from Home Doesn't Work," *The Atlantic*, October 3, 2017, https://www.theatlantic.com/magazine/archive/2017/11/when-working-from-home-doesnt-work/540660/.

4. Paul Krugman, "The Pandemic and the Future City," *New York Times*, March 15, 2021, https://www.nytimes.com/2021/03/15/opinion/cities-covid-remote-work.html.

5. Richard Baldwin, *The Globotics Upheaval: Globalization, Robotics, and the Future of Work* (New York: Oxford University Press, 2019).

6. Robert J. Gordon, *Is US Economic Growth Over? Faltering Innovation Confronts the Six Headwinds*, Centre for Economic Policy Research, Policy Insight no. 63, September 2012, cepr.org/sites/default/files/policy_insights/PolicyInsight63.pdf.

Chapter 1. Short-Run Gains for Workers

1. Chip Cutter, "Even Warren Buffett Wonders if People Will Return to Offices," *Wall Street Journal*, May 4, 2020, https://www.wsj.com/articles/even-warren-buffett-wonders-if-people-will-return-to-offices-11588597506.

2. Jose Maria Barrero, Nicholas Bloom, and Steven J. Davis, "Why Working from Home Will Stick" (working paper 2020-174, University of Chicago, Becker Friedman Institute for Economics, 2020).

3. Dingel and Neiman, "How Many Jobs."

4. Peter Linneman and Philip E. Graves, "Migration and Job Change: A Multinomial Logit Approach," *Journal of Urban Economics* 14, no. 3 (1983): 263–79; Robert H. Topel and Michael P. Ward, "Job Mobility and the Careers of Young Men," *Quarterly Journal of Economics* 107, no. 2 (1992): 439–79; Jorge De La Roca and Diego Puga, "Learning by Working in Big Cities," *Review of Economic Studies* 84, no. 1 (2017): 106–42.

5. Derek Neal, "The Complexity of Job Mobility among Young Men," *Journal of Labor Economics* 17, no. 2 (April 1999): 237–61; Topel and Ward, "Careers of Young Men."

6. Sydney Trent, "Dreading or Dreaming of a Return to the Office in 2021," *Washington Post*, December 28, 2020, https://www.washingtonpost.com /local/social-issues/return-to-office-work-from-home-coronavirus/2020/12 /27/9796d0c8-43da-11eb-b0e4-0f182923a025_story.html.

7. Susan Rohwedder and Robert J. Willis, "Mental Retirement," *Journal of Economic Perspectives* 24, no. 1 (2010): 119–38.

8. Emma Aguila, Orazio Attanasio, and Costas Meghir, "Changes in Consumption at Retirement: Evidence from Panel Data," *Review of Economics and Statistics* 93, no. 3 (2011): 1094–99.

9. John Ameriks, Joseph Briggs, Andrew Caplin, Minjoon Lee, Matthew D. Shapiro, and Christopher Tonetti, "Older Americans Would Work Longer if Jobs Were Flexible," *American Economic Journal: Macroeconomics* 12, no. 1 (2020): 174–209.

10. Mitchell L. Moss and Carson Qing, *The Emergence of the "Super-Commuter,"* Rudin Center for Transportation, New York University Wagner School of Public Service, 2012, https://wagner.nyu.edu/files/rudincenter/ supercommuter_report.pdf.

11. Romic Aevaz, "2019 ACS Survey: While Most Americans' Commuting Trends Are Unchanged, Teleworking Continues to Grow, and Driving Alone Dips in Some Major Cities," Eno Center for Transportation, October 18, 2019, https://www.enotrans.org/article/2018-acs-survey-while-most-americans

-commuting-trends-are-unchanged-teleworking-continues-to-grow-and
-driving-alone-dips-in-some-major-cities/.

12. Enrico Moretti, "Real Wage Inequality," *American Economic Journal: Applied Economics* 5, no. 1 (2013): 65–103.

13. Donald C. Shoup, "The High Cost of Free Parking," *Journal of Planning Education and Research* 17, no. 1 (1997): 3–20.

14. Björn Hårsman and John M. Quigley, "Political and Public Acceptability of Congestion Pricing: Ideology and Self-Interest," *Journal of Policy Analysis and Management* 29, no. 4 (2010): 854–74.

15. Nathaniel Baum-Snow, Matthew E. Kahn, and Richard Voith, "Effects of Urban Rail Transit Expansions: Evidence from Sixteen Cities, 1970–2000," *Brookings-Wharton Papers on Urban Affairs* (2005): 147–206.

16. Daniel S. Hamermesh, Harley Frazis, and Jay Stewart, "Data Watch: The American Time Use Survey," *Journal of Economic Perspectives* 19, no. 1 (2005): 221–32; Daniel S. Hamermesh, "Timing, Togetherness and Time Windfalls," in *Family, Household and Work*, edited by Klaus F. Zimmerman and Michael Volger, 1–23 (Berlin: Springer, 2003); Daniel S. Hamermesh, "Time to Eat: Household Production under Increasing Income Inequality," *American Journal of Agricultural Economics* 89, no. 4 (2007): 852–63; F. T. Juster and F. P. Stafford, "The Allocation of Time: Empirical Findings, Behavioral Models, and Problems of Measurement," *Journal of Economic Literature* 29, no. 2 (June 1991): 471–522.

17. Kenneth A. Small, Clifford Winston, and Jia Yan, "Uncovering the Distribution of Motorists' Preferences for Travel Time and Reliability," *Econometrica* 73, no. 4 (2005): 1367–82.

18. US Bureau of Labor Statistics, *American Time Use Survey: May to December 2019 and 2020 Results*, https://www.bls.gov/news.release/pdf/atus.pdf.

19. Sara Raley, Suzanne M. Bianchi, and Wendy Wang, "When Do Fathers Care? Mothers' Economic Contribution and Fathers' Involvement in Child Care," *American Journal of Sociology* 117, no. 5 (2012): 1422–59; Erin L. Kelly, Phyllis Moen, J. Michael Oakes, Wen Fan, Cassandra Okechukwu, Kelly D. Davis, Leslie B. Hammer, et al., "Changing Work and Work-Family Conflict: Evidence from the Work, Family, and Health Network," *American Sociological Review* 79, no. 3 (2014): 485–516; Tammy D. Allen, Ryan C. Johnson, Kaitlin M. Kiburz, and Kristen M. Shockley, "Work-Family Conflict and Flexible Work Ar-

rangements: Deconstructing Flexibility," *Personnel Psychology* 66, no. 2 (2013): 345–76; Bryce Covert, "Write a Book? Sure, Work from Home. Care for a Child? Nope," *New York Times*, June 25, 2020, https://www.nytimes.com/2020/06/25/opinion/coronavirus-remote-work-gender-gap.html.

20. Kendall Houghton, *Childcare and the New Part-Time: Gender Gaps in Long-Hour Professions*, Job Market Paper, version of November 2, 2020.

21. Timothy D. Golden, John F. Veiga, and Zeki Simsek, "Telecommuting's Differential Impact on Work-Family Conflict: Is There No Place Like Home?," *Journal of Applied Psychology* 91, no. 6 (2006): 1340.

22. Michael L. Anderson, Fangwen Lu, Yiran Zhang, Jun Yang, and Ping Qin, "Superstitions, Street Traffic, and Subjective Well-Being," *Journal of Public Economics* 142 (2016): 1–10.

23. John Calfee and Clifford Winston, "The Value of Automobile Travel Time: Implications for Congestion Policy," *Journal of Public Economics* 69, no. 1 (1998): 83–102.

24. Nicholas Bloom, James Liang, John Roberts, and Zhichun Jenny Ying, "Does Working from Home Work? Evidence from a Chinese Experiment," *Quarterly Journal of Economics* 130, no. 1 (2015): 165–218.

25. Michael Gibbs, Friederike Mengel, and Christoph Siemroth, "Work from Home and Productivity: Evidence from Personnel and Analytics Data on IT Professionals" (working paper 2021-56, University of Chicago, Becker Friedman Institute for Economics, 2021).

26. Matthis Doepke and Fabrizio Zilibotti, *Love, Money, and Parenting: How Economics Explains the Way We Raise Our Kids* (Princeton, NJ: Princeton University Press, 2019); Robert Frank, *Falling Behind: How Rising Inequality Harms the Middle Class* (Berkeley: University of California Press, 2013).

27. V. Kerry Smith, *Time and the Valuation of Environmental Resources*, Discussion Papers 10485, Resources for the Future (1997), DOI: 10.22004/ag.econ.10485; Simon Georges-Kot, Dominique Goux, and Eric Maurin, "Following the Crowd: Leisure Complementarities beyond the Household," *Journal of Labor Economics* 35, no. 4 (2017): 1061–88.

28. Denise DiPasquale and Edward L. Glaeser, "Incentives and Social Capital: Are Homeowners Better Citizens?," *Journal of Urban Economics* 45, no. 2 (1999): 354–84.

29. Robert D. Putnam, *Bowling Alone: The Collapse and Revival of American Community* (New York: Simon and Schuster, 2000).

30. Dora L. Costa and Matthew E. Kahn, "Understanding the American Decline in Social Capital," *Kyklos* 56, no. 1 (2003): 17–46.

31. Edward L. Glaeser, David Laibson, and Bruce Sacerdote, "An Economic Approach to Social Capital," *Economic Journal* 112, no. 483 (2002): F437–58.

32. Cong Sun, Siqi Zheng, Jianghao Wang, and Matthew E. Kahn, "Does Clean Air Increase the Demand for the Consumer City? Evidence from Beijing," *Journal of Regional Science* 59, no. 3 (2019): 409–34.

33. James H. Cardon, Eric R. Eide, Kerk L. Phillips, and Mark H. Showalter, "A Model of Sleep, Leisure and Work over the Business Cycle," *Journal of Economic Dynamics and Control* 95 (2018): 19–36.

34. William J. Carrington, "The Alaskan Labor Market during the Pipeline Era," *Journal of Political Economy* 104, no. 1 (1996): 186–218; Robert A. Margo, "Wages in California during the Gold Rush," in Margo, *Wages and Labor Markets in the United States, 1820–1860* (Chicago: University of Chicago Press, 2009); James Feyrer, Erin T. Mansur, and Bruce Sacerdote, "Geographic Dispersion of Economic Shocks: Evidence from the Fracking Revolution," *American Economic Review* 107, no. 4 (2017): 1313–34; Thomas DeLeire, Paul Eliason, and Christopher Timmins, "Measuring the Employment Impacts of Shale Gas Development" (unpublished manuscript, McCourt School of Public Policy, Georgetown University, 2014); Melissa S. Kearney and Riley Wilson, "Male Earnings, Marriageable Men, and Nonmarital Fertility: Evidence from the Fracking Boom," *Review of Economics and Statistics* 100, no. 4 (2018): 678–90.

35. Robert J. Shiller, *The New Financial Order: Risk in the 21st Century* (Princeton, NJ: Princeton University Press, 2009).

36. Robert J. Shiller, "Whatever Happened to Wage Insurance?," Project Syndicate, March 21, 2006, https://www.project-syndicate.org/commentary/whatever-happened-to-wage-insurance?barrier=accesspaylog.

37. Raven Molloy, Christopher L. Smith, and Abigail Wozniak, "Internal Migration in the United States," *Journal of Economic Perspectives* 25, no. 3 (2011): 173–96.

38. Raven K. Saks and Abigail Wozniak, "Labor Reallocation over the

Business Cycle: New Evidence from Internal Migration," *Journal of Labor Economics* 29, no. 4 (2011): 697–739.

39. Ihsaan Bassier, Arindrajit Dube, and Suresh Naidu, "Monopsony in Movers: The Elasticity of Labor Supply to Firm Wage Policies" (working paper 27755, National Bureau of Economic Research, 2020).

40. Gregor Aisch, Robert Gebeloff, and Kevin Quealy, "Where We Came From and Where We Went, State by State," *New York Times,* August 14, 2014, https://www.nytimes.com/interactive/2014/08/13/upshot/where-people-in -each-state-were-born.html.

41. Alexandre Mas and Amanda Pallais, "Valuing Alternative Work Arrangements," *American Economic Review* 107, no. 12 (2017): 3722–59; Liliana E. Pezzin, Robert A. Pollak, and Barbara S. Schone, "Long-Term Care of the Disabled Elderly: Do Children Increase Caregiving by Spouses?," *Review of Economics of the Household* 7, no. 3 (2009): 323–39; Janice Compton and Robert A. Pollak, "Family Proximity, Childcare, and Women's Labor Force Attachment," *Journal of Urban Economics* 79 (2014): 72–90.

42. Janice Compton and Robert A. Pollak, "Proximity and Co-residence of Adult Children and Their Parents in the United States: Descriptions and Correlates," *Annals of Economics and Statistics/Annales d'Économie et de Statistique* 117/118 (2015): 91–114.

Chapter 2. Medium-Term Gains for Workers

1. Robert G. Wood, Mary E. Corcoran, and Paul N. Courant, "Pay Differences among the Highly Paid: The Male-Female Earnings Gap in Lawyers' Salaries," *Journal of Labor Economics* 11, no. 3 (1993): 417–41.

2. Marianne Bertrand, Claudia Goldin, and Lawrence F. Katz, "Dynamics of the Gender Gap for Young Professionals in the Financial and Corporate Sectors," *American Economic Journal: Applied Economics* 2, no. 3 (2010): 228–55, at 228.

3. Yoram Ben-Porath, "The F-Connection: Families, Friends, and Firms and the Organization of Exchange," *Population and Development Review* 6, no. 1 (1980): 1–30; Michael A. Zabek, *Local Ties in Spatial Equilibrium,* Finance and Economics Discussion Series 2019-080 (Washington, DC: Board of Governors of the Federal Reserve System, 2019).

4. Upwork, "Upwork Report Finds Up to 23 Million Americans Plan to Relocate amid Rising Remote Work Trends," 2020, https://www.Upwork.com/
press/releases/Upwork-report-finds-up-to-23-million-americans-plan-to
-relocate-amid-rising-remote-work-trends.

5. Siqi Zheng and Matthew E. Kahn, "China's Bullet Trains Facilitate Market Integration and Mitigate the Cost of Megacity Growth," *Proceedings of the
National Academy of Sciences* 110, no. 14 (2013): E1248–53.

6. Nathaniel Baum-Snow, "Did Highways Cause Suburbanization?,"
Quarterly Journal of Economics 122, no. 2 (2007): 775–805; Jeffrey Brinkman
and Jeffrey Lin, "Freeway Revolts!" (working paper 19-29, FRB of Philadelphia Working Paper, 2019).

7. Carmen Carrión Flores and Elena G. Irwin, "Determinants of Residential Land-Use Conversion and Sprawl at the Rural-Urban Fringe," *American
Journal of Agricultural Economics* 86, no. 4 (2004): 889–904.

8. Jan Brueckner, Matthew E. Kahn, and Gary C. Lin, "A New Spatial He-
donic Equilibrium in the Emerging Work-from-Home Economy?" (working paper 28526, National Bureau of Economic Research, March 2021); Christopher
T. Stanton and Pratyush Tiwari, "Housing Consumption and the Cost of Remote Work" (working paper 28483, National Bureau of Economic Research,
February 2021).

9. Rakesh Kochhar and Richard Fry, "Wealth Inequality Has Widened
along Racial, Ethnic Lines since End of Great Recession," *Pew Research Center*
12, no. 104 (2014): 121–45.

10. Matthew E. Kahn, "Racial and Ethnic Differences in the Financial Returns to Home Purchases from 2007 to 2020" (working paper 28759, National
Bureau of Economic Research, May 2021).

11. Matthew E. Kahn, "Does Sprawl Reduce the Black/White Housing
Consumption Gap?," *Housing Policy Debate* 12, no. 1 (2001): 77–86.

12. Lisa J. Dettling and Melissa S. Kearney, "House Prices and Birth Rates:
The Impact of the Real Estate Market on the Decision to Have a Baby," *Journal
of Public Economics* 110 (2014): 82–100; Jessamyn Schaller, "Booms, Busts, and
Fertility Testing the Becker Model Using Gender-Specific Labor Demand,"
Journal of Human Resources 51, no. 1 (2016): 1–29.

13. Jess Gaspar and Edward L. Glaeser, "Information Technology and the
Future of Cities," *Journal of Urban Economics* 43, no. 1 (1998): 136–56.

14. Statista, "Regional Distribution of the U.S. Population from 1790–2019" (Statista Research Department, January 20, 2021), https://www.statista.com/statistics/240766/regional-distribution-of-the-us-population/.

15. Dora L. Costa and Matthew E. Kahn, "The Rising Price of Nonmarket Goods," *American Economic Review* 93, no. 2 (2003): 227–32.

16. Matthew E. Kahn, "Demographic Change and the Demand for Environmental Regulation," *Journal of Policy Analysis and Management* 21, no. 1 (2002): 45–62.

17. Matthew E. Kahn, "Do Liberal Cities Limit New Housing Development? Evidence from California," *Journal of Urban Economics* 69, no. 2 (2011): 223–28.

18. David Graeber, *Bullshit Jobs: The Rise of Pointless Work, and What We Can Do about It* (New York: Penguin, 2019).

19. Robin Bleiweis, "Quick Facts about the Gender Wage Gap" (Center for American Progress, March 24, 2020), https://www.americanprogress.org/issues/women/reports/2020/03/24/482141/quick-facts-gender-wage-gap/; Mitra Toossi and Teresa L. Morisi, *Women in the Workforce before, during, and after the Great Recession* (U.S. Bureau of Labor Statistics, 2017), https://ecommons.cornell.edu/bitstream/handle/1813/78334/BLS_Women_in_the_Workforce_Great_Recession.pdf.

20. Marianne Bertrand, "Gender in the Twenty-First Century," *AEA Papers and Proceedings* 110 (2020): 1–24; Henrik Kleven, Camille Landais, Johanna Posch, Andreas Steinhauer, and Josef Zweimüller, "Child Penalties across Countries: Evidence and Explanations," *AEA Papers and Proceedings* 109 (2019): 122–26.

21. Francine D. Blau and Lawrence M. Kahn, "The Gender Wage Gap: Extent, Trends, and Explanations," *Journal of Economic Literature* 55, no. 3 (2017): 789–865.

22. Zoë B. Cullen and Ricardo Perez-Truglia, "The Old Boys' Club: Schmoozing and the Gender Gap" (working paper 26530, National Bureau of Economic Research, 2019).

23. Dan A. Black, Natalia Kolesnikova, and Lowell J. Taylor, "Why Do So Few Women Work in New York (and So Many in Minneapolis)? Labor Supply of Married Women across US Cities," *Journal of Urban Economics* 79 (2014): 59–

71; William R. Johnson, "House Prices and Female Labor Force Participation," *Journal of Urban Economics* 82 (2014): 1–11.

24. Thomas Le Barbanchon, Roland Rathelot, and Alexandra Roulet, "Gender Differences in Job Search: Trading Off Commute against Wage," *Quarterly Journal of Economics* 136, no. 1 (2021): 381–426.

25. Ghazala Azmat and Rosa Ferrer, "Gender Gaps in Performance: Evidence from Young Lawyers," *Journal of Political Economy* 125, no. 5 (2017): 1306–55; George A. Akerlof and Rachel E. Kranton, "Economics and Identity," *Quarterly Journal of Economics* 115, no. 3 (2000): 715–53; John Cogan, "Fixed Costs and Labor Supply" (working paper 0484, National Bureau of Economic Research, June 1980); Jérôme Adda, Christian Dustmann, and Katrien Stevens, "The Career Costs of Children," *Journal of Political Economy* 125, no. 2 (2017): 293–337.

26. Karen V. Lombard, "Female Self-Employment and Demand for Flexible, Nonstandard Work Schedules," *Economic Inquiry* 39, no. 2 (2001): 214–37; M. Keith Chen, Peter E. Rossi, Judith A. Chevalier, and Emily Oehlsen, "The Value of Flexible Work: Evidence from Uber Drivers," *Journal of Political Economy* 127, no. 6 (2019): 2735–94.

27. Martin Halla, Julia Schmieder, and Andrea Weber, "Job Displacement, Family Dynamics, and Spousal Labor Supply," *American Economic Journal: Applied Economics* 12, no. 4 (2020): 253–87.

28. Claudia Goldin and Lawrence F. Katz, "The Cost of Workplace Flexibility for High-Powered Professionals," *Annals of the American Academy of Political and Social Science* 638, no. 1 (2011): 45–67, at 55.

29. V. Joseph Hotz, Per Johansson, and Arizo Karimi, *Parenthood, Family Friendly Firms, and the Gender Gaps in Early Work Career* (Cambridge, MA: National Bureau of Economic Research, 2017); Lonnie Golden, "Flexible Work Schedules: What Are We Trading Off to Get Them," *Monthly Labor Review* 124 (2001): 50; Claudia Goldin and Lawrence F. Katz, "A Most Egalitarian Profession: Pharmacy and the Evolution of a Family-Friendly Occupation," *Journal of Labor Economics* 34, no. 3 (2016): 705–46; Rebecca Korzec, "Working on the Mommy-Track: Motherhood and Women Lawyers," *Hastings Women's Law Journal* 8 (1997): 117.

30. Goldin and Katz, "The Cost of Workplace Flexibility," 55.

31. Le Barbanchon, Rathelot, and Roulet, "Gender Differences in Job Search"; Louis-Philippe Beland, Abel Brodeur, Joanne Haddad, and Derek Mikola, "COVID-19, Family Stress and Domestic Violence: Remote Work, Isolation and Bargaining Power" (IZA discussion paper 13332, Institute of Labor Economics, June 2020).

32. Ilyana Kuziemko, Jessica Pan, Jenny Shen, and Ebonya Washington, "The Mommy Effect: Do Women Anticipate the Employment Effects of Motherhood?" (working paper 24740, National Bureau of Economic Research, 2018); Elizabeth L. Doran, Ann P. Bartel, and Jane Waldfogel, "Gender in the Labor Market: The Role of Equal Opportunity and Family-Friendly Policies," *RSF: The Russell Sage Foundation Journal of the Social Sciences* 5, no. 5 (2019): 168–97; Kleven et al., "Child Penalties."

33. Aarti Ramaswami, George F. Dreher, Robert Bretz, and Carolyn Wiethoff, "The Interactive Effects of Gender and Mentoring on Career Attainment: Making the Case for Female Lawyers," *Journal of Career Development* 37, no. 4 (2010): 692–716; Dora L. Costa and Matthew E. Kahn, "Power Couples: Changes in the Locational Choice of the College Educated, 1940–1990," *Quarterly Journal of Economics* 115, no. 4 (2000): 1287–315.

34. Claudia Goldin, "The Quiet Revolution That Transformed Women's Employment, Education, and Family," *American Economic Review* 96, no. 2 (2006): 1–21; Lisa J. Dettling, "Broadband in the Labor Market: The Impact of Residential High-Speed Internet on Married Women's Labor Force Participation," *ILR Review* 70, no. 2 (2017): 451–82; David L. Chambers, "Accommodation and Satisfaction: Women and Men Lawyers and the Balance of Work and Family," *Law & Social Inquiry* 14, no. 2 (1989): 251–87.

35. Gary Stanley Becker, *A Treatise on the Family* (Cambridge, MA: Harvard University Press, 2009).

36. Marianne Bertrand, Patricia Cortés, Claudia Olivetti, and Jessica Pan, "Social Norms, Labor Market Opportunities, and the Marriage Gap for Skilled Women" (working paper 22015, National Bureau of Economic Research, 2016); Marianne Bertrand, Jessica Pan, and Emir Kamenica, "Gender Identity and Relative Income within Households," *Quarterly Journal of Economics* 130, no. 2 (2015): 571–614; Linda N. Edwards and Elizabeth Field-Hendrey, "Home-Based Work and Women's Labor Force Decisions," *Journal of Labor Economics* 20, no. 1 (2002): 170–200; Paula England, Jonathan Bearak, Michelle J. Budig,

and Melissa J. Hodges, "Do Highly Paid, Highly Skilled Women Experience the Largest Motherhood Penalty?," *American Sociological Review* 81, no. 6 (2016): 1161–89.

37. Natalia Zinovyeva and Maryna Tverdostup, "Gender Identity, Co-working Spouses and Relative Income within Households" (IZA discussion paper 11757, Institute of Labor Economics, August 2018); Bertrand, Pan, and Kamenica, "Gender Identity and Relative Income."

38. Gary S. Becker, "Human Capital, Effort, and the Sexual Division of Labor," *Journal of Labor Economics* 3, no. 1, part 2 (1985): S33–58.

39. Lena Edlund, Cecilia Machado, and Maria Micaela Sviatschi, "Gentrification and the Rising Returns to Skill" (working paper 21729, National Bureau of Economic Research, 2015).

40. Patrick Bayer, Hanming Fang, and Robert McMillan, "Separate When Equal? Racial Inequality and Residential Segregation," *Journal of Urban Economics* 82 (2014): 32–48; Joel Waldfogel, "The Median Voter and the Median Consumer: Local Private Goods and Population Composition," *Journal of Urban Economics* 63, no. 2 (2008): 567–82; John F. Kain, "The Spatial Mismatch Hypothesis: Three Decades Later," *Housing Policy Debate* 3, no. 2 (1992): 371–460.

41. William Julius Wilson, *When Work Disappears: The World of the New Urban Poor* (New York: Vintage, 2011).

42. Gene Balk, "Percentage of Black Residents in Seattle Is at Its Lowest Point in 50 Years," *Seattle Times*, June 16, 2020, https://www.seattletimes.com/seattle-news/data/percentage-of-blacks-living-in-seattle-at-lowest-point-in-50-years/.

43. Alberto Alesina, Stefanie Stantcheva, and Edoardo Teso, "Intergenerational Mobility and Preferences for Redistribution," *American Economic Review* 108, no. 2 (2018): 521–54.

44. "Pinterest Announces Termination of Future Lease Contract," *Business Wire*, August 28, 2020, https://www.businesswire.com/news/home/20200828005364/en/Pinterest-Announces-Termination-of-Future-Lease-Contract.

45. Ulises Ali Mejias, "Doing Faculty Diversity Differently," *Inside Higher Ed*, October 20, 2020, https://www.insidehighered.com/views/2020/10/20/increase-diversity-colleges-should-allow-more-faculty-color-teach-remotely-opinion.

46. Nick Bilton, "'Tech Workers Are Never Going Back to the Office': The Pandemic Housing-Market Explosion Could Upend Silicon Valley as We Know It," *Vanity Fair*, October 22, 2020, https://www.vanityfair.com/news/2020/10/the-pandemic-housing-market-explosion-could-upend-silicon-valley.

47. Edward L. Glaeser, Matthew E. Kahn, and Jordan Rappaport, "Why Do the Poor Live in Cities? The Role of Public Transportation," *Journal of Urban Economics* 63, no. 1 (2008): 1–24.

48. Julie Berry Cullen and Steven D. Levitt, "Crime, Urban Flight, and the Consequences for Cities," *Review of Economics and Statistics* 81, no. 2 (1999): 159–69.

Chapter 3. How Will Firms Adapt?

1. Joshua D. Coval and Tobias J. Moskowitz, "The Geography of Investment: Informed Trading and Asset Prices," *Journal of Political Economy* 109, no. 4 (2001): 811–41; Chris Forman and Avi Goldfarb, "Concentration and Agglomeration of IT Innovation and Entrepreneurship: Evidence from Patenting" (working paper 27338, National Bureau of Economic Research, 2020); Heiko Gerlach, Thomas Rønde, and Konrad Stahl, "Labor Pooling in R&D Intensive Industries," *Journal of Urban Economics* 65, no. 1 (2009): 99–111; Guy Dumais, Glenn Ellison, and Edward L. Glaeser, "Geographic Concentration as a Dynamic Process," *Review of Economics and Statistics* 84, no. 2 (2002): 193–204; Henry G. Overman and Diego Puga, *Labor Pooling as a Source of Agglomeration: An Empirical Investigation* (Chicago: University of Chicago Press, 2010).

2. Enrico Moretti, *The New Geography of Jobs* (Boston: Houghton Mifflin Harcourt, 2012).

3. Danlei Zhang, Pengyu Zhu, and Yanmei Ye, "The Effects of E-commerce on the Demand for Commercial Real Estate," *Cities* 51 (2016): 106–20.

4. Matthew Haag, "Manhattan Faces a Reckoning if Working from Home Becomes the Norm," *New York Times*, May 12, 2020, https://www.nytimes.com/2020/05/12/nyregion/coronavirus-work-from-home.html.

5. Brad Smith, "Investing to Grow Right Here at Home," *Official Microsoft Blog*, November 28, 2017, blogs.microsoft.com/blog/2017/11/28/investing-grow-right-home/.

6. Dan Frommer, "Apple Says Its New Office Is the 'World's Largest Natu-

rally Ventilated Building,'" *Vox*, February 22, 2017, https://www.vox.com/2017/2/22/14696882/apple-park-ventilation; Matthew E. Kahn and Pei Li, "Air Pollution Lowers High Skill Public Sector Worker Productivity in China," *Environmental Research Letters* 15, no. 8 (2020): article 084003.

7. Elizabeth Dwoskin, "Americans Might Never Go Back to the Office, and Twitter Is Leading the Charge," *Washington Post*, October 1, 2020, https://www.washingtonpost.com/technology/2020/10/01/twitter-work-from-home/?arc404=true.

8. Mohammad Arzaghi and J. Vernon Henderson, "Networking Off Madison Avenue," *Review of Economic Studies* 75, no. 4 (2008): 1011–38; Stuart S. Rosenthal and William C. Strange, "The Attenuation of Human Capital Spillovers," *Journal of Urban Economics* 64, no. 2 (2008): 373–89; Moretti, *The New Geography of Jobs*; Stuart S. Rosenthal and William C. Strange, "Evidence on the Nature and Sources of Agglomeration Economies," in *Handbook of Regional and Urban Economics*, vol. 4, *Cities and Geography*, ed. J. Vernon Henderson and Jacques-François Thisse, 2119–71 (Elsevier, 2004); Laura Bliss, "The Flight of the Techies Won't Be the End of Silicon Valley," *Bloomberg*, August 18, 2020, https://www.bloomberg.com/news/newsletters/2020-08-18/is-silicon-valley-over-don-t-count-on-it.

9. Tripp Mickle, "Google Adopts Hybrid Workweek, With 20% of Its Employees to Work Remotely," *Wall Street Journal*, May 5, 2021, https://www.wsj.com/articles/google-shifts-to-hybrid-workweek-allowing-20-of-its-employees-to-work-remotely-11620240694?mod=flipboard.

10. "Coronavirus Information: Information for Staff," Johns Hopkins University, Office of Communications, https://covidinfo.jhu.edu/information-for-staff/.

11. Eric D. Gould, B. Peter Pashigian, and Canice J. Prendergast, "Contracts, Externalities, and Incentives in Shopping Malls," *Review of Economics and Statistics* 87, no. 3 (2005): 411–22; Christian Catalini, Christian Fons-Rosen, and Patrick Gaule, "Did Cheaper Flights Change the Direction of Science?" (IZA discussion paper 9897, Institute of Labor Economics, April 2016); Esteban Rossi-Hansberg, Pierre-Daniel Sarte, and Raymond Owens, "Firm Fragmentation and Urban Patterns," *International Economic Review* 50, no. 1 (2009): 143–86.

12. Nathaniel Baum-Snow, "Did Highways Cause Suburbanization?,"

Quarterly Journal of Economics 122, no. 2 (2007): 775–805; Edward L. Glaeser and Matthew E. Kahn, "Decentralized Employment and the Transformation of the American City" (working paper 8117, National Bureau of Economic Research, 2001).

13. Christian Catalini, Christian Fons-Rosen, and Patrick Gaulé, "How Do Travel Costs Shape Collaboration?," *Management Science* 66, no. 8 (2020): 3340–60.

14. Xiaofang Dong, Siqi Zheng, and Matthew E. Kahn, "The Role of Transportation Speed in Facilitating High Skilled Teamwork across Cities," *Journal of Urban Economics* 115 (2020): article 103212.

15. Sebastian Herrera, "Amazon Bets on Office-Based Work with Expansion in Major Cities," *Wall Street Journal*, August 18, 2020, https://www.wsj.com/articles/amazon-bets-on-office-based-work-with-expansion-in-major-cities-11597741203.

16. Gilles Duranton and Diego Puga, "Nursery Cities: Urban Diversity, Process Innovation, and the Life Cycle of Products," *American Economic Review* 91, no. 5 (2001): 1454–77.

17. Siqi Zheng, Weizeng Sun, Jianfeng Wu, and Matthew E. Kahn, "The Birth of Edge Cities in China: Measuring the Effects of Industrial Parks Policy," *Journal of Urban Economics* 100 (2017): 80–103.

18. Kim-Mai Cutler, "DATA: Post-Pandemic Silicon Valley Isn't a Place," *View from Initialized*, January 26, 2021, https://blog.initialized.com/2021/01/data-post-pandemic-silicon-valley-isnt-a-place.

19. N. G. Lietz and S. Bracken, "Why WeWork Won't," *Harvard Business School Working Knowledge* (September 18, 2019).

20. Moretti, "Real Wage Inequality."

21. Daniel M. G. Raff and Lawrence H. Summers, "Did Henry Ford Pay Efficiency Wages?," *Journal of Labor Economics* 5, no. 4, part 2 (1987): S57–86.

22. Arizo V. Karimi, Joseph Hotz, and Per Johansson, "Family Friendly Firms? Worker Mobility, Firm Attributes and Wage Trajectories of Women and Men" (discussion paper, Institute for Evaluation of Labour Market and Education Policy, 2016).

23. Stefen Künn, Christian Seel, and Dainis Zegners, "Cognitive Performance in the Home Office-Evidence from Professional Chess" (IZA discussion paper 13491, Institute of Labor Economics, July 2020).

24. Bloom, Liang, Roberts, and Ying, "Does Working from Home Work?"

25. Alan Blinder, "Offshoring: The Next Industrial Revolution," *Offshoring* (2007): 1000–1017; Alan S. Blinder and Alan B. Krueger, "Alternative Measures of Offshorability: A Survey Approach," *Journal of Labor Economics* 31, no. S1 (2013): S97–128.

26. Michael Storper and Anthony J. Venables, "Buzz: Face-to-Face Contact and the Urban Economy," *Journal of Economic Geography* 4, no. 4 (2004): 351–70.

27. Mark Thoma, "The Death of Distance Has Been Greatly Exaggerated," *Economist's View*, November 27, 2007, https://economistsview.typepad.com/economistsview/2007/11/the-death-of-di.html.

28. Kyoung-Hee Yu and Frank Levy, "Offshoring Professional Services: Institutions and Professional Control," *British Journal of Industrial Relations* 48, no. 4 (2010): 758–83.

29. Alan S. Blinder, "Offshoring: Big Deal, or Business as Usual?," in Jagdish Bhagwati and Alan S. Blinder, *Offshoring of American Jobs: What Response from US Economic Policy*, 19–60 (Cambridge, MA: MIT Press, 2009).

30. Nicholas Bloom, Mirko Draca, and John Van Reenen, "Trade Induced Technical Change? The Impact of Chinese Imports on Innovation, IT and Productivity," *Review of Economic Studies* 83, no. 1 (2016): 87–117.

Chapter 4. The Rise of Remote Work and Superstar Cities

1. Joel Connelly and Grant Hindsley, "Seattle in the 1970s: From Big City to Big-Time Metropolis," *SeattlePI.com*, February 7, 2018, https://www.seattlepi.com/local/seattle-history/article/Connelly-The-1970-s-a-decade-where-nothing-in-12544348.php.

2. "All-Transactions House Price Index for King County, WA," FRED, February 23, 2021, https://fred.stlouisfed.org/series/ATNHPIUS53033A.

3. "General Fund Revenue Overview," Figure 9, City of Seattle, 2020, https://www.seattle.gov/Documents/Departments/FinanceDepartment/20proposedbudget/General_Fund_Revenue_Overview.pdf.

4. Arjun Ramani and Nick Bloom, "The Donut Effect: How COVID-19 Shapes Real Estate," *SIEPR Policy Brief*, January 2021.

5. "Apple and Google Buses under Fire in Silicon Valley," BBC News, January 18, 2018, https://www.bbc.com/news/technology-42738709.

6. "Issued Building Permit Stats," Seattle.gov, accessed May 23, 2021, http://www.seattle.gov/sdci/resources/issued-building-permit-stats.

7. Chris McGreal, "Is Bezos Holding Seattle Hostage? The Cost of Being Amazon's Home," *The Guardian*, July 4, 2018, https://www.theguardian .com/cities/2018/jul/04/is-bezos-holding-seattle-hostage-the-cost-of-being -amazons-home.

8. Jim Brunner and Benjamin Romano, "Amazon's Growing Spending on Seattle Politics Includes a Spate of Donations from Jeff Bezos' 'S Team,'" *Seattle Times*, November 8, 2019, https://www.seattletimes.com/seattle-news/ politics/amazons-growing-spending-on-seattle-politics-includes-a-spate-of -donations-from-jeff-bezos-s-team/.

9. Daniel Beekman and Jim Brunner, "Amazon Drops Additional $1 Million-Plus into Seattle City Council Races, with Ballots Out This Week," *Seattle Times*, October 16, 2019, https://www.seattletimes.com/seattle-news /politics/amazon-drops-additional-1-million-plus-into-seattle-city-council -races-with-ballots-mailing-this-week/.

10. Daniel Beekman and Jim Brunner, "Seattle City Council to Consider Repeal of Head Tax Less Than a Month after Approving It," *Seattle Times*, June 12, 2018, https://www.seattletimes.com/seattle-news/politics/seattle-council -to-consider-repeal-of-head-tax-less-than-a-month-after-approving-it/.

11. Brunner and Romano, "Amazon's Growing Spending."

12. David Kroman, "Pressure vs. Collaboration: What Put Seattle's Payroll Tax over the Top?," *Crosscut*, January 4, 2021, https://crosscut.com/2020/07/ what-seattles-new-payroll-tax-says-about-citys-politics.

13. Daniel Beekman, "Seattle City Council Votes in Committee to Advance New Tax on Big Businesses," *Seattle Times*, July 1, 2020, https://www .seattletimes.com/seattle-news/politics/seattle-city-council-votes-in-com mittee-to-advance-new-tax-on-big-businesses/; "Tax Amazon," Seattle.gov, April 17, 2020, https://www.seattle.gov/council/meet-the-council/kshama -sawant/tax-amazon.

14. "Seattle Will, Indeed, 'Tax Amazon' as $200M+ JumpStart Tax on Big Businesses Approved," *Capitol Hill Seattle Blog*, July 7, 2020, https://www

.capitolhillseattle.com/2020/07/seattle-will-indeed-tax-amazon-as-200m-jumpstart-tax-on-big-businesses-approved/.

15. David Wehner, "Facebook Commits $1 Billion and Partners with the State of California to Address Housing Affordability," Facebook Newsroom, October 22, 2019, https://about.fb.com/news/2019/10/facebook-commits-1-billion-to-address-housing-affordability/.

16. Monica Nickelsburg, "Facebook Launches $1B Affordable Housing Initiative, Joining Tech Peers Trying to Close the Gap," *GeekWire*, October 23, 2019, https://www.geekwire.com/2019/facebook-launches-1b-affordable-housing-initiative-joining-tech-peers-trying-close-gap/.

17. New Detroit Committee, "A Crisis of People," May 1968, Box 1, Folder Progress Reports, Joseph L. Hudson Papers, Bentley Historical Library, University of Michigan, https://policing.umhistorylabs.lsa.umich.edu/s/detroitunderfire/item/5059; "New Detroit Committee," Detroit Under Fire, accessed May 23, 2021, https://policing.umhistorylabs.lsa.umich.edu/s/detroitunderfire/page/new-detroit-committee.

18. Elizabeth Brayer, *George Eastman: A Biography* (Rochester, NY: University of Rochester Press, 2006).

19. "Amazon Launches $2 Billion Housing Equity Fund to Preserve and Create over 20,000 Affordable Homes," Amazon, January 6, 2021, https://www.aboutamazon.com/news/community/amazon-launches-2-billion-housing-equity-fund-to-preserve-and-create-over-20-000-affordable-homes.

20. Enrico Moretti, "Human Capital Externalities in Cities," in *Handbook of Regional and Urban Economics*, vol. 4, *Cities and Geography*, edited by J. Vernon Henderson and Jacques-François Thisse, 2243–91 (Elsevier, 2004).

21. Rune Fitjar and Andrés Rodríguez-Pose, "Marshall Was Wrong: Nothing Is in the Air," VOX, CEPR Policy Portal, accessed May 23, 2021, https://voxeu.org/article/marshall-was-wrong-nothing-air.

22. Matthew E. Kahn, "Racial and Ethnic Differences in the Financial Returns to Home Purchases from 2007 to 2020" (working paper 28759, National Bureau of Economic Research, 2021).

23. Haag, "Manhattan Faces a Reckoning."

24. Richard Hornbeck and Daniel Keniston, "Creative Destruction: Barriers to Urban Growth and the Great Boston Fire of 1872," *American Economic Review* 107, no. 6 (2017): 1365–98.

25. Philipp Ager, Katherine Eriksson, Casper Worm Hansen, and Lars Lønstrup, "How the 1906 San Francisco Earthquake Shaped Economic Activity in the American West," *Explorations in Economic History* 77 (2020): article 101342.

26. Christine Meisner Rosen, *The Limits of Power: Great Fires and the Process of City Growth in America* (Cambridge: Cambridge University Press, 2003).

27. James Siodla, "Razing San Francisco: The 1906 Disaster as a Natural Experiment in Urban Redevelopment," *Journal of Urban Economics* 89 (2015): 48–61.

28. Hornbeck and Keniston, "Creative Destruction."

29. Donald R. Davis and David E. Weinstein, "Bones, Bombs, and Break Points: The Geography of Economic Activity," *American Economic Review* 92, no. 5 (2002): 1269–89.

30. Edward L. Glaeser, "Urban Colossus: Why Is New York America's Largest City?" (working paper 11398, National Bureau of Economic Research, 2005).

31. Alberto Abadie and Sofia Dermisi, "Is Terrorism Eroding Agglomeration Economies in Central Business Districts? Lessons from the Office Real Estate Market in Downtown Chicago," *Journal of Urban Economics* 64, no. 2 (2008): 451–63; Edwin S. Mill, "Terrorism and US Real Estate," *Journal of Urban Economics* 51, no. 2 (2002): 198–204.

32. Abadie and Dermisi, "Is Terrorism Eroding."

33. Bill Hethcock, "1,800 Companies Left California in a Year—with Most Bound for Texas," Bizjournals.com, December 13, 2018, https://www .bizjournals.com/dallas/news/2018/12/13/1-800-companies-left-california -in-a-year-with.html.

34. US Census Bureau, 2017 American Community Survey, 1-Year Estimates, State-to-State Migration Flows.

35. Joel Kotkin and Marshall Toplansky, *Beyond Feudalism: A Strategy to Restore California's Middle Class* (research brief, Center for Demographics and Policy, Chapman University, 2020), https://www.chapman.edu/communica- tion/_files/beyond-feudalism-web-sm.pdf.

36. Jared Walczak and Janelle Cammenga, "2021 State Business Tax Climate Index," Tax Foundation, March 8, 2021, https://taxfoundation.org/2021 -state-business-tax-climate-index/.

37. Pacific Research Institute, "Why California's Most Coveted Industries Aren't Coming to the Golden State," February 2018.

38. Joel Kotkin and Marshall Toplansky, "Op-Ed: The Roots of California's Tattered Economy Were Planted Long before the Coronavirus Arrived," *Los Angeles Times*, October 25, 2020, https://www.latimes.com/opinion/story/2020 -10-25/california-economy-weakness-unemployment-tech-industries.

39. Joe Lonsdale, "California, Love It and Leave It," *Wall Street Journal*, November 15, 2020, https://www.wsj.com/articles/california-love-it-and -leave-it-11605472619.

40. Katherine Bindley, "Remote Work Is Reshaping San Francisco, as Tech Workers Flee and Rents Fall," *Wall Street Journal*, August 14, 2020, https://www.wsj.com/articles/remote-work-is-reshaping-san-francisco-as -tech-workers-flee-and-rents-fall-11597413602.

41. Paul Krugman, "History versus Expectations," *Quarterly Journal of Economics* 106, no. 2 (1991): 651–67.

42. Matthew Haag, "Manhattan Emptied Out during the Pandemic; But Big Tech Is Moving In," *New York Times*, October 13, 2020, https://www.nytimes .com/2020/10/13/nyregion/big-tech-nyc-office-space.html?referringSource= articleShare.

43. Edward L. Glaeser and Joshua D. Gottlieb, "Urban Resurgence and the Consumer City," *Urban Studies* 43, no. 8 (2006): 1275–99; Edward L. Glaeser and Matthew E. Kahn, "Sprawl and Urban Growth," in *Handbook of Regional and Urban Economics*, vol. 4, *Cities and Geography*, edited by J. Vernon Henderson and Jacques-François Thisse, 2481–527 (Elsevier, 2004); William A. Fischel, *The Economics of Zoning Laws: A Property Rights Approach to American Land Use Controls* (Baltimore: Johns Hopkins University Press, 1987); Edward L. Glaeser, Joseph Gyourko, and Raven Saks, "Why Is Manhattan So Expensive? Regulation and the Rise in Housing Prices," *Journal of Law and Economics* 48, no. 2 (2005): 331–69.

44. Joseph Gyourko, Christopher Mayer, and Todd Sinai, "Superstar Cities," *American Economic Journal: Economic Policy* 5, no. 4 (2013): 167–99.

45. Simeon Djankov, Rafael La Porta, Florencio Lopez-de-Silanes, and Andrei Shleifer, "The Regulation of Entry," *Quarterly Journal of Economics* 117, no. 1 (2002): 1–37.

46. Matt Boone, "San Francisco Rent Prices Down 31% as Residents

Leave for More Space, Cheaper Housing amid Pandemic," ABC7 San Francisco (KGO-TV), October 18, 2020, https://abc7news.com/sf-rent-prices-dropping-covid-19-housing-realtorcom-report/7032535/; Becca Savransky, "Study: Seattle Saw Third Largest Drop in Rent Prices since Start of Pandemic," SeattlePI .com, May 19, 2021, https://www.seattlepi.com/realestate/slideshow/seattle-third-largest-drop-rent-prices-since-covid-210364.php.

47. David Genesove and Christopher Mayer, "Loss Aversion and Seller Behavior: Evidence from the Housing Market," *Quarterly Journal of Economics* 116, no. 4 (2001): 1233–60.

48. Jane Jacobs, "Downtown Is for People," in *The Exploding Metropolis*, edited by William H. Whyte, 168 (Doubleday, 1958).

49. Vicki Been, Ingrid Gould Ellen, Michael Gedal, Edward Glaeser, and Brian J. McCabe, "Preserving History or Restricting Development? The Heterogeneous Effects of Historic Districts on Local Housing Markets in New York City," *Journal of Urban Economics* 92 (2016): 16–30.

Chapter 5. New Opportunities for Other Areas

1. Henrik Jacobsen Kleven, Camille Landais, and Emmanuel Saez, "Taxation and International Migration of Superstars: Evidence from the European Football Market," *American Economic Review* 103, no. 5 (2013): 1892–924.

2. Brian Costa, "How a Florida Town Became the Nexus of the Golf Universe," *Wall Street Journal*, March 3, 2016, https://www.wsj.com/articles/how-a-florida-town-became-the-nexus-of-the-golf-universe-1457026763.

3. Laura Saunders, "Remote-Working from a Different State? Beware of a Tax Surprise," *Wall Street Journal*, May 29, 2020, https://www.wsj.com/articles/remote-working-from-a-different-state-beware-of-a-tax-surprise-11590744601.

4. Romano, "Mayor Durkan Says Amazon's Relationship."

5. Freakonomics, "Can 'Charter Cities' Change the World? A Q&A with Paul Romer," Freakonomics, September 29, 2009, https://freakonomics.com/2009/09/29/can-charter-cities-change-the-world-a-qa-with-paul-romer/.

6. Colleen de Bellefonds, "Why the Yellow Vests in France Are Different from Other Western Protests," *U.S. News & World Report*, December 7, 2018,

https://www.usnews.com/news/best-countries/articles/2018-12-07/frances
-yellow-vests-movement-reveals-countrys-growing-divisions.

7. Matthew J. Holian and Matthew E. Kahn, "Household Demand for Low Carbon Policies: Evidence from California," *Journal of the Association of Environmental and Resource Economists* 2, no. 2 (2015): 205–34.

8. Neal E. Boudette and Coral Davenport, "G.M. Will Sell Only Zero-Emission Vehicles by 2035," *New York Times*, January 28, 2021, https://www.nytimes.com/2021/01/28/business/gm-zero-emission-vehicles.html.

9. Environmental Protection Agency, "Sources of Greenhouse Gas Emissions," April 14, 2021, https://www.epa.gov/ghgemissions/sources-greenhouse-gas-emissions.

10. Stephen P. Holland, Erin T. Mansur, Nicholas Z. Muller, and Andrew J. Yates, "Are There Environmental Benefits from Driving Electric Vehicles? The Importance of Local Factors," *American Economic Review* 106, no. 12 (2016): 3700–729; Magali A. Delmas, Matthew E. Kahn, and Stephen L. Locke, "The Private and Social Consequences of Purchasing an Electric Vehicle and Solar Panels: Evidence from California," *Research in Economics* 71, no. 2 (2017): 225–35; Holian and Kahn, "Household Demand for Low Carbon Policies"; Katherine Bindley, "Tech Workers Take to the Mountains, Bringing Silicon Valley with Them," *Wall Street Journal*, November 1, 2020, https://www.wsj.com/articles/tech-workers-take-to-the-mountains-bringing-silicon-valley-with-them-11604242802.

11. Alissa Walker, "Climate-Change-Related Lawsuit Nixes Huge California Development," Curbed.com, April 20, 2021, https://www.curbed.com/2021/04/tejon-ranch-judge-ruling-wildfire.html.

12. Enrico Moretti, "Fires Aren't the Only Threat to the California Dream," *New York Times*, November 3, 2017, https://www.nytimes.com/2017/11/03/opinion/california-fires-housing.html.

13. Patrick Baylis and Judson Boomhower, "Moral Hazard, Wildfires, and the Economic Incidence of Natural Disasters" (working paper 26550, National Bureau of Economic Research, 2019).

14. Patrick Baylis and Judson Boomhower, *Building Codes and Community Resilience to Natural Disasters*, April 2021, patrickbaylis.com/pdf/buildingcodes-apr2021.pdf.

15. 2017 Census of Agriculture, US Department of Agriculture, webpage last modified March 16, 2021, https://www.nass.usda.gov/AgCensus/index.php.

16. Chang-Tai Hsieh and Enrico Moretti, "Housing Constraints and Spatial Misallocation," *American Economic Journal: Macroeconomics* 11, no. 2 (2019): 1–39.

17. California Department of Food and Agriculture, "Links to County Crop Reports," accessed May 23, 2021, https://www.cdfa.ca.gov/exec/county/CountyCropReports.html.

18. California Department of Food and Agriculture, "Links to County Crop Reports," accessed May 23, 2021, https://www.cdfa.ca.gov/exec/county/CountyCropReports.html.

19. California Department of Food and Agriculture, *California County Agricultural Commissioners' Reports Crop Year 2016-2017*, December 28, 2018, https://www.cdfa.ca.gov/statistics/pdfs/2017cropyearactboo.pdf.

20. Matthew J. Kotchen and Shawn M. Powers, "Explaining the Appearance and Success of Voter Referenda for Open-Space Conservation," *Journal of Environmental Economics and Management* 52, no. 1 (2006): 373–90; Novato City Council, "City of Novato General Plan," March 8, 1996, http://www.novato.org/home/showdocument?id=3049.

21. "Irrigation and Water Use," Economic Research Service, US Department of Agriculture, September 23, 2019, https://www.ers.usda.gov/topics/farm-practices-management/irrigation-water-use.

22. Michael I. Cragg and Matthew E. Kahn, "Climate Consumption and Climate Pricing from 1940 to 1990," *Regional Science and Urban Economics* 29, no. 4 (1999): 519–39.

23. Jordan Rappaport, "The Increasing Importance of Quality of Life," *Journal of Economic Geography* 9, no. 6 (2009): 779–804; Jennifer Roback, "Wages, Rents, and the Quality of Life," *Journal of Political Economy* 90, no. 6 (1982): 1257–78; Richard Rogerson and Johanna Wallenius, "Household Time Use among Older Couples: Evidence and Implications for Labor Supply Parameters," *Quarterly Journal of Economics* 134, no. 2 (2019): 1079–120.

24. Leah Platt Boustan, Matthew E. Kahn, Paul W. Rhode, and Maria Lucia Yanguas, "The Effect of Natural Disasters on Economic Activity in US

Counties: A Century of Data," *Journal of Urban Economics* 118 (2020): article 103257.

25. "Charleston Peninsula Coastal Flood Risk Management Study," Charleston District, US Army Corps of Engineers, accessed May 23, 2021, https://www.sac.usace.army.mil/Missions/Civil-Works/Supplemental -Funding/Charleston-Peninsula-Study/.

26. "2021 Best Tech Startups in Carlsbad," *Tech Tribune*, January 5, 2021, http://thetechtribune.com/10-best-tech-startups-in-carlsbad/; Gerald A. Carlino and Albert Saiz, "Beautiful City: Leisure Amenities and Urban Growth," *Journal of Regional Science* 59, no. 3 (2019): 369–408; Jordan Rappaport and Jeffrey D. Sachs, "The United States as a Coastal Nation," *Journal of Economic Growth* 8, no. 1 (2003): 5–46.

27. Kelly Pohl, "Growth Inevitable, Will Need Thoughtful Response," *Bozeman Daily Chronicle*, August 26, 2020, https://www.bozemandailychron icle.com/opinions/guest_columnists/growth-inevitable-will-need-thoughtful -response/article_7dc35ff9-4635-5883-a4c4-17104ef1caa9.html.

28. Jeff Zillgitt, "The Utah Jazz Have a New Owner: At Age 42, Ryan Smith Is a Tech Billionaire Committed to Sticking Around," *USA Today*, December 18, 2020, https://www.usatoday.com/story/sports/nba/jazz/2020/12/18/utah -jazz-new-owner-ryan-smith/3956955001/.

29. Greg Howard, "The Migration Accelerator: Labor Mobility, Housing, and Demand," *American Economic Journal: Macroeconomics* 12, no. 4 (2020): 147–79.

30. Edward L. Glaeser, Jed Kolko, and Albert Saiz, "Consumer City," *Journal of Economic Geography* 1, no. 1 (2001): 27–50; Joel Waldfogel, "The Median Voter and the Median Consumer: Local Private Goods and Population Composition," *Journal of Urban Economics* 63, no. 2 (2008): 567–82.

31. Paul Stafford, "The 30 Most Charming Small Cities in the USA," *TravelMag*, April 5, 2021, https://www.travelmag.com/articles/small-cities-usa/.

32. City of Berkeley, Departments of Planning and Development and Health, Housing & Community Services, *City of Berkeley 2015-2023 Housing Element*, https://www.cityofberkeley.info/uploadedFiles/Planning_and _Development/Level_3_-_Commissions/Commission_for_Planning/2015 -2023%20Berkeley%20Housing%20Element_FINAL.pdf.

33. Kahn, "Liberal Cities"; William Marble and Clayton Nall, "Where Self-Interest Trumps Ideology: Liberal Homeowners and Local Opposition to Housing Development," March 19, 2019, https://www.dropbox.com /s/ocpefxjmqhrgkqg/interest35.pdf.

34. Sarah Holder, "The 5 Cities Ready to Build with Remote Workers in Mind," *Bloomberg.com*, January 26, 2021, https://www.bloomberg.com/news/ articles/2021-01-26/how-small-cities-are-trying-to-lure-remote-workers.

35. Liz Farmer, "The New Company Town: How Rochester, New York, Is Angling to Be a Remote Work Hub," Lincoln Institute of Land Policy, May 17, 2021, https://www.lincolninst.edu/publications/articles/2021-05-new-com pany-town-how-rochester-new-york-is-angling-to-be-remote-work-hub.

36. Gyourko, Mayer, and Sinai, "Superstar Cities."

37. Edward L. Glaeser and Joseph Gyourko, "Urban Decline and Durable Housing," *Journal of Political Economy* 113, no. 2 (2005): 345–75.

38. Jan K. Brueckner and Stuart S. Rosenthal, "Gentrification and Neighborhood Housing Cycles: Will America's Future Downtowns Be Rich?," *Review of Economics and Statistics* 91, no. 4 (2009): 725–43.

39. "The World Is Spiky," *Atlantic Monthly*, October 2005, available at http://www.creativeclass.com/rfcgdb/articles/other-2005-The%20World %20is%20Spiky.pdf.

40. "The Kirwan Commission and Education Reform in Maryland," Baltimore Community Foundation, accessed May 26, 2021, http://education.bal timorecommunityfoundation.org/.

41. "Policy Solutions to the American Dream," Opportunity Insights, November 19, 2020, https://opportunityinsights.org/.

42. www.heckmanequation.org.

43. F. Douglas Scutchfield and C. William Keck, "Deaths of Despair: Why? What to Do?," *American Journal of Public Health* 107, no. 10 (2017): 1564; Anne Case and Angus Deaton, *Deaths of Despair and the Future of Capitalism* (Princeton, NJ: Princeton University Press, 2020).

44. Victor Couture, Benjamin Faber, Yizhen Gu, and Lizhi Liu, "E-commerce Integration and Economic Development: Evidence from China" (working paper 24383, National Bureau of Economic Research, 2018); Edward L. Glaeser and Naomi Hausman, "The Spatial Mismatch between Innovation and Joblessness," *Innovation Policy and the Economy* 20, no. 1 (2020): 233–99.

45. Patrick Ruffini, "How Permanent Work-from-Home Could Help Repair America's Partisan Divide," *Medium*, June 10, 2020, https://gen.medium.com/permanent-work-from-home-could-end-americas-big-sort-e0ed9cf7686d.

46. Waldfogel, "The Median Voter."

47. Emmy M. Cho and Ariel H. Kim, "Nearly a Quarter of Rural Americans Unable to Receive Medical Care during Pandemic, School of Public Health Poll Finds," *Harvard Crimson*, October 6, 2020, https://www.thecrimson.com/article/2020/10/26/rural-america-pandemic-healthcare-access/; Lillian Rizzo, "Americans Working from Home Face Internet Usage Limits," *Wall Street Journal*, October 25, 2020, https://www.wsj.com/articles/americans-working-from-home-face-internet-usage-limits-11603638000.

48. Fast Company, "Remote Work Can't Change Everything until We Fix This $80 Billion Problem," *Medium*, November 30, 2020, https://medium.com/fast-company/remote-work-cant-change-everything-until-we-fix-this-80-billion-problem-f4e7486c3f23.

49. Victor Couture, Benjamin Faber, Yizhen Gu, and Lizhi Liu, "Connecting the Countryside via E-commerce: Evidence from China" (working paper 24384, National Bureau of Economic Research, 2018).

50. "Telehealth Use in Rural Healthcare," RHIhub, accessed May 26, 2021, https://www.ruralhealthinfo.org/topics/telehealth; "Barriers to Telehealth in Rural Areas," RHIhub, accessed May 26, 2021, https://www.ruralhealthinfo.org/toolkits/telehealth/1/barriers.

51. Isaiah Mayersen, "Amazon Can Now Deliver Half of Its Own Packages, to the Tune of 2.5 Billion Packages and Growing," TechSpot, December 14, 2019, https://www.techspot.com/news/83195-amazon-can-now-deliver-half-own-packages.html.

52. Benjamin Austin, Edward Glaeser, and Lawrence H. Summers, "Saving the Heartland: Place-Based Policies in 21st Century America," Brookings Institution, March 8, 2018, https://www.brookings.edu/bpea-articles/saving-the-heartland-place-based-policies-in-21st-century-america.

53. "Minden, West Virginia: A Brief History of 'The Most Toxic Town in the US,'" Ecospears, April 15, 2019, https://ecospears.com/minden-west-virginia-a-brief-history-of-the-most-toxic-town-in-the-us/.

54. Email correspondence from Brad Humphreys.

Conclusion

1. Jess Gaspar and Edward L. Glaeser, "Information Technology and the Future of Cities," *Journal of Urban Economics* 43, no. 1 (1998): 136–56.

2. Edward L. Glaeser, *Triumph of the City: How Our Greatest Invention Makes Us Richer, Smarter, Greener, Healthier and Happier* (New York: Penguin, 2011); Edward L. Glaeser, "Are Cities Dying?," *Journal of Economic Perspectives* 12, no. 2 (1998): 139–60.

3. Gyourko, Mayer, and Sinai, "Superstar Cities."

4. "How the Pandemic Reversed Old Migration Patterns in Europe," *The Economist*, January 28, 2021, https://www.economist.com/europe/2021/01/30/how-the-pandemic-reversed-old-migration-patterns-in-europe.

5. Gharad Byran, Shyamal Chowdhury, and Ahmed Mushfiq Mobarak, "Underinvestment in a Profitable Technology: The Case of Seasonal Migration in Bangladesh," *Econometrica* 82, no. 5 (2014): 1671–748; Robert Jensen and Nolan H. Miller, "Keepin' 'em Down on the Farm: Migration and Strategic Investment in Children's Schooling" (working paper 23122, National Bureau of Economic Research, 2017).

6. Daniel Garrote Sanchez, Nicolas Gomez Parra, Caglar Ozden, Bob Rijkers, Mariana Viollaz, and Hernan Winkler, "Who on Earth Can Work from Home?," *World Bank Research Observer* 36, no. 1 (2021).

7. Eric Andrew-Gee, "Remote Work Has Boosted Canada's Hot Housing Market, But How Long Will the Boom Last?," *Globe and Mail*, May 3, 2021, https://www.theglobeandmail.com/canada/article-dont-expect-the-pandemics-dramatic-remote-work-shift-to-be-permanent.

8. Charles I. Jones and Peter J. Klenow, "Beyond GDP? Welfare across Countries and Time," *American Economic Review* 106, no. 9 (2016): 2426–57.

9. Stephen J. Macekura, "The Mismeasure of Progress," in Macekura, *The Mismeasure of Progress: Economic Growth and Its Critics* (Chicago: University of Chicago Press, 2020).

10. Joseph Stiglitz, "GDP Is the Wrong Tool for Measuring What Matters," *Scientific American* 323, no. 2 (August 2020): 24–31, https://www.scientificamerican.com/article/gdp-is-the-wrong-tool-for-measuring-what-matters.

11. Daniel Kahneman and Alan B. Krueger, "Developments in the Measurement of Subjective Well-Being," *Journal of Economic Perspectives* 20, no. 1 (2006): 3–24; Alan B. Krueger and Andreas I. Mueller, "Time Use, Emotional

Well-Being, and Unemployment: Evidence from Longitudinal Data," *American Economic Review* 102, no. 3 (2012): 594–99; R. A. Easterlin, "Life Cycle Happiness and Its Sources: Intersections of Psychology, Economics, and Demography," *Journal of Economic Psychology* 27, no. 4 (August 2006): 463–82; Sonja Lyubomirsky, Kennon M. Sheldon, and David Schkade, "Pursuing Happiness: The Architecture of Sustainable Change," *Review of General Psychology* 9, no. 2 (2005): 111–31.

12. Blau and Kahn, "The Gender Wage Gap."

13. Claudia Goldin and Robert A. Margo, "The Great Compression: The Wage Structure in the United States at Mid-century," *Quarterly Journal of Economics* 107, no. 1 (1992): 1–34.

Recommended Reading

Ameriks, John, Joseph Briggs, Andrew Caplin, Minjoon Lee, Matthew D. Shapiro, and Christopher Tonetti. "Older Americans Would Work Longer if Jobs Were Flexible." *American Economic Journal: Macroeconomics* 12, no. 1 (2020): 174–209.

Austin, Benjamin, Edward Glaeser, and Lawrence H. Summers, "Saving the Heartland: Place-Based Policies in 21st Century America." *Brookings Papers on Economic Activity*, 151–255. Brookings Institution, March 8, 2018. https://www.brookings.edu/bpea-articles/saving-the-heartland-place -based-policies-in-21st-century-america.

Autor, David H. "Work of the Past, Work of the Future." *AEA Papers and Proceedings* 109 (2019): 1–32.

Autor, David H., David Dorn, and Gordon H. Hanson. "The China Syndrome: Local Labor Market Effects of Import Competition in the United States." *American Economic Review* 103, no. 6 (2013): 2121–68.

Azmat, Ghazala, and Rosa Ferrer. "Gender Gaps in Performance: Evidence from Young Lawyers." *Journal of Political Economy* 125, no. 5 (2017): 1306–55.

Baldwin, Richard. *The Globotics Upheaval: Globalization, Robotics, and the Future of Work.* New York: Oxford University Press, 2019.

Barrero, Jose Maria, Nicholas Bloom, and Steven J. Davis. "Why Working from Home Will Stick." University of Chicago, Becker Friedman Institute for Economics Working Paper 2020-174 (2020).

Becker, Gary S. "A Theory of the Allocation of Time." *Economic Journal* 75, no. 299 (1965): 493–517.

———. *A Treatise on the Family*. Cambridge, MA: Harvard University Press, 2009.

Been, Vicki, Ingrid Gould Ellen, Michael Gedal, Edward Glaeser, and Brian J. McCabe. "Preserving History or Restricting Development? The Heterogeneous Effects of Historic Districts on Local Housing Markets in New York City." *Journal of Urban Economics* 92 (2016): 16–30.

Bertrand, Marianne, Claudia Goldin, and Lawrence F. Katz. "Dynamics of the Gender Gap for Young Professionals in the Financial and Corporate Sectors." *American Economic Journal: Applied Economics* 2, no. 3 (2010): 228–55.

Bertrand, Marianne, Emir Kamenica, and Jessica Pan. "Gender Identity and Relative Income within Households." *Quarterly Journal of Economics* 130, no. 2 (2015): 571–614.

Black, Dan A., Natalia Kolesnikova, and Lowell J. Taylor. "Why Do So Few Women Work in New York (and So Many in Minneapolis)? Labor Supply of Married Women across US Cities." *Journal of Urban Economics* 79 (2014): 59–71.

Blau, F. D., and L. M. Kahn. "The Gender Wage Gap: Extent, Trends, and Explanations." *Journal of Economic Literature* 55, no. 3 (September 2017): 789–865.

Blinder, A. S. "Offshoring: The Next Industrial Revolution?" *Foreign Affairs* 85, no. 2 (March/April 2006): 113–28.

Bloom, N., J. Liang, J. Roberts, and Z. J. Ying. "Does Working from Home Work? Evidence from a Chinese Experiment." *Quarterly Journal of Economics* 130, no. 1 (February 2015): 165–218.

Carlino, Gerald A., and Albert Saiz. "Beautiful City: Leisure Amenities and Urban Growth." *Journal of Regional Science* 59, no. 3 (2019): 369–408.

Compton, Janice, and Robert A. Pollak. "Family Proximity, Childcare, and Women's Labor Force Attachment." *Journal of Urban Economics* 79 (2014): 72–90.

Costa, Dora L., and Matthew E. Kahn. "Power Couples: Changes in the Locational Choice of the College Educated, 1940–1990." *Quarterly Journal of Economics* 115, no. 4 (2000): 1287–315.

———. "Understanding the American Decline in Social Capital." *Kyklos* 56, no. 1 (2003): 17–46.

Cullen, Julie Berry, and Steven D. Levitt. "Crime, Urban Flight, and the Consequences for Cities." *Review of Economics and Statistics* 81, no. 2 (1999): 159–69.

Ellison, Glenn, Edward L. Glaeser, and William R. Kerr. "What Causes Industry Agglomeration? Evidence from Coagglomeration Patterns." *American Economic Review* 100, no. 3 (2010): 1195–213.

Fischel, William A. *The Homevoter Hypothesis.* Cambridge, MA: Harvard University Press, 2009.

Fisman, Ray, and Tim Sullivan. *The Org: The Underlying Logic of the Office.* Updated edition. Princeton, NJ: Princeton University Press, 2015.

Gaspar, Jess, and Edward L. Glaeser. "Information Technology and the Future of Cities." *Journal of Urban Economics* 43, no. 1 (1998): 136–56.

Gibbs, Michael, Friederike Mengel, and Christoph Siemroth. "Work from Home and Productivity: Evidence from Personnel and Analytics Data on IT Professionals." University of Chicago, Becker Friedman Institute for Economics Working Paper 2021-56 (2021).

Glaeser, Edward L., and Matthew E. Kahn. "The Greenness of Cities: Carbon Dioxide Emissions and Urban Development." *Journal of Urban Economics* 67, no. 3 (2010): 404–18.

Glaeser, Edward L., Matthew E. Kahn, and Jordan Rappaport. "Why Do the Poor Live in Cities? The Role of Public Transportation." *Journal of Urban Economics* 63, no. 1 (2008): 1–24.

Glaeser, Edward L., Jed Kolko, and Albert Saiz. "Consumer City." *Journal of Economic Geography* 1, no. 1 (2001): 27–50.

Glaeser, Edward L., and David C. Mare. "Cities and Skills." *Journal of Labor Economics* 19, no. 2 (2001): 316–42.

Goldin, Claudia, and Lawrence F. Katz. "The Cost of Workplace Flexibility for High-Powered Professionals." *Annals of the American Academy of Political and Social Science* 638, no. 1 (2011): 45–67.

———. "A Most Egalitarian Profession: Pharmacy and the Evolution of a Family-Friendly Occupation." *Journal of Labor Economics* 34, no. 3 (2016): 705–46.

Goldin, Claudia, and Robert A. Margo. "The Great Compression: The Wage Structure in the United States at Mid-century." *Quarterly Journal of Economics* 107, no. 1 (1992): 1–34.

Graeber, David. "Bullshit Jobs: The Rise of Pointless Work, and What We Can Do about It." New York: Penguin, 2019.

Hamermesh, Daniel S., Harley Frazis, and Jay Stewart. "Data Watch: The American Time Use Survey." *Journal of Economic Perspectives* 19, no. 1 (2005): 221–32.

Hårsman, Björn, and John M. Quigley. "Political and Public Acceptability of Congestion Pricing: Ideology and Self-Interest." *Journal of Policy Analysis and Management* 29, no. 4 (2010): 854–74.

Herkenhoff, Kyle F., Lee E. Ohanian, and Edward C. Prescott. "Tarnishing the Golden and Empire States: Land-Use Restrictions and the US Economic Slowdown." *Journal of Monetary Economics* 93 (January 2018): 89–109.

Hsieh, Chang-Tai, and Enrico Moretti. "Housing Constraints and Spatial Misallocation." *American Economic Journal: Macroeconomics* 11, no. 2 (2019): 1–39.

Kahn, Matthew E. *Climatopolis: How Our Cities Will Thrive in the Hotter Future.* New York: Basic Books, 2013.

———. "Do Liberal Cities Limit New Housing Development? Evidence from California." *Journal of Urban Economics* 69, no. 2 (2011): 223–28.

———. "Gentrification Trends in New Transit-Oriented Communities: Evidence from 14 Cities That Expanded and Built Rail Transit Systems." *Real Estate Economics* 35, no. 2 (2007): 155–82.

———. *Racial and Ethnic Differences in the Financial Returns to Home Purchases from 2007 to 2020.* No. w28759. Cambridge, MA: National Bureau of Economic Research, 2021.

———. "Urban Growth and Climate Change." *Annual Review of Resource Economics* 1, no. 1 (2009): 333–50.

Kain, John F. "The Spatial Mismatch Hypothesis: Three Decades Later." *Housing Policy Debate* 3, no. 2 (1992): 371–460.

Kerr, William R., and Frédéric Robert-Nicoud. "Tech Clusters." *Journal of Economic Perspectives* 34, no. 3 (2020): 50–76.

Krugman, Paul. "History versus Expectations." *Quarterly Journal of Economics* 106, no. 2 (1991): 651–67.

———. "The Pandemic and the Future City." *New York Times*, March 15, 2021.

https://www.nytimes.com/2021/03/15/opinion/cities-covid-remote-work
.html.

Moretti, Enrico. *The New Geography of Jobs*. Boston: Houghton Mifflin Harcourt, 2012.

Moretti, Enrico, and Daniel J. Wilson. "The Effect of State Taxes on the Geographical Location of Top Earners: Evidence from Star Scientists." *American Economic Review* 107, no. 7 (2017): 1858–903.

Moss, Mitchell L., and Carson Qing. *The Emergence of the "Super-Commuter."* Rudin Center for Transportation, New York University Wagner School of Public Service, 2012.

Putnam, Robert D., *Bowling Alone: The Collapse and Revival of American Community*. New York: Simon and Schuster, 2000.

Rappaport, Jordan. "The Increasing Importance of Quality of Life." *Journal of Economic Geography* 9, no. 6 (2009): 779–804.

Roca, Jorge De La, and Diego Puga. "Learning by Working in Big Cities." *Review of Economic Studies* 84, no. 1 (2017): 106–42.

Rohwedder, Susan, and Robert J. Willis. "Mental Retirement." *Journal of Economic Perspectives* 24, no. 1 (2010): 119–38.

Rosenthal, Stuart S., and William C. Strange. "Evidence on the Nature and Sources of Agglomeration Economies." In *Handbook of Regional and Urban Economics*, vol. 4, *Cities and Geography*, edited by J. Vernon Henderson and Jacques-François Thisse, 2119–71. Elsevier, 2004.

Topel, Robert H., and Michael P. Ward. "Job Mobility and the Careers of Young Men." *Quarterly Journal of Economics* 107, no. 2 (1992): 439–79.

Index

Abadie, Alberto, 133

adaptation, varying capacities for, 23, 115

affordable housing, Facebook's program for, 124

African Americans: disproportionate residence in city center neighborhoods, 57; housing choices, racial wealth gap and, 56–57; preference for living in cities with high percentages of black residents, and limited job and education opportunities, 82; and rising real estate prices in superstar cities, lack of gain from, 130–31; and WFH, access to more affordable housing through, 57

African Americans, in large postindustrial cities: increased opportunities with WFH, 10, 15–16, 81–83; as large pool of potential workers, 80–81; lost manufacturing jobs, 79; reasons for limited opportunities, 79–81

African American unemployment: companies' increased interest in

diverse workforce and, 81–82; effect of WFH on, 81–83; lack of local high-paying technology and finance jobs, 80–81, 82; and lack of working role models, 79–80, 81; move of jobs to suburbs and, 79; reduction of, through WFH, 79–80; and spatial mismatch hypothesis, 79

Airbnb: and exurban families' access to city culture and amenities, 57; and visits to environmentalist worker communities, 61

air travel, low-cost: and decentralization of firms, 91, 97; and scientific and academic collaborations, increase in, 97; and visits to potential new homes, 166

Amazon: corporate campus, recently built, 1, 92; decentralization of, 97–98, 101; hiring of African Americans and, 81; Housing Equity Fund of, 127; HQ2 in Virginia, 82, 92; move into Seattle politics, 123; and Seattle's economic boom, 119; Seattle's efforts

Amazon *(continued)*
    to tax, 14, 122–24; and shopping malls, effect on, 91; and WFH's effect on productivity, monitoring and adjusting as needed, 129–30

American Time Use Survey, 36–37

Apple: corporate campus, recently-built, 1, 89, 93; and rising rents in Seattle, local anger about, 121

Arizona, California residents and businesses moving to, 135

Atlanta: percentage of commuters using cars, 31; suburbs with cheaper housing in, 53, 54–55, 57

automakers in Detroit, funding of programs in response to 1967 riots, 125–26

Baltimore: concentration of poor people in city center, 86; and deindustrialization, failure to recover from, 169, 170–71; disadvantages of minority children raised in, 172; Great Fire, redevelopment following, 132; high number of low-income residents, as challenge, 95; housing in, as investment, viability of, 171; increased job opportunities with WFH, 82; lack of high-paying technology and finance jobs, 80–81; large African American population in, 10, 80; low housing prices in, 169, 170; poor housing, health risks of, 57; population decline, 15–16, 95, 169, 186; as postindustrial city, 13, 169–70; potential benefits from new WFH residents, 15–16, 80, 169, 171–73,

186; quality-of-life challenges in, 170–71; and WFH at Johns Hopkins University, concerns about effects of, 94–95; and WFH commuters to Washington, DC, 170; and WFH power couples, 76–77, 78. *See also* cities, postindustrial

beautiful places: ability to move to, and increase in inequality, 163; attractiveness as locations for firms with WFH workers, 180; availability of information on, 166; large number in US, 163, 177–78; marketing of, to WFH workers, 166; possibility of moving to, with WFH flexibility, 163; risks faced by early movers to, 177; with room for new WFH workers, examples of, 178–79. *See also* climate, pleasing

beautiful places, development in: and balance of growth and quality of life, 165–66, 180–81, 186; determining proper balance of development and preservation, 164; developers' anticipation of WFH workers' moves to, 163, 164; and environmental costs, incentives to limit, 164–65; and evolution of consumer city, 167; and need for infrastructure improvements, 186–87; potential resistance to, 163; use of market price incentives to shape, 164. *See also* environmentalist communities

Becker, Gary, 4, 77

behavioral economics, new boom in, 28

benefits: cost effectiveness of WFH as, 104; various types of, 104-5

Bentonville, Arkansas, recruiting of WFH workers, 168-69

Berkeley, California, obstacles to housing construction in, 61, 168

Biden administration: and climate change, 62; and infrastructure investment, 16; proposed heavy regulation of large firms, 127; reduced greenhouse gas emissions as goal of, 151

Big Data: and ability to assess place-based risk, 161-62; and determining proper balance of development and preservation, 164; and measurement of quality of life, 17, 27-28; and monitoring of WFH functionality, 75, 110-11

billionaires, US, in California, 134, 143

Bloom, Bick, 23

Boston: economic boom in, as driven by specific industries, 119; fire of 1872, redevelopment following, 132, 133; high cost of housing in, 29, 31-32, 56; as high-productivity city, 80; investment in urban infrastructure in, 3-4, 13; limited housing construction in, and rise in real estate prices, 121; long commutes in, 29, 30; low level of African American property ownership in, 130; as majority white, 80; percentage of commuters using cars, 31; public transportation in, 30, 33, 35; and supercommuters, 30; weather affecting commutes in, 34. *See also* cities, superstar

Bowling Alone (Putnam), 42, 149

Boyd, Virgil, 125

Bozeman, Montana: attractiveness to WFH workers and firms, 165, 166; boom in, and balance of growth and quality of life, 165-66; desirability of, for people with residence portfolio, 160-61; quality of life in, 143

Brattle Group, 106

Bren, Donald, 177

broadband access: inequality of, 179; need for expansion in rural areas, 174-75

Buffett, Warren, 23, 115

Bullshit Jobs (Graeber), 66

California: attractive aspects of, 134; green electricity grid in, 152; high cost of housing in, 56; and housing construction, obstacles to, 135, 168; Northern, and climate change, 62

California, exodus of firms and individuals from, 134-36; crime rates and, 136; high levels of regulation and, 135, 136; housing prices and, 135; poor performance in jobs creation, 135; poor performance in secondary education, 135; tax rates and, 134, 135; WFH and, 135-36

California, high income tax rates in, 143-44; and exodus of firms and individuals, 134, 135; popularity despite, 143

capital access, for women vs. men, 68

capitalism, and mismatch of workers and jobs, 66–67

carbon mitigation policies, urban progressives' support for, 153

carbon tax, increased opportunity for, with reduced reliance of fossil fuels, 153–54

career development, potential costs of WFH to, 12, 38, 63–64, 108

cars, electric: carbon footprint, variation with source of electricity, 152; and reduced environmental costs of sprawl, 152

cars, modern, increased fuel efficiency of, 151

Charleston, South Carolina, climate-resilience measures in, 162

charter cities. *See* cities, new (charter cities)

Chetty, Raj, 172–73

Chicago: fire of 1871, redevelopment following, 132; percentage of commuters using cars, 31, 33; public transportation in, 30, 35; range of job opportunities in, 76; vacancy rate in downtown commercial buildings after 9/11 attacks, 133–34; weather affecting commutes in, 34. *See also* cities, superstar

chief economists of firms, and design and evaluation of WFH, 112

childcare: more-equitable sharing of, in WFH, 37, 73; time per day spent on, 37

children: gains from parents' WFH, 40–41; and increased inequality with WFH, 41. *See also* family; women, and motherhood

China: commute to good schools in, 34; competition with European firms, Italian response to, 114; effect of WFH in, 187; study on effects of access to e-commerce, 175; study on increased scientific collaborations with low-cost air fares, 97; study on pollution's effect on decision-making, 93; study on pollution's effect on pleasure of time spent with friends, 41, 43; study on productivity of new industrial parks in, 101; study on stress effects of commuting, 37; study on WFH and productivity, 38–39, 111

Chrysler Motor Company, funding of programs in response to Detroit riots of 1967, 125–26

cities: change in fortune over time, 119–20; disasters in, and silver lining of redevelopment opportunities, 131–33; growth, expectations and, 136–37; megacities, effect of WFH on, 188; over 50,000 population, number in US, 167; places competing for WFH workers, 166, 168–69; raising of taxes on corporations, and risk of corporate flight, 13–14; smaller carbon footprint of residents in, 150. *See also* economic growth centers

cities, attraction of: decreased crime and, 137; "greening" and, 137; as likely to continue, 3–4, 7; quality of life fundamentals and, 137–38; for young people, 6–7, 25–26, 137

cities, high productivity. *See* cities, superstar

cities, new (charter cities), 145–50;

and communities for specific lifestyles, 149; growth of, and economies of scale, 147–48; importance of good schools to viability of, 145–47; importance of sufficient public goods to viability of, 145–46; and opportunity to implement well-designed government, 145; potential rise of, with WFH mobility, 145; and risk of creating isolated groups of like-minded people, 149–50. *See also* schools in new (charter) cities

cities, postindustrial: deindustrialization's effect on, 169; economic decline, and homes' loss of value, 46, 48; economic stagnation of, as problem before pandemic, 2; isolation of urban poor in, 85–86; lack of high-paying technology and finance jobs, 80–81, 82; large pool of African American potential workers, 80–81; population loss in, 15, 169; potential benefits from new WFH residents, 15–16, 169, 171–73, 186; residents' increased opportunities with WFH, 10, 15, 46–49, 79–83, 186; and urban poor, effect of influx of WFH workers on, 171–72; WFH workers in, and increased tax base, 80. *See also* African Americans, in large postindustrial cities; Baltimore

cities, superstar: as expensive to live in, 80; heavy investment in commercial real estate, 13; high cost of housing in, 29; and "knowledge in the air" as positive externality in, 128–29; limited housing construc-

tion, and rise in real estate prices, 121–22; long commutes in, 29–30; as majority white, 80; major tech firms' ongoing investment in, 137; ongoing attractiveness for consumers and tourists, 137; relocations of major companies, news stories on, 131; and rising rents, local anger about, 121; as unappealing to African American workers, 80; and WFH, lower rents and increased number of young workers as likely effect of, 14

cities, superstar, effect of WFH on: decreased demand for city space, and return to affordability, 4, 54–55, 56, 141, 185, 186; increased competition to attract and retain talent, 119; increase in firms' ability to threaten departure, 124; loss of skilled workers, potential macroeconomic productivity losses from, 127–31; as potentially positive, 129; reduced incentive for civic engagement in host cities, 127

cities, superstar, large companies driving booms in, 119–20; city officials' efforts to tax, 122–24; defensive move into political arena, 123; relationship with city, vs. past norms, 125–27

city, location in: as benefit for startup firms, 11–12, 98–100; effect of information technology on demand for, 58; young people's preference for, 6–7, 25–26

city center neighborhoods: African Americans' disproportionate residence in, 57; health risks in, 57 civic engagement: benefits of, 41–42; firms' reduced incentive for, with WFH, 127; as gain from WFH, 5, 41–44

Cleveland: disadvantages of minority children raised in, 172; large African American population in, 10, 80; low housing prices in, 170; as postindustrial city, 13, 169–70; potential economic growth from WFH residents, 80, 169. *See also* cities, postindustrial

climate, pleasing: creation of environmentalist communities in, 60; and high housing prices, 58–59; rising demand to live in, 58, 160–61. *See also* beautiful places; environmentalist communities

climate change: areas likely to suffer damage from, 62; and assessment of place-based risk, 161–62, 191; and climate-resilient locations, demand for housing in, 161–62, 191; and climate-resilient places, natural vs. man-made forms of, 162; design of housing to accommodate, 154; environmental restrictions on new construction and, 155; and flight from at-risk places, 162; and increased regulatory costs of construction, 155; migration due to, 62; migration due to, political effects of, 62–63; and WFH workers' freedom to migrate, 63, 191

Coastal Risk Consulting, 161

collaborations, scientific and academic, increase in, with low-cost air travel, 97

college graduates, number of, as indication of cities' attractiveness, 138

colleges and universities: diversity goals of, African Americans' location preference and, 82–83; and WFH, effects on surrounding community as concern, 94–95

Colorado, California residents and businesses moving to, 136

Columbia Center (building), 120

Common, 168

commuting: disutility of, as matter of individual preference, 37; as necessitated by inadequate housing supply near workplaces, 30, 31; reverse, 29; and trade-off between time and housing costs, 36

commuting, reducing through WFH: decreased traffic volume and, 33–35; equivalence to faster transportation technology, 54–55; money saved by workers, 36; and public transportation revenues, 35; time saved by workers, 35–36; uses of time saved by, 36–37

commuting by car: as more likely for residents of suburbs, 31; as percentage of all commuters, 31

commuting by public transportation: improvements in, as means of reducing car traffic, 31; as more likely for residents of cities, 31; as more time-consuming and uncomfortable than by car, 30; reduced revenue from WFH, impact of, 35

commuting time, 29–35; accidents and weather and, 34; as constraint on work and home location, 7–8, 16, 54, 193–94; length of, and level of interest in WFH, 38; limits on, and cost of housing, 9; for middle class in productive cities, as very high, 29–30, 36; as problem before pandemic, 2, 4; suburb-to-city commute as longest, 29, 36; supercommuters, 30; women's strong preference for shorter commute, 69

commuting time, reducing: and increase in discretionary trips, 34; quality of life improvements from, 4, 5, 33, 195–96; road pricing as method for, 31, 32–33, 99, 122, 164; through improved public transportation, 32. *See also* commuting, reducing through WFH

companies. *See* firms

compensation, factors affecting, 105. *See also* pay

contingencies, increased ability to address, with WFH flexibility, 6, 7, 17, 34, 50, 184, 187, 190–91, 194

coordination problem: beautiful places and, 60; high human capital cities and, 99; in rural areas, developers' role in solving, 177

corporate campuses, recently-built, 89, 91–93; emphasis on health and quality of life, 93; as little used after pandemic, 1; as place-based bet, 11

Costa, Dora, 42, 58–59

costs and risks of WFH: career development costs, 12, 38, 63–64, 108; competition from immigrants as, 189; feeling "out of the loop" as,

18, 63, 64, 65–66, 109, 111; foreign competition as, 3, 12, 18, 47, 53, 113–15, 184, 189; lack of connection with boss as, 63–64, 65, 105, 107–8; loss of face-to-face interaction as, 53, 63–64, 109; minimization through preparation, 3, 53, 184–85; reduced mentoring opportunities as, 25, 107; and work assignments, less-desirable, 63, 64–65

costs and risks of WFH, strategies to reduce: experimentation to find winning formulas, 12–13, 40, 64, 108–9, 111–12, 129–30; interviewing of departing employees and candidates declining job offers, 109; redesign of mentoring relationship, 107, 112; rules limiting competition for boss's favor, 64, 65; strategies to replace face-to-face interactions, 90, 109–10, 112, 129; work assignment using artificial intelligence, 65–66

costs to firms of WFH: damage to corporate culture as, 12, 26, 107, 108; difficulties in evaluating workers' output as, 108, 180–81; reduced loyalty as, 25, 105, 106, 107

COVID-19 pandemic: and emptying of expensive commercial offices, 1–2; home schooling in, 148; impact on aged, 51; and new awareness of disease risk in dense areas, 151; new technology allowing business to continue despite, 90; and rising real estate prices in suburban fringes, 120; and social

COVID-19 pandemic *(continued)*
experiment in WFH, 2, 89–90,
184; and suddenness of change to
WFH, 39, 40; and Western wildfires, 62
crime, as incentive for leaving cities, 85, 86
CTRIP travel agency, WFH at, and
efficiency, 38–39
Cutler, Kim-Mai, 102

Dallas: Amazon regional office in,
97; and supercommuters, 30
decentralization. *See* firms, decentralization (fragmentation) of
Denver, Amazon regional office in, 97
Dermisi, Sofia, 133
Detroit: Amazon regional office in,
97; deindustrialization in, 46; failure to recover from deindustrialization, 14; isolation of urban poor
in, 86; large African American
population in, 10, 80; low housing
prices in, 86, 170; as postindustrial
city, 13, 169–70; potential benefits
from new WFH residents, 169,
171–72; riots of 1967, funding of
programs in response to, 125–26.
See also cities, postindustrial
disasters, silver lining of redevelopment opportunities in, 131–33. *See
also* shocks, major
diversity: companies' interest in, 81–
82; universities' interest in, 82–83
diversity, WFH's accommodation of,
4, 19, 98; and choice of location
by WFH workers, 63, 184; market
economies and, 149

double bottom-line mentality: of
major firms, 124; of nonprofits,
94–95

Eastman, George, philanthropy of,
126–27
economic downturns, local, flexibility of WFH and, 46–49
economic growth centers: factors affecting location of, 5, 15; increased
number of, with spreading out of
workforce, 5, 15; and locals' blocking of growth with land use regulations, 5, 15, 61, 122, 141, 144–45,
163–64; rise in home prices in,
15; strategies for attracting WFH
workers, 14–15. *See also* beautiful
places
economic inequality, decrease in,
1945–65, 196
education level: and desire for green
lifestyle, 59; of neighbors, positive
externalities of, 174; of residents,
as indication of cities' attractiveness, 138; of WFH workers, 23–24
entertainment industry, clustering in
Hollywood region, 91
environmental costs of sprawl, 150–
56; carbon footprint increase with
decreased population density,
150–51; reduction of, with electric cars, 152, 153; reduction of,
with new solar-powered carbon-
neutral homes, 152–54; use of incentives to limit, 164–65
environmentalist communities: attraction of green businesses, 60;
attraction of more like-minded

people to, 60; creation in beautiful places, with WFH flexibility, 60; as demonstration projects, 61; green government policies in, 60–61; tendency to lock down growth, 61–62. *See also* beautiful places, development in

environmentalists, blocking of new construction in boom cities, 122

equity and inclusion effects from WFH: measurement of, 196; as open question, 131

Europe, effect of WFH in, 187

experience good, working from home as, 2, 38–39

exurban fringe, high cost of housing pushing city residents into, 155–56

Facebook: affordable housing program, 124; corporate campus, recently-built, 1, 92; and interaction of people with opposing views, 150

face-to-face interactions: building into WFH environment, 108–9, 112, 129–30; and building of friendship and altruism within organization, 108; and career growth, 25; decline of, with cell phone use, 42; and effect of WFH in Europe, 187; firms' separation of activities requiring and not requiring, 95–96; importance for career advancement, 12, 74; importance for new worker training, 25, 107, 129; importance for young workers, 25, 107; loss of, with WFH, 53, 63–64, 109; as nec-

essary in service industries, 85; with neighbors, and increased civic engagement, 41–44; ongoing importance in business, 13; as potentially important to a firm's success, 12; shutdown during pandemic, as social experiment in WFH, 2, 89–90, 184; with skilled people, and increased productivity of educated workers, 128; startup firms' need for, 99–100; for WFH workers, maximizing quality of, 58

face-to-face interactions, replacing with remote versions: development of methods for, 109–10, 112; effectiveness of, as key factor in success of WFH, 129; effectiveness of, as open question, 90

fair society, and employees' ability to choose WFH, 39

family: and African American ties to postindustrial cities, 10; caring for, flexibility of WFH and, 8–9, 17, 190–91; distant, flexibility to maintain ties with, through WFH, 6, 49–50; increased time with, through WFH, 5, 41–42, 100; increased time with, value to workers, 106; large, as incentive to find cheaper housing, 29, 57, 68; locating near, WFH and, 16, 49–51. *See also* marriage; women, and motherhood

farmland conversion to housing, 156–60; economic benefits of, 157–58; environmentalists' concerns about, 156 farmland in Silicon Valley region: amount of, 157; crop types and value, 157–58; decline in acreage and farm size, 157; high water usage, 159–60

farmland in Silicon Valley region, conversion to housing: economic benefits of, 157–58; effect on food prices, 159; strategy to protect biodiversity in, 158–59; and water conservation, 159–60

Filmhub, as decentralized startup, 102

finance industry: clustering in New York City, 91; in Manhattan, large amount of commercial real estate used by, 91

firms: increased interest in diverse workforce, 81–82; large, Biden's proposed heavy regulation of, 127

firms, decentralization (fragmentation) of, 95–98; and ability to hire from nationwide talent base, 180; advances in information technology and, 96; Amazon and, 97–98; and competition with centralized firms, 102–3; effect on geographical clustering of firms, 101; flexibility of, 103; and monitoring of firm's performance, 110–11; recent decentralized startup firms, 101–2; and reduction or elimination of permanent office space, 100–104; and separation of activities requiring city center interactions from those performable anywhere, 95–96; transportation infrastructure improvements and, 96–97;

venture capital suppliers and, 103; Wall Street firms and, 133

firms, major: double bottom-line mentality of, 124; incentives for increasing job satisfaction among workers, 93; worker preferences for WFH, 93

firms offering WFH: attractiveness of beautiful places as locations for, 180; competitive edge in attracting workers, 104, 106–7, 112–13; increase in, news stories on, 131; and loyalty of happy workers, 180; and WFH as nontaxed benefit, 104

firms' relationship with host cities: norms of twentieth century in, 125–27; recent tensions in, 122–24

firms with WFH workers: building of face-to-face interactions into system, 108–9, 112, 129–30; company culture and profitability and, 8; costs of failing to adapt, 11–12; experimentation to find winning WFH formula, 12–13, 40, 64, 108–9, 111–12, 129–30; flexibility in location, 8; higher costs of communication and coordination in, 39; and location, tradeoffs in, 11–13; and reduction or elimination of permanent office space, 100–104; short-term rentals of office space as needed, 100, 103–4; and wages competitive with foreign workers, 12, 113. *See also* costs and risks of WFH, strategies to reduce; gains for firms from WFH; productivity in WFH

First Base, 100

First Street Foundation, 161

flexibility: of decentralization firms, 103; and gains in well-being, 192

flexibility, increased with WFH, 4, 6; and ability to address contingencies, 6, 7, 17, 34, 50, 184, 187, 190–91, 194; and ability to avoid consequences of local economic downturns, 46–49; and ability to choose housing location, 59, 85, 181, 184–85; and ability to pursue one's own vision of the good life, 17, 57, 183, 193, 194; measuring workers' valuation of, 194–95; and women's ability to balance motherhood and career, 52. *See also* housing location chosen by WFH workers; spreading out of workforce

Florida: attractiveness as low-tax area, 14; competition for WFH workers, 119; as desirable WFH location, 27; individuals and businesses moving to, 142–43; rising demand for residence in, 160

football players, European, preference for homes in low-tax countries, 142

Ford, Harrison, 183

Ford Motor Company, funding of programs in response to 1967 Detroit riots, 125–26

foreign competition with WFH workers, 3, 12, 18, 47, 53, 113–15, 184, 189; and downward pressure on wages, 12, 113–14, 189; and future technology able to mimic face-to-face interactions, 113; investment in new skills to counter, 113, 114–15, 189; populist response to, 115; and WFH option as compensation for lower pay, 12, 17, 113–14, 189

France, data on women's commuting preferences in, 69

freelancer work: online platforms to match jobs with, 44–46; opportunities for, in WFH environment, 44

Friedman, Thomas, 113

friends: effect of pollution on pleasure of time spent with, 41, 43; greater engagement with, as gain from WFH, 41–44

fuel efficiency, and rebound effect, 55

gains for firms from WFH, 100–104; increased leverage over cities as, 124; savings on office costs, 100–104

gains to workers from WFH, 191–96; measurement of well-being and, 191–92, 194–96; medium-term games, 7–11; for middle-aged workers, 26–27; for older workers, 27–28; reduced commuting time as, 5, 33–34; short-run gains, 5–7; social engagement in one's neighborhood as, 41–44; variation with individual, 2–3, 6–7, 9, 17, 57, 173, 193, 194; for younger workers, 25–26, 193. *See also* personal freedom; quality of life improvements in WFH; well-being gains from WFH

gasoline tax increases, strong opposition from people reliant on cars,
151–52

Gaspar, Jess, 58

General Motors, funding of programs in response to 1967 riots in
Detroit, 125–26

geographic portfolios, seasonal:
Harrison Ford and, 183; for WFH
workers, 160–61, 183

gig economy: health insurance and,
189–90; WFH as form of, 189–90

Glaeser, Edward, 58

Goldilocks effect, 165, 166

Goldin, Claudia, 73

Goldman Sachs, potential move of
asset management arm to Florida, 143

golfers, professional, residence in
low-tax Florida, 142–43

Google: corporate campus, recently-
built, 1; and rising rents in San
Francisco, local anger about, 121;
WFH policies of, 93–94

Gordon, Robert, 17–18

Graeber, David, 66

green energy grids, dependence on
cheap, effective batteries, 152–53

greenhouse gas emission, lowering of: as goal of Biden administration, 151; through gas tax increases, opposition to, 151–52

green lifestyle: education level as indicator of interest in, 59; rising interest in, 59. See also environmentalist communities

gross domestic product (GDP), vs.
well-being, 192, 196

growth, regulation by pricing of resources, 61, 164

Harrison, George, "Taxman" song
by, 142

Harvard and Beyond (H&B) survey, 73

health insurance, and WFH gig
economy jobs, 189–90

Heckman, James, 172–73

high tech industry, clustering in Silicon Valley region, 91

home schooling, WFH parents and,
148–49

hometowns: college graduates' distance from, 50–51; possibility of
return to, with WFH, 49–51

household chores: more-equitable
sharing of, in WFH, 5, 37; and multitasking during WFH, 37

housing construction: blocking of,
by property owners in nice areas,
5, 15, 61, 122, 141, 144–45, 163–64;
building for adaptability to climate change, 154; in California,
difficulty of, 135, 168; environmental restrictions on, 155; near
water, desirability of, 59; and non-
WFH workers' benefits from WFH
workers' migration, 84; shaping of
new economic geography by, 181;
urban, complications of, 9. See also
climate, pleasing

housing in new (charter) cities:
building for adaptability to climate change, 154; economies
of scale in, 154; environmental restrictions on new construc-

tion and, 155; new solar-powered carbon-neutral homes in, 152–54
housing in superstar cities: conversion of commercial property into, obstacles to, 138–40; high cost of, 9, 13, 29, 31–32, 56, 104, 121–22, 135, 155–56, 186; increased cost with decreased commuting time, 31–32; need for increased amount of, 138
housing location chosen by WFH workers: access to leisure activities and, 160; demand for climate-resilient places, 161–62; dependence on individual choice, 9, 14, 59, 143, 149, 181, 186; environmentalists' congregation in beautiful places, 59–60; firms dedicated to finding, 168; flexibility in choice of, 59, 85, 181, 184–85; good hospitals and, 160; places competing for selection as, 166, 168–69; potential economic growth in, 15–16; preference for warm-weather locations, 160–61; strategies for attracting WFH workers, 14–15; unlinking of work and home location and, 7–8, 16–17, 54–55, 76, 162, 184–85, 193–94; and "voting with your feet," 62, 85, 138, 149, 162. *See also* spreading out of workforce
housing prices: in California, as well above national average, 135; climate as factor in, 58–59; decline with distance from city, spreading out of workforce and, 53–54, 84; racial wealth gap and, 56–57; in Sun Belt, affordability of, 160
housing prices in cities: groups ben-

efiting from reduction of, 56–57; high cost of, 29, 32, 104, 121–22; lowering of, through new construction, 121–22, 138; lowering of, with departure of WFH workers, 4, 54–55, 56, 141, 185, 186; and pushing of residents into exurban fringe, 155–56
Houston: suburbs with cheaper housing in, 57; and supercommuters, 30
Humphreys, Brad, 179–80
Hurricane Sandy (2012), New York's recovery from, 133

immigrants: benefit from reduction of city housing prices, 56–57; competition with WFH workers, 189
income inequality, rising real estate prices in superstar cities and, 130–31
income per capita, vs. well-being, 192
India: competition for US jobs, 113; effect of WFH in, 188
industries, key, geographical clustering of, 91; decline of, in WFH environment, 91; as draw for new firms, 91
inequality: in ability to move to beautiful places, 163; in broadband access, 179; in children's gains from parents' WFH, 41; economic, decrease from 1945 to 1965, 196; rising real estate prices in superstar cities and, 130–31; from spreading out of workforce with WFH, 179–80, 181; in wealth, and reduced housing choices, 56–57

information technology: and CO-VID-19 lockdowns, continuation of business despite, 90; effect on demand for city living, 58; enabling of WFH by, 53; and firms' ability to fragment operations, 96; and foreign workers' ability to compete for US jobs, 113; and reduced need for physical office, 110

infrastructure: Biden administration investment in, 16; need for, in growing beautiful places, 186–87; in rural areas, needed improvements in, 16; successful cities' investment in, 3–4, 13; synergies with private investments, 16; transportation, WFH and, 96–97

internet, and interaction of people with opposing views, 150

internet broadband access: inequality of, 179; need for expansion in rural areas, 174–75

Ireland, effect of WFH in, 188–89

Italy, response to Chinese competition, 114

Jackson Hole, Wyoming, as beautiful place, 163–67

Jacobs, Jane, 128, 130, 140–41

Japan, smaller carbon footprints in, 150

J. L. Hudson Company, and 1967 riots in Detroit, 126

jobs, matching of worker with, as poor in many cases, 66–67

jobs, matching of worker with, using artificial intelligence, 65–66; online platforms for, and destruction of good jobs, 189–90; online plat-forms for, effectiveness of, 44–46; suburban residents' benefit from, 67–68. *See also* Upwork

jobs tied to physical locations: and constraints of work and home location, 7–8, 16, 193–94; and increased cost of maintaining ties with distant family and friends, 6, 49

Johns Hopkins University, effects of WFH on surrounding community as concern, 94–95

Jupiter, 161

Kain, John, 79

Katz, Lawrence F., 73

Khan Academy, 148, 177

Kirwa Commission, 172

Kodak Company, and philanthropy in Rochester, New York, 126–27

Krugman, Paul, 3, 136

labor pooling, startup companies and, 98–99

Las Vegas: increasing sophistication of, 167; rising demand for residence in, 160

leisure activities: as better with friends, 41; time spent on specific types of, 36–37

Leonard, Kawhi, 196

livelihood insurance, Shiller's proposal for, 47–48

Los Angeles: and environmental issues, increased costs of construction due to, 155; good quality of life in, 143; percentage of commuters using cars, 31; real estate boom in, 134 loyalty: buying of, as reason for higher pay, 105; monitoring of workers and, 106; WFH workers and, 25, 105, 106, 107, 180

Lucas, Robert, 154

Manhattan: Amazon regional office in, 81; large amount of commercial real estate used by financial firms, 91; past downturns weathered by, 14. *See also* New York City

market economies, and accommodation of diversity, 149. *See also* diversity, WFH's accommodation of

market price incentives, in determining proper balance of development and preservation, 164

marriage: effect of WFH on, 77–78; and relationship-specific investment, 77; similar education levels of spouses as typical in, 75; strain on, with woman's income greater than man's, 77–78; with two working spouses, reduced specialization in, 78. *See also* power couples

Marshall, Alfred, 128

Maryland, and cost of early education programs, 172

Merrell, Allen, 125

Michigan Bell, and Detroit riots of 1967, 126

Micka, Allie, 26

Microsoft: corporate campus, recently built, 92–93; and Seattle's economic boom, 119

middle-aged people: and local economic downturns, flexibility of WFH and, 48; office-based work as less important to, 26–27; reluc-

tance to move in search of work, 48, 49

Midwestern US, increasing population of, 58

Minden, West Virginia, 179

minimum wage, high, and reduced demand for workers in suburban and exurban areas, 84

minorities: benefit from reduction of city housing prices, 56–57; children raised in postindustrial cities, and cycle of poverty, 172–73; increased opportunities with WFH, 10; limited opportunities for, as problem before pandemic, 2; value of affordable city housing to, 138. *See also* African Americans

monitoring of workers: with computer monitoring systems, 105–6; and potential employee resentment, 106; as unnecessary with happy workers, 180–81

Moretti, Enrico, 155–56

Morgenfeld, Todd, 81–82

Moses, Robert, 140

Mosqueda, Teresa, 123

Mount Vernon, Washington, as example of beautiful place with room for WFH workers, 178

musicians, as early WFH workers, 142

Musk, Elon, 134

MySwimPro, as decentralized startup, 102

NAACP, programs in response to 1967 riots in Detroit, 125

National Bureau of Economic Research (NBER), 56

natural resource extraction, lingering damage to some towns from, 179

NBER. *See* National Bureau of Economic Research

New Detroit Committee, 125–26

new jobs, ability to experiment with, as benefit of WFH, 44–45

New Orleans, recruiting of WFH workers, 168–69

New York City: Amazon regional office in, 97; difficult commutes in, 9; economic boom in, as driven by specific industries, 119; features valued by young people, 137; high home prices in, 9; as high-productivity city, 13, 186; investment in urban infrastructure in, 3–4, 13; major tech firms' ongoing investment in, 137; ongoing growth, expectations and, 137; past major shocks, recovery from, 131, 133; percentage of commuters using cars, 31; preservation of historical neighborhoods in, 140–41; public transportation in, 30, 33, 35; range of job opportunities in, 76; and supercommuters, 30; talent in, as attraction for talent, 137; zoning laws as obstacle to building use changes, 138–39. *See also* cities, superstar; Manhattan

New Yorkers, retirement to Florida, WFH and, 27

NIMBY issue: environmentalist communities and, 61; moving to beautiful places and, 163

non-WFH workers: impact of WFH on, 10–11, 83–86; possible retraining as WFH-eligible employees, 85; and reduced commuting times with increase in WFH, 34–35. *See also* service-sector workers

Northeastern US, declining population of, 58

Oakland, California, population increase vs. housing stock, 156

Ogden, Utah, recruiting of WFH workers, 168–69

older workers: benefits of WFH for, 27–28; quality of life, need for more data on, 27–28

Pacific Research Institute, 135

parents, aging, flexibility to care for, with WFH, 6, 9, 16, 51

pay: needed to attract workers, firm's reputation and, 106–7, 111; for WFH workers, reputation of firm and, 106–7; for workers in expensive cities, cost of rents as drain on, 32, 104

pay, gender gap in: increase with age, 73–74; reasons for, 52, 67–68; variation by country, 67–68

pay reductions with WFH, 12, 17, 104–7; and ability to compete with foreign workers, 12, 113–14, 189; and WFH quality of life gains as compensation for lower pay, 113–14, 189

Pei Li, 93

personal freedom, expansion of: with increased choice of where to work and live, 7, 8–9, 16–17, 19,

quality of life *(continued)*
built corporate campuses, 93;
housing prices and, 138; vs. income, 146; locations' marketing
of, 166, 168–69; locations with,
as likely destinations for WFH
workers, 186; measurement of, 17,
27–28, 37–38; new WFH communities' setting of rules for, 60–62;
postindustrial cities and, 170–71;
and property owners blocking
of new construction in desirable
places, 5, 15, 61, 122, 141, 144–45,
163–64; variation by location, 143;
willingness to pay for, 143. *See also*
well-being
quality of life improvements in
WFH: as compensation for pay
reductions, 113–14, 189; freedom
to choose work location and, 9,
186; leisure time improvements
and, 18; personal preference and,
59; potential inequality and, 181;
reduced commuting time as, 4,
5, 33, 195–96; related service-sector jobs and, 17, 18, 83–86; role
of infrastructure in, 16, 18; rural
America and, 173–76; for stay-at-
home spouses, 71; testing of locations and, 148; and "voting with
your feet," 62, 85, 138, 149, 162;
workers' experience of, during
pandemic, 2, 89. *See also* flexibility, increased with WFH; gains
to workers from WFH; minorities, increased opportunities with
WFH; well-being gains from
WFH; women, increased opportunities with WFH

real estate, commercial, 90–95; and
clustering of industries, 91; converting into new housing, obstacles to, 138–40; as currently
under-used, 3–4; high cost vs. benefits of, 11, 90; owners' reluctance
to sell at loss, 138
real estate, commercial, future demand for: dependence on need
for face-to-face interactions, 91,
99–100; as likely ongoing but reduced, 13
real estate, commercial, high
rents for: likely decrease, post-
pandemic, 4; and likely move of
some companies, 8; as problem
before pandemic, 2
real estate prices: rise in cities with
superstar firms, and income inequality, 130–31; rise in suburban
fringe areas during COVID-19
pandemic, 120; shifts in, with
more WFH, 4–5; in superstar cities, high cost of, 32, 104. *See also*
housing prices; housing prices in
cities
rebound effect, commuting and, 55
recruitment, effect of firm's reputation on, 106–7, 111
Remote, as decentralized startup, 102
Republicans, opposition to gas tax
increases, 152
reputation: effect of employee satisfaction on, 106; effect on hiring,
106–7, 111; firms' relations with
city and, 124
road pricing: cities now using, 32;
as method for reducing commuting time, 31, 32–33, 99, 122; and

action of people with opposing views, 150

South Korea, effect of WFH in, 188

spatial mismatch hypothesis, 79

sports teams, professional, economic gains from, 176

spreading out of workforce: facilitation of, by transportation improvements, 54; more affordable housing outside city as draw for, 53–54; and reduced exposure to urban pollution and disease, 150–51. *See also* environmental costs of sprawl

spreading out of workforce with WFH: and access to more-affordable housing, 54, 57; and diversity of choices in location, 184; and economic growth centers, increased number of, 5, 15; effect equivalent to faster transportation technology, 54–55; and exurban families' access to city culture and amenities, 57; and lower rents in small cities, 181; and new cities, potential rise of, 145; potential for increased inequality from, 179–80, 181; and service-sector workers, opportunities for, 5, 10–11, 17–18, 83–85, 167, 181, 185, 196; and urban housing prices, reduction of, 4, 54–55, 56, 141, 185, 186; and urban poor, further isolation of, 85–86. *See also* housing location chosen by WFH workers

startup firms: choice of location, guesswork in, 101; effect of de-centralization of firms on, as unknown, 100–101; fully decentralized, 101–2

startup firms, benefits of urban location for, 11–12, 98–100; as diminished in WFH environment, 99; and importance of learning and networking, 99; labor pooling and, 98–99; large pool of college graduates as, 99; need for face-to-face interactions and, 99–100

statistical discrimination, women in workforce and, 71–72

St. Louis: large number of African Americans in, 80; low housing prices in, 170; potential economic growth from WFH residents, 169

Stockholm, road pricing in, 32

stress effects of commuting, studies on, 37

suburban residents, and internet-matched remote work, benefits from, 67–68

suburban women, and internet-matched WFH, benefits from, 68–71

suburbs, wealthy: resistance to new construction, 144–45; small number of rental properties or poor people in, 147

Sun Belt: cheaper housing prices in, 160; rising demand to live in, 58, 160

taxes on income: high, residents' willingness to pay, 143; individuals moving to avoid, 142; states with

housing choices for minorities, 56–57

well-being: firms' incentives for considering, 111; vs. GDP, 192, 196; internet access and, 175. *See also* quality of life

well-being gains from WFH, 143; discovery of, during pandemic, 89; expansion of personal freedom and, 143, 149; freedom to relocate to desirable area and, 149; insufficient data on, 37–38; measurement of, 37, 39, 191–92, 194–96; reduction of commute and, 43. *See also* flexibility, increased with WFH; personal freedom, expansion of; quality of life improvements in WFH

western US, and climate change, forest fires and, 62, 155

West Virginia: broadband access, inequality of, 179; and influx of WFH workers, potential for increased inequality from, 179–80; opportunity zones in, 176

WeWork model of space rental, 100, 103–4

WFH. *See* working from home

Williams, Ardine, 137

Wilson, William Julius, 79

women: improvements from WFH, measurement of, 196; increased opportunities with WFH, 10; limited opportunities for, as problem before pandemic, 2; and self-employment, increase in, 70; strong preference for shorter commute, 69; and WFH income, benefits of, 71; workforce partici-

pation, increase in, with WFH, 68–71; and work-life balance, fields chosen to facilitate, 71

women, and motherhood: career costs of, 52, 67–69, 71–72, 74; flexibility of WFH and, 52; value of preparation for WFH, 73–74; WFH as option to reduce career costs of, 70, 72–73, 74–75

women, in workforce: earnings penalties for job interruption, by advanced degree type, 73; firms' incentives for retention of, 74; and reduced civic engagement, 42; and statistical discrimination, 71–72

workers: areas with small number of, and exploitation, 48–49; dislike of work in many cases, 66–67; dissatisfied, shirking of work by, 105; motivating, proper balance of carrots and sticks in, 105–6; superstar, special privileges given to, 196

workers, treatment of: effect on reputation, 106; proper balance of carrots and sticks, 105–6

working from home (WFH): allowing employees to choose, 39, 40, 111; counties with highest percentage of workers eligible for, 24–25; education level of WFH workers, 23–24; as an experience good, 2, 38–39; future percentage of workforce engaged in, 1, 3, 193; as gig economy, 189–90; groups benefiting from, 52; and home schooling, 148–49; impact in China, 187; impact in developing countries, 188;

working from home *(continued)*
impact in Europe, 187; impact in
Ireland, 188–89; impact in South
Korea, 188; lessons learned in,
impact on future work, 2; as likely
to continue, 18–19; personality
types suitable for, 28–29; potentially disastrous problems with, as
unlikely, 18–19; stigma on, before
COVID-19 lockdowns, 89–90;
types of jobs suited for, 24; workers' preferences for, 23–24, 38;
workers themselves as best judge
of suitability for, 40, 111
working from home (WFH), unlocking full potential of: as goal, 2; individual preparation and, 3, 53,
184–85; workers' role in, 51. *See
also* costs and risks of WFH, strategies to reduce
World Is Flat, The (Friedman), 113

Yellow Vest protests in France,
151–52
young people: advantages of working in city for, 6–7, 25–26; features
of New York valued by, 137; job
switching by, 25; preference for
office-based work, 25–26, 93, 192;
value of affordable city housing
to, 138

zoning and land-use laws: for development of beautiful places, 164;
as obstacle to conversion of commercial properties to residential use, 138–39; property owners' blocking of new construction
with, 5, 15, 61, 122, 141, 144–45,
163–64; proposed revisions of,
164
zoom, communication on, benefits
only for established workers, 26–27